Psychology Revivals

Analytical Psychology and the English Mind

Originally published in 1950, the name of the late Dr H.G. Baynes was already well-known as a leading exponent of and translator of the writings of Professor C.G. Jung, as author and as psychotherapist.

The essay which gives it title to this varied and interesting collection of writings, shows clearly Dr Baynes's gift for illuminating a familiar subject with fresh insight drawn from his wide knowledge of the unconscious mind. He can make the unconscious real to us, and can convince us that myth and dream are expressions of vital problems of the human soul.

The collection includes material to interest many types of reader, from *The British Journal of Medical Psychology*, from *Folk-Lore*, from The Society for Psychical Research. But perhaps most full of interest for the majority of readers are the first three chapters of an unfinished book – *What It Is All About*; here we find an admirable introduction, given with a wealth of illustration, to the main concepts of Professor Jung's analytical psychology.

Dr Baynes made Professor Jung's thought his own, without loss of his own originality. He can touch with significance any subject on which he writes, whether it be the problem of the individual or the kindred problems of humanity.

Analytical Psychology and the English Mind

and other papers

H.G. Baynes

Routledge
Taylor & Francis Group
LONDON AND NEW YORK

First published in 1950
by Methuen & Co. Ltd

This edition first published in 2015 by Routledge
27 Church Road, Hove BN3 2FA

and by Routledge
711 Third Avenue, New York, NY 10017

Routledge is an imprint of the Taylor & Francis Group, an informa business

Publisher's Note
The publisher has gone to great lengths to ensure the quality of this reprint but points out that some imperfections in the original copies may be apparent.

Disclaimer
The publisher has made every effort to trace copyright holders and welcomes correspondence from those they have been unable to contact.

ISBN: 978-1-138-85562-5 (hbk)
ISBN: 978-1-315-72024-1 (ebk)

ANALYTICAL PSYCHOLOGY AND THE ENGLISH MIND

and other papers by

H. G. BAYNES

with a foreword by
C. G. JUNG

METHUEN & CO., LTD. LONDON
36 Essex Street, Strand, W.C.2

First published in 1950

CATALOGUE NO. 5156/U

PRINTED IN GREAT BRITAIN

Foreword

I write these few introductory words to this collection of essays and lectures in affectionate memory of their author. The late H. G. Baynes was my assistant for several years, my travelling companion on our African expedition, and my faithful friend till his all too early death, which has left a painful gap in the circle of his friends and colleagues.

His first published work was his most excellent translation of my book *Psychological Types*. Later he became well known as the author of two important works, *Mythology of the Soul* and *Germany Possessed*. The first of these deals with the daily reality of the psychotherapist, and the second with contemporary events.

In *Mythology of the Soul* the author uses raw material—such as the psychotherapist meets with daily in his consulting hours—as a clue to guide the reader through the maze of individual reflections, opinions, interpretations and attempts at explanation which a psychologist gathers in the course of his experience. The empirical material stimulates such considerations and they are also indispensable in order to integrate it in consciousness.

Germany Possessed is concerned with the great contemporary problems which form a direct challenge to the psychologically minded doctor. This book made the author known to a very wide public.

His shorter writings, which have been collected in this present volume, deal with the complex psychic conditions characteristic of medical psychology. Psychology is thus a discipline which obliges the medical psychologist to deal with complex psychic factors, for the psychotherapeutic process can only take place on this level. Therefore analytical psychology is also rightly called 'complex psychology'.

A simplifying theory is naturally exceedingly popular in this highly complicated field, but the author has wisely resisted any such temptation. In its place he has drawn from a really remarkable wealth of theoretical and practical points of view, and has opened up possibilities and connections worthy of further discussion.

H. G. Baynes left us too soon. May this volume, which he has left to us, become a milestone on the road of psychological research.

C. G. Jung

Acknowledgments

I should like, in the first place, to express my indebtedness to Professor C. G. Jung, for writing the Foreword.

My warmest thanks are also due to Miss Toni Wolff and Miss Ina Jephson for their help in reading the manuscripts and for many excellent suggestions; and to Mr. Rex Littleboy for his help in reading the proofs.

I am indebted to Verlag von Julius Springer, Berlin, for allowing me to include the essay 'Analytical Psychology and the English Mind' originally published in *Die Kulturelle Bedeutung der Komplexen Psychologie*; to *The British Journal of Medical Psychology* for permission to include the essays 'Freud versus Jung' and 'The Importance of Dream Analysis for Psychological Development'; to the Society for Psychical Research for permission to include the two papers 'The Ghost as a Psychic Phenomenon' and 'Jung's Conception of the Structure of Personality in Relation to Psychical Research'; and to the Folk Lore Society for permission to include the essay 'On the Psychological Origins of Divine Kingship'.

ANNE BAYNES

Reed House, West Byfleet
September 1949

Contents

Foreword by C. G. Jung *page* v

1. The Unconscious as the Real Object of Psychology 1
2. A Demonstration of Analytical Practice 19
3. Analytical Psychology and the English Mind 34
4. The Provisional Life 61
5. The Psychological Background of the Parent-Child Relation 76
6. Freud versus Jung 97
7. The Importance of Dream-analysis for Psychological Development 130
8. The Ghost as a Psychic Phenomenon 154
9. Jung's Conception of the Structure of Personality in relation to Psychical Research 168
10. On the Psychological Origins of Divine Kingship 180
11. What it is all about 204

Index 239

The Unconscious as the Real Object of Psychology[1]

I am told that my title is hard to swallow; for how can a thing that is unconscious be an object of science? There is an advantage in a provocative title in the fact that it forces us to take stock of our terms. This one has the added advantage of introducing our theme. My main argument or thesis is that extraverted science, religion and education deal in great detail with the relatively inessential containers of human interest, while ignoring the essential things. The intellect, with all its satellites, is overfed with a surfeit of fact, while the soul is parched of meaning. If we follow the centrifugal intellectual movement in any direction we come upon all the manifold objects of natural science. But the essential meaning of things is at the centre, not at the circumference. Our culture is like an ever-expanding ring, with a hollow centre.

Analytical psychology is the one introverting science: its direction is towards the centre. All the essential things which extraverted culture has overlooked are to be found as pregnant contents of the unconscious. It is an empirical fact that the unconscious is overcharged with the vital human contents which our civilized consciousness lacks. This is why it is almost unbearably true to say that the unconscious is the real object of psychology.

But there is another sense in which we can say that the unconscious is the real *object* of our science; in as much as the products of unconscious activity are projected spontaneously upon the field of consciousness without contamination or critical interference.

The word 'object' means literally something that is thrown before the mind. In apprehending the object the subjective variable can never be ruled out, since the mind must always be the recipient in every act of cognition. But by insisting upon the verification of observations by several minds and by introducing invariable mechanism for the purpose of recording objective processes, science has to a large extent excluded the irrational, spontaneous psyche from the scientific field. Psyche, it should be remembered, is the Greek word for butterfly.

[1] Paper read at a public meeting of the Analytical Psychology Club, London, on 9 December 1938.

Thus it comes about that the great body of science consists of facts which invite no difference of opinion or feeling, and offer no field for the free projection of psychic images.

We have accepted this mechanization of knowledge fatalistically; even, perhaps, with a smothered sigh, asserting it to be a great triumph of the human intellect. Yet we remember with delight that the awakening of science in the mind of primitive man, when he first began to inquire into the meaning of dreams or tried to probe the riddle of human fate, was a winged flight, unaided by any apparatus whatsoever, except such as nature had thought fit to provide.

Both dream-interpretation and astrology were intuitive sciences concerned, at bottom, with the problem of individual fate, and both were based on the assumption that objects in the external universe, like the stars and the special objects pertaining to augury and divination, were just as relevant to human destiny as the objects of the inner world appearing in dreams.

To these first scientific inquirers, the world of matter was as mysterious as the world of the mind. The starry heavens presented an uncharted field upon which the impersonal contents of the unconscious could be projected. Dream-imagery presented another objective field upon which the human mind could project its meaningful interpretations. Later, alchemy found or created the field of chemical processes, upon which the mystical quest for the imperishable value could be projected.

In the beginning of culture the scientific attitude was indistinguishable from the religious. We have evidence, for instance, in the early Sumerian epic *Gilgamish*, that the gods rewarded Uta-Napishtim with the unprecedented boon of immortality, because he was not only wise enough to attend to the dream (imparted to the walls of the Reed hut by Ea, to warn him of the coming deluge), but was also faithful enough to act upon it. Ea-Oannes explains:[1]

Sooth, indeed 'twas not I of the Great Gods the secret revealed,
[But] to th' Abounding in Wisdom[2] vouchsafed I a dream, and [in this wise]
He of the gods heard the secret. Deliberate, now, on his counsel
[Then] to the Ark came up Enlil; [3]my hand did he grasp, and uplifted

[1] Citations are from R. Campbell Thompson's translation *The Epic of Gilgamish* (Luzac & Co. 1928).

[2] Uta-Napishtim, the Chaldean Noah.

[3] The god of storm and destruction who had been the original instigator of the deluge.

Me, even me, and my wife, too, he raised, and, bent-kneed beside me,
Made her to kneel; our foreheads he touched as he stood there between us,
Blessing us; 'Uta-Napishtim hath hitherto only been mortal,
Now, indeed, Uta-Napishtim and [also] his wife shall be equal
Like to us gods; in the distance afar at the mouth of the rivers
Uta-Napishtim shall dwell.'

In this passage we are informed that the scientific quest of dream-interpretation was united in the same person and in the same act with true religious piety—piety to which even Enlil, the originator of the deluge, was prompted to do honour.

Not to confound magic with religion, we could say that in the moment when that individual man emerged from his little necessitous cave and first wondered: 'I made this fire—then who made the sun?' or some such deeply questing thought—in that moment the first scientific inquiry and the first truly religious feeling were united.

There are indications in the Gilgamish epos that the early science of astrology was also associated with a ritual of religious initiation. Out of astrology grew the still more amazing science of astronomy. Although ostensibly the objective field of the two sciences was the same, their real aims were poles asunder. The astrologers were not, in fact, interested in the real nature of the stars, and only incidentally in their objective behaviour. For them the stars were the gods. The macrocosm without and the microcosm within were both infinite, but the latter was in some way dependent upon the former. Therefore all that could be learned about the one revealed the nature of the other.

Similarly, as we now understand, the alchemists were not interested in the nature of matter as such, but only in so far as it was the vessel or vehicle of the primordial contents of the unconscious which they projected into it.

Now it is a fact of the greatest importance to psychology that as soon as the primordial or intuitive sciences, astrology and alchemy, were superseded by the scientific disciplines of astronomy and chemistry, the former practically disappeared. Astrology, it is true, managed to survive in the somewhat dingy purlieus of occultism, but without a genuine scientific status. While alchemy was relegated to the cultural museum as a curious mediaeval conceit.

The third of the great intuitive sciences of antiquity, namely, dream-interpretation, was never superseded; it remained outcast on the shores of the primitive world until the beginning of the present century, when the dream was rediscovered by Freud, as a possible object of science.

The importance of the disappearance of these primordial forerunners of science will begin to emerge when we consider that in no case was the real object of the primordial science satisfied or fulfilled by that which superseded it. Our understanding of the factors which constitute human fate, for example, has not been materially advanced by astronomy. Nor has the individuating passion which expressed itself, somewhat confusedly, in alchemy, been answered or satisfied by chemistry. Coming to dream-interpretation—our little Cinderella among her queenly sisters—I cannot believe that the realistic imagination of early man, which conceived the *mana* dream as the voice of the Great Spirit, could ever feel satisfied with the wish-fulfilment theory of mechanistic science.

We know beyond the shadow of a doubt that these forces or contents of the primordial psyche which have not been expressed and fulfilled on the conscious level, will be found latent but living in the unconscious. The primordial mind is inextinguishable and it cannot be cheated or swindled. If the intellect is so constructed that it can only make reality clearly visible to itself with the aid of mechanisms wherewith to measure, weigh and number the objective universe, it does not follow that the ultimate truth is therefore a mechanism. It only tends to confirm the self-evident truth that, if in our search for reality we exclude every other function of the mind but the one which venerates the machine, we are likely to conclude that the universe is, in fact, a machine.

It is essential that we recognize the god we actually serve, since this determines the aspect reality will eventually assume in our eyes. This truth was demonstrated by Sir James Jeans, who confessed that the only mind which could have conceived and created the universe which astronomy revealed was that of a mathematician.

Let me not be misunderstood. I am committed to the scientific *Weltanschauung*, as every educated man of the West must be. We have no choice: the universe which the scientific intellect discovered is altogether more comprehensive and intelligible than the one our forefathers believed in. We cannot go back on that. But those of us who have to do with the unconscious are made profoundly aware, on the one hand, of the one-sidedness of consciousness and, on the other, of certain primordial elements of the mind which this one-sidedness has repressed.

We are aware that no vital element of the mind is ever obliterated. We know how a certain content can lie dormant in the primordial psyche for centuries; until at last, when the repressive conscious influence is exhausted, it leaps suddenly into life again to shout its native truth to the heavens.

An instance of this is clearly demonstrable in the Nazi revolution. We must remember that the pagan Teutons—the ancestors of modern Germany—were bundled into the Church at the point of the sword, during the totalitarian phase of the Holy Roman Empire. Also that the pagan Wotan worship did not go over into Christianity, whereas the Druidic religion in this country accepted the Christian graft without great difficulty. Pagan Germany was repressed by the conqueror and lay dormant for centuries, until, reawakened, it rose once again and proclaimed its rather queer truth to a startled world.

What happened in Germany is only one item in the transitional upheavals of the present epoch. Christendom is essentially a millennial formation. The crusading, extraverted momentum of Christianity was an attempt to overleap the slow process of evolution and to supersede, with the Christian ideology, everything that had gone before. In the long run, however, the evolutionary process resumes its own gait. For a time it seemed to be jostled on one side by the millennial rush of Christianity: but now we have the backwash, and things which nineteenth-century optimism regarded as past and done with emerge once more from the unconscious, demanding their place in life.

This does not mean that we must return to paganism or try to unlearn our scientific knowledge. No return is feasible. Even in Germany, in spite of the mediaeval pogroms and the brutal intolerance; in spite of the holy Roman-Berlin Axis, the Wotan-worship, the new *furor teutonicus* which staggered the world like a typhoon—in spite of all this self-evident regression to the former unfulfilled transition, we cannot say that it is a mere historical *rechute*. We know it is not. The German nation was by no means demoralized. It went back with deep instinctive purpose to recover a primitive soul which it left behind with those blond pagan heroes of long ago. If only the nation had known what it was seeking, it might have found a leader of a different sort; one who could have conducted that great enterprise without leading the whole nation into dishonour.

I have to mention this tragic example because the Germans are not the only people who left part of their soul behind. Those distant quests of the primordial mind have still to be reckoned with. Superseded by scientific disciplines, their essential longing has never been satisfied. These contents of the general unconscious come up again because science has given no answer and no profound study to the essential problems of individual being. Only those things are finally superseded which have been lived out and therewith exhausted of meaning. The primitive form may be superseded but not the essential content.

Take, for instance, the mystery-rites of antiquity which were superseded by the Christian mass. All the pagan mystery-cults were chthonian or earth-cults. The presiding deities were feminine: Demeter, Kore, Hecate, Isis, etc. Pluto, the god of the underworld, is really a secondary figure. The central figure is the great mother, the earth-goddess upon whom the whole fertility of the earth, the cattle and the human family depends.

With the advent of Christianity, the father deity, or logos-principle, superseded the *magna mater*, and lent an exclusively masculine character to Christian theology. But during the Middle Ages the essential content of the pagan mystery religions came up in the form of the cult of the Virgin, who took over from her pagan forerunners qualities of fertile motherhood.

Throughout the history of culture we can trace this resurgence of the essential content of an earlier cult emerging in the characteristic framework of the later form.

Alchemy presents a rather different problem. In one very real sense, alchemy is the chemistry of the Middle Ages: in another it is a concealed religion. The idea of the transmutation of base metals into noble ones arose probably among the Alexandrine Greeks in the early centuries of the Christian Era. In the writing of Zosimus and Synesius we can trace an obvious derivation from the Persian adepts. In Greece the idea of transmutation had a philosophical basis. This central philosophical core was of the utmost value to the developing science of Chemistry, for it focused and unified scientific effort which, without this centralizing principle, was always liable to spend itself on mere empirical acquaintance with a mass of disconnected technical processes.

Now it is boldly assumed by scientific thinkers that this energizing psychical core of the alchemical apple was concerned, at bottom, with the science of chemistry. Liebig asserted, for example, that

'Alchemy was never at any time anything different from Chemistry'. It is one of the most remarkable features of our successful extraverted culture that it blithely assumes everything which preceded it to be merely a preparatory step in its enlightened progress.

Let us disinfect our minds of this charming arrogance and look once again at the origins of alchemy to see if the expectations with which it started have been fulfilled by the science of chemistry. Numerous legends cluster around its origin. According to one tradition it was founded by the Egyptian god Hermes (Thoth): hence alchemy was called the hermetic art. Another legend asserts that the fallen angels taught the principles of alchemy to the women they married, their instruction being recorded in a book called Chema. A similar story appears in the Book of Enoch, and Tertullian has much to say about the wicked angels who revealed to men the knowledge of gold and silver, of lustrous stones and of the power of herbs, and who introduced the arts of astrology and magic upon the earth. Another legend, from Arabic sources, asserts that alchemy was revealed by God to Moses and Aaron.

Very early in the Greek tradition we find the philosophical theory of the *prima materia*, the elementary substance which was identical in all bodies, but which received its individual form by the adjunction of qualities expressed by the Aristotelian elements—earth, fire, air and water. Thus we find alchemy in its first inspired flight revealing the familiar quarternary symbolism of individuation. The legends of its origin from divine or infernal sources are tantamount to a clear statement that the central idea of alchemy came in the form of a revelation from the collective unconscious. The first projections of profound philosophical ideas, from the primordial unconscious into the temporal sphere of human existence, tend to bring about strange admixtures, which are so far beyond the limits of contemporary understanding that they are liable to be explained away as fantastic aberrations of the human mind.

A somewhat similar example occurred in Egypt in the religion of Aton. It arose like a queer exotic island in the main stream of Egyptian culture, revealed through the royal mediumship of Akhnahton (Amenhotep IV); but because of the conservative hostility and lack of understanding in the contemporary mind of Egypt, it subsided once again into the unconscious. Its essential content emerged again in the Christian revelation, and became the energizing mystical core of the succeeding wave of culture.

Alchemy, then, contained an admixture of opposing elements. It was the spirit, or germ, of a new religion in conflict with scientific materialism. But the spirit of the new religion was not so much a faith as a way or method whereby the supreme individual value could be transformed out of common human elements. The elixir, or philosophers' stone, by whose virtue the transmutation could take place, was a mystical substance, corresponding with that spiritual key to life which Christ called the Kingdom of Heaven. In every mystical religion the goal is also the means. Through the power of the Kingdom or elixir we can attain unto the Kingdom: or because of the love of God in man, man is able to love God.

But the essence of alchemy was concerned with the discovery of the way by which the divine work could be achieved. From this standpoint alchemy can be regarded as the Yoga-system of the West; inasmuch as all the various systems of Yoga are concerned primarily with the teaching and practice of a specific method of spiritual development rather than with precise forms of faith.

When we claim alchemy as the forerunner of the individuation process, the meaning and symbolism of which was discovered by Jung among the ignored contents of the unconscious, we must not overlook the tremendous difference which lies in the fact that the alchemists projected all this symbolism into matter, whereas we are in a position to appreciate it as a psychological process.

The alchemists inhabited a very different world from ours. Matter, though mysterious to us, was profoundly more mysterious to them. The primordial unconscious can be apprehended only by means of projection, and projection of the unconscious is possible only on a relatively unknown or mysterious object. So long as the field of heaven was unexplored and the nature of its denizens unknown, it presented an unrivalled field for the projection of primordial unconscious contents. Astrology resulted from that projection of inherited or instinctual wisdom.

In the same way the soul-image or anima of a man is liable to be projected upon a woman who is still sufficiently unformed or undifferentiated to be able to personify the primordial mystery of woman.

It is important to realize that these projections of the unconscious, which science finally succeeded in detaching from the objective field upon which they were projected, are not mere subjective contaminations which need to be scoured away. They are the very essence of our human reality, the factors upon which our fate hangs and which we absolutely need to know if we are to succeed in our individual experiment.

These are the things which have formed the central pillar of Chinese and Hindu philosophy. The *Yi King*, or Book of Changes, is an inexhaustible fountain of Chinese wisdom. It has been distilled through the centuries and the finest minds of Chinese culture have put into the Yi the inspirations that were generated while reflecting on the problem of individual fate. It is an unfathomable store of tortoise-wisdom, revealed from the unconscious, as is shown by the legend of its origin. For it is said that: 'the river Lo produced the writing. This writing was given on the back of a tortoise which came up out of the river Lo and showed it to the Great Yu, while he was engaged in his celebrated work of draining off the waters of the flood. To the sage it suggested the Great Plan, which was a treatise of Physics, Astrology, Divination, Morals, Politics and Religion, which served as the model for the government of the kingdom.'

What, then, has our extraverted science to say concerning this problem of fate? Which branch of science is detailed to handle this problem? Is it possible that it has been overlooked? What do the philosophers say about it? Originally, in early Greek thought, fate was personified in the *moira*, the allotted portion or lot to which both gods and men were subject. But to-day fate is an abstraction which nobody cares to discuss.

It is not hard to arrive at the intellectual conclusion that a man's individual fate comprises the sum of his unconscious determinants. Having reached this conclusion, we might then proceed to argue that, were it possible to extend and deepen our knowledge of these unconscious determinants, we might possibly begin to modify our fate. But these determining factors, upon which our very fate hangs, are those we have so busily excluded as superstitious admixtures disturbing the purity of our scientific vision.

The answer of Christendom to this whole problem is to believe in the redeeming power of Christ. To have faith is enough. To some the devout Christian would even be lacking in faith if he were to seek a way, a method, a body of real knowledge concerning the process of deliverance. But in India, whose chief product has always been religion, the period of faith is reserved for childhood. There are many different methods and many different schools; but they are all concerned with the one goal, namely, spiritual development, or the intensification of consciousness.

In the West, alchemy was the one outstanding attempt to discover a method of psychological metamorphosis; but because of the mediaeval ignorance concerning the nature of matter, the results of that early psychological research are hopelessly contaminated with seemingly irrelevant chemical admixtures.

The first intuitive sciences roamed over the whole field of human fate, the practitioner attempting, as it were, to find by which star in the heavens this individual could safely steer his course. With the arrival of alchemy, a definite body of teaching, concerned with the royal way, began to be built up. There is a world of difference between the primitive canoe or coracle which has to go with the wind, and the well-built ship with rudder, keel and sail, with which one can hold to a course in spite of contrary winds. With the development of civilization, the practical primitive standpoint which paid attention to dreams as plain intuitive statements, was lost; but with the advent of alchemy a relatively coherent attempt was made to use the primitive materials of the unconscious in the creation of a vessel worthy of the royal quest of individuation.

The primitive form invariably tends to disappear when a more differentiated function emerges. As an illustration of this principle I will mention an example from my own experience. When camping with Jung on the slopes of Mt. Elgon, a very old medicine man or *laibon* of the Masai people, in answer to an inquiry about dreams, told us that in former times he used always to dream when a murder was committed or cattle were stolen or people fell sick, the dream pointing to the cause or the culprit. 'But now', he said sadly, 'the District Commissioner sees to all that; it is his *showri* and my dreams are not needed any more.' Here the cultural form, which superseded the primitive, performs the same function to better purpose.

It is the proud boast of science that it serves knowledge for its own sake, quite apart from any possible effect its findings could have upon human life. This absolutely pure attitude of science is born of the aim to achieve strict detachment from all subjective considerations. Even psycho-analysis affects to pursue a sterilized scientific investigation, in which warm-blooded subjective factors are never permitted to show their heads. Actually, this inhuman detachment of science from the real problems of human life is an affectation of superiority which must be criticized; because as soon as man creates something which affects to be above and beyond human life and its problems, that thing soon begins to destroy our dearest values. Everything we make into a god, and place above man, is liable to become a Frankenstein's monster.

Let us come back, then, to our original truth, namely, that that which serves man and furthers his real interests is the true object of science.

To take a case in point, let us ask ourselves which is more germane to the real object of science: a vast collection of primitive belief, custom and ritual such, for example, as Frazer provides in his *Golden Bough*; or a profound attempt to understand and use such material such as Jung gives us in his *Psychology of the Unconscious*? Both, naturally, are necessary: for the psychologist cannot ask 'Why?' until the scientific collector has asked 'How?' But which of the two asks the question most pertinent to human interests and human reality—the extraverted collector or the introverted investigator?

Let us survey the so-called psychological field itself. Look at the literature of this science which, by definition, is the 'science of the nature, functions and phenomena of the human soul or mind'. Observe the questions asked of candidates who wish to qualify in psychological knowledge in our universities and academies. Go into a psychological laboratory and examine all the apparatus for testing the faculties and functions of the mind. Do you ever find one single allusion to the human soul, or to the problems of human fate? In other words, the one thing which is absolutely excluded from mechanistic or scientific psychology is the human psyche.

I am fully aware of the invaluable work done in the experimental field of the special senses, in mental testing, in the mechanical drainage of the neurotic systems by psycho-analysis, and in the extension of biology and physiology into the sphere of mental processes—all are valuable contributions to that outer ring of our civilized citadel. But we must realize that mechanically mediated information can throw no light upon that central darkness which the primitive sciences of dream-interpretation and astrology originally set out to penetrate.

Let us take an analogy from another fateful field. Among excessively extraverted cultures we are liable to find tragic marriage failures, due neither to bad will, vice, cruelty nor ignorance; but rather to an inability to attend to the essential things. Individual cases will inevitably occur to our minds; cases which, because of their shining extraverted façade, expect to pass for ideally happy marriages. In one case I have in mind the husband was successful, self-confident, talkative; the wife was quiet, introverted, shadowy, and almost obliterated by her overwhelmingly successful husband. As a partnership they presented an unbroken front and no one would have suspected that within the fortifications all was not well. For, because of the ever-expanding outer ring, there was no living centre at the heart. The husband had no intimate relation with his wife; he was too busy ever to spend any time with her: he gave no chance for talking or discussing problems together, and naturally there was no time for holidays, or common interests. Because of the absence of *rapport* the instinctual relation also fell into abeyance. So long as they were doing things together and keeping a bold face to the world they were able to conceal the hollow at the centre. But the soul of the marriage had really flown away.

I have used a poignant example to express my feeling about the real object of psychology. I can see and can evaluate the extraverted ring of solid achievement already built up by our Cinderella science, but I still must turn an anxious eye to the island in the centre where the marooned soul of man waits in unconsidered neglect. But already, thanks to the genius of C. G. Jung, this introverted island begins to yield its riches to those who, like Orpheus, cannot exist without a soul.

But is it a fact that our extraverted, objective habit of mind has created a psychology which excludes the psyche? For where, you may ask, is the psyche to be found, if not in authorized text-books on psychology? If neither introspection nor the intelligence test can reveal it, nor any experiment upon the mental faculties, nor those dubious allies, hypnosis and suggestion, where then can it be found? So long as the scientist is present with his marvellous apparatus, the soul hides herself. But if for a moment the scientist could forget about his results, or the scepticism of his learned colleagues, and would cast a longing glance over his shoulder, he might catch a glimpse of his soul as she waits expectantly on the island he fears to visit.

But how can a thing that is so elusive ever become the real object of psychology? The soul becomes elusive when the rationalistic pantechnicon appears. It will not be caught and held in a rigid frame, and it dances away from the precise formula. Yet the soul is objective in the true primitive sense, for is there not a dream-image thrown upon a screen for us to look at? And do not the denizens of the dream live and move and speak and act in a completely independent, objective way? Are they not entirely indifferent to, and therefore detached from, our subjective volition or control? Furthermore, a dream or a fantasy can be terribly real, in the sense that it may change the whole course and meaning of one's life.

We can see then, that we have found a function of the mind which spontaneously produces images upon the plane of phenomena; images which are informed with their own independent activity and take part in a drama, the source and outcome of which are outside our knowledge and control. In many dreams these living objects speak: sometimes in commanding, sometimes in appealing or persuasive tones.

The imagery of dreams must be regarded as objective in the fullest sense of the word, i.e. as something that is thrown before the mind. Once we can overleap our inherent extraverted habit of assuming that the world of objects is outside us, it is possible to regard the dream, in fact, as a truly objective process. Clearly we have to do with an inner world of objects as well as an outer; and this inner world is the realm of the primordial human soul, speaking to us in the primordial language of pictures.

What, in fact, does the dream say? Let us begin with Freud's theory of wish-fulfilment: the dream figures and personalities are, when all is said and done, personifications of the libido, and what is the libido but an organic stream of energy, desire, command or interest? When, therefore, vital energy which has been lying dormant in the unconscious, leaps in a manifest form upon the plains of sense, it is achieving a certain fulfilment. In this rather restricted sense Freud's original formulation can be regarded as the foundation stone of our science; but we must also confess that all human behaviour and the whole output of culture can just as well be included in the same formula. So nothing very definite has actually been said.

Jung was more cautious in his formulation. He did not attempt to make a key-formula for the dream, but he defined the soul, or anima, as the personification of the unconscious, and the function of the soul as the function of relation to the contents of the collective unconscious. This formulation tells us more, and at the same time is more conservative than that of Freud.

Jung, according to my idea, is the true psychological empiricist, because he listens all the time to what the dream is saying, and is correspondingly economical with theory. He also teaches his pupils to listen and not to assume.

Everyone tends to be frightened when he begins to listen seriously to his dreams. He fears he will not be able to understand and so forgets to listen. It is much the same when one is living in a foreign country; one can begin to hear what people are saying only when one allows oneself to suppose that it is possible to understand what is actually being said.

Fearing he may not understand, a novice begins to invent clever interpretations and to think that at last he has plumbed the mystery of the soul. Others are too frightened to think at all about their dreams. At the back of this fear lies the presupposition that there must be some absolutely authentic interpretation and that, therefore, whatever one says or thinks will be wrong. In other cases it is simply fear of the irrational, primitive element which produces an intellectual eclipse.

It is a simple truth that anyone who will patiently learn to understand the primordial picture language of the dream, and will then be humanly and humbly receptive to what the dream is saying, can discover the key to his own soul. But although the soul is relative to this actual person, with all his individual morbidities and particularities, it is none the less *the* human soul: the soul with its historical and prehistorical continuity, its future extension, its acquired wisdom, and its instinctual interplay with the forces of nature. It is both the infinitely great and the infinitely small; it is both the personal and the impersonal, the primordial and the cultural, the source of man's weakness, as well as the generator of his greatest power.

In conclusion let me recount a dream which came to me just before I began to reflect upon this paper:

I was standing on a cliff at the edge of the sea, with a companion. I saw a porpoise out in the bay—or was it perhaps a whale?

The whale came nearer, moving deliberately, in great curves, like a porpoise. Then it was beneath us, stretched at full length in the white foam of the breakers, as they came rolling in to a little cove on our right.

Then it was on the beach basking in the sun. Now it was vast, and covered with hairs, and, in a close-up of a piece of the skin, I observed numbers of flies. I wondered if any of the flies (or fleas) would come on to us. It was a warm sunny day, and the feeling of the dream was exhilarating.

I must explain that when I first began to ponder on how to present the so-called unconscious as the object of psychology, the picture which first occurred to my waking mind was a peaceful lagoon of clear water, full of its familiar denizens. Into this tranquil scene a whale or a shark suddenly irrupted, scattering the rightful inhabitants in all directions.

The lagoon would, of course, be the personal unconscious, while the sea beyond would be the impersonal, primordial unconscious; and a primordial content or image may sometimes break through from the impersonal into the personal unconscious. Now, this representation came to me in much the same way as the dream came, but the dream was very much more vivid and impressive than the waking image.

I want to mention this instance because of the hubristic modern illusion (which is remarkably contagious) that consciousness makes thoughts and even determines dreams. The rational egoist would immediately assume, therefore, that he invented the idea of the whale breaking through into the lagoon and that the dream-mind chose to reiterate the same idea—as though dreams were mere echoes of consciousness.

This rationalization is, of course, simply an umbrella put up to preserve the mind against the impact of something which might prove overwhelming. Let us make a few criticisms.

In the dream the scene is not a lagoon, but a bay of the open sea. I am at once reminded of an occasion when my wife and I were in a small boat off the west coast of Scotland and a whale came up quite near us, behaving in much the same fashion as the whale in my dream. In my waking picture I imagined great commotion and even storm following the irruption of the whale. In the dream there is no disturbance at all; the whale seems to be enjoying himself, claiming his place in the sun like anyone else. Finally, the dream focuses upon the hairs and upon the flies or fleas which inhabit the whale's skin. This feature is an innovation of the dream which a rationalist might fail to observe.

What, then, is the significance of this improvisation? First, I must give an association which is simple and clear. I have often had the fantasy of the earth as a vast animal: the forests and vegetation are its hair, and all men and animals are parasites enjoying the hospitality of the indifferent pachyderm. You will have observed the ambivalency in my doubt whether they are, in fact, flies or fleas. Fleas, being bloodsuckers, have a worse reputation than flies, though both are unpleasant.

To my mind the most indicative thing is the presence of the two planes or levels in the structure of the dream. There is, for instance, the open sea and the little cave beside us; there is the cliff, whence one gets a broadly extended view, and the beach where one can only see what is just in front of one. There is the vast animal and the close-up of hair and fly. All the way through we get a repetition of the general and the particular as two aspects of one and the same scene, not as two arbitrarily divided worlds. At one moment I am viewing the whale, at another a particular fly sitting on a particular hair. I don't see them both at one and the same time, but I can accommodate my vision and my mind to the two aspects without any feeling of contradiction.

Here is a direct experience of the unconscious which means something in the meaning and flow of my life. But without even touching on that inner significance, the dream provides, at the psychological moment, a perfect example of the relation between the archetypal forces of the collective unconscious and the personal levels of the mind.

If the whale comes into the orbit of my life, I can do nothing about it except participate in the exhilaration, or the cataclysm, caused by his emergence. But my knowledge that the mighty one is moving does help me to adjust my mind to the events that are taking place. For if I were to attempt to explain all the disturbances and affliction and emotions which come upon me in terms of flea- or fly-determinants, omitting the whale from my universe altogether, as your rationalist will always tend to do, I should probably go insane. For a world in which there are no powers greater or more powerful than the ego is, in fact, a crazy world. But one would not wish to be visited by the whale in one's private and personal domain, nor to be taken by him down into the depths, as Moby Dick took his insane pursuer. Either would spell insanity.

I have attempted to show that the real object of psychology is concerned with the same quest which started human science on its long journey: in other words, with the vital problems of the human soul. Natural science has, so far, entirely omitted to concern itself with those problems, committed as it is to a quantitative and mechanistic conception of the universe. The unconscious primordial mind, in which are to be found all those living contents of the soul which have not been lived out, is liable to erupt like a volcano as soon as the repressive civilized crust wears thin. Just as in the personal unconscious we find the ghosts of tendencies or periods which were not lived out at their proper time, so in the general unconscious we must suppose cultural ghosts to lie dormant, waiting for the moment when they can flow once again into the stream of events.

Unless we are completely blinded by the dictatorship of the intellect, it is these living contents of the unconscious which constitute the real object of psychology. But apart from their profound significance for our lives, the contents of the unconscious also achieve projection upon the field of consciousness in a truly objective fashion. They are spontaneous, unique, and independent of subjective interference; they are the native phenomena of the psychic field and, as such, are the true objects of psychology.

I have tried to put before you the general problem of the unconscious, in so far as this hinges upon the extraverted one-sidedness of contemporary consciousness.

To those of us whose *métier* it is to try to understand the activities of the unconscious in the lives of our patients, it is refreshing to open our sails to a wide impersonal breeze. It is my belief that not only the psychology of the future, but that history, philosophy, politics, morals, education and religion, besides the humanistic branches of natural science, will have to take the unconscious seriously into account as an objective field of phenomena. But so far as our personal lives are concerned, it is the activity of the unconscious as the inexhaustible womb of possibilities which matters most. No theoretical description of the soul could have real meaning for us unless we have had in our lives the actual experience of the soul's intervention, either in the form of a vision, a command, a voice in the heart, a dream, a revelation or a mystical exaltation.

A problem of immense philosophical implication faces those of us who are in a position to watch both the amazing appropriateness of the soul's activity and the way in which the truth, thrown upon the dream-screen, seems to be adjusted to the understanding of the conscious personality. What kind of intelligence is it that intervenes in this way in our conscious life? And from what kind of premisses or standpoint are dreams produced?

One of the symbols of the unconscious is the Grail, the inexhaustible cruse, the vessel of abundance. Such questions as those we have just asked rise above the inexhaustible vessel like fragrant steam from a noble brew.

A Demonstration of Analytical Practice[1]

Myself when young did eagerly frequent
Doctor and Saint, and heard great Argument
About it and about: but evermore,
Came out by the same Door where in I went.
OMAR KHAYYAM

This was also my experience until one evening, many years ago, I went to call upon Dr. Jung in his home by the edge of the lake of Zürich. He did not try to teach, to illuminate, or to impress. In fact he made no effort of any kind. But what he said had for me the character of a rare natural experience, as though for a moment I had stood on the rim of the known world and looked over the edge into the source from which all living forms had sprung. I entered a door that seemed like many similar doors from which I had emerged unscathed. But this one was the last; I could not leave it. I had been gripped by a view which went to the roots of mental life, and this experience changed the course of my life.

The question is often asked: 'Why cannot you tell us quite simply what analysis really is? There is so much discussion and argument between this school and that; but no one will tell us what analysis means in terms of actual experience.' I shall do my best to answer this question here; but first I must ask: 'Are you a *bona fide* traveller? Or do you seek this information in order to gain a certain respite from the real task of coming to terms with yourself?' This question is rather like a customs' official who asks to see your passport before letting you cross the frontier. All the same, it is necessary; for it is only possible to explain the purpose and meaning of the analytical experience to someone with the real need to understand. An academic curiosity alone will never give you the key to the understanding of Jung's ideas.

What, then, are the kinds of difficulties or symptoms which force a man to realize that the analytical experience could be relevant to his life? I will give a few examples.

The first is a doctor who is worried because his practice is declining.

[1] Paper read at a public meeting of the Analytical Psychology Club at Friends' House, London, N.W.1, on 11 June 1937.

He knows that his professional knowledge is well grounded. He has tried to keep in touch with the important advances in medical science. The practice was a good one, and he can see no reason why it should fall off. What he does not worry about is the fact that he has lost affection for his wife, that he is deeply involved with another woman, and that he is keeping this other relationship in a watertight compartment, as though it concerned nobody but himself.

The second case is a woman who finds that her work, in the editorial department of a journal, has become intensely distasteful. The colleagues with whom she is thrown in daily contact irritate her beyond bearing. She dislikes any contact with her own family. But worst of all, she is borne down by an icy depression which has not only closed every avenue of outward expression, but seems to freeze the very springs of feeling and vitality.

The third is a man of fifty who would like to marry, but cannot find the right woman. He has no difficulty at all in making casual erotic encounters; in fact this has been his chief hobby. But none of the women he frequents can he conceive as a possible partner for life.

The fourth is a professional woman of forty-two who is plagued by migraine. The attacks are becoming more frequent and all the drugs that she has been accustomed to take to relieve the pain have lost their efficacy. Thus she never knows from one day to the next whether she will be able to keep her engagements or be incapacitated. She is also distressed, because the increasing demands of her profession seem to leave her neither time nor energy for the needs of her personal life.

The fifth is a young woman of twenty-two who has deliberately encouraged an intimacy with a fellow student of her own age in order to gain a certain independence from a too solicitous mother. Now this man wants to marry her and she suddenly realizes that she has no real interest in him. She even finds that his claim upon her has become more tiresome than that of the mother.

The sixth is the case of a clergyman who married when very young 'in order to save himself from temptation', and now he has fallen deeply in love with a married woman of his congregation. Yet he had won his name as a preacher by his passionate defence of the sanctity of marriage and his stern denunciation of adultery.

There is, of course, no end to the difficulties which can bring a man or woman to the fateful question: 'What then is the meaning of it all? Why has my life gone wrong?' It may be an artist who finds he can never bring off the work he longs to create. Or it may be a civil servant with great natural gifts, who ruins every opportunity by assuming hostile feelings and motives in everyone with whom he has personal dealings. It may be an impediment in thought, or in speech; a difficulty in attention, so that concentration on the work in hand becomes impossible; or a bitter sense of frustration, due to a sense that, always, when the desired object is about to be grasped, fate intervenes and snatches it away. It may be pains of the body, or distress of the mind; it may be fear of death, of insanity, or of suicide, or it may be the longing to find something real and satisfying in life. But whatever the nature of the difficulty, at bottom there lurks the doubt, the fatal undermining doubt, in the validity of the self.

Neurosis is a general problem of rational civilized man, and we do not understand it aright if we think of it only in relation to the pathological case. It is not necessary to assume that everyone with a problem needs anaylsis, though I believe that everyone can become more competent in the art of living by a knowledgeable acquaintance with his own psychology. When a man has this, we say he has common sense. The experience which analysis involves is specifically for those who have come to the end of their tether. A man tries this way and that, but always he encounters the same tormenting doubt or difficulty, and the feeling that some intangible obstacle is crippling his life. If the source of the difficulty lay within the grasp of consciousness he could put his hand upon it, and find a rational solution.

It was this realization that prompted the pioneers of modern psychology to explore the subterranean part of the mind, which they then called the unconscious. We know what is meant by consciousness, though we cannot define it. It is simply the illuminated stage or field in which certain perceptions, ideas, feelings, and any other kind of mental content, are presented to the ego. This naturally changes from moment to moment as the stream of mental life flows within the orbit of attention; therefore what is conscious one moment may be unconscious the next.

The unconscious is also a relative condition. But when we use it in psychological description we mean the sum of all those root processes and instinctual mechanisms from which the contents of consciousness arise, as well as the deep affective determinants of our being which never become conscious at all. The conscious function is on the whole rational, civilized, and highly centralized. We associate will, purpose, attention, ethical standards, moral judgments and a host of other integrative and ideal qualities, with consciousness. The unconscious, on the other hand, is on the whole irrational, dynamic, more loosely organized and more primitive in its mode of functioning. But the two qualities which are especially characteristic of unconscious activity are (1) that it tends to play a compensatory and complementary role in relation to consciousness, and (2) that its activity is involuntary, independent and purposive in and for itself. This means that, in so far as any part or aspect of my personality is unconscious, it is beyond the control of my conscious will. But just as soon as I have been able to extend my consciousness to include the part that was hitherto unconscious, I can assimilate it, and therewith bring it into relation with the needs and claims of other functions.

Now suppose I find some intangible obstacle hindering me, and I cannot discover what it is by conscious introspection. What do I do next? I turn my attention inwards and I begin to watch for some movement of the unconscious, very much as a salmon-fisher watches for the fish to run. I shall probably get a dream; or perhaps a flight of rather arresting images will appear spontaneously in my mind. Now I take this dream, or fantasy, and I begin to reflect about it. Probably some neighbouring or associated images will begin to insinuate themselves. I take note of these too. Then I begin to ask certain questions. Why am I behaving in this fashion in the dream? Why is the house I dreamed of unfinished? Why is that figure that comes against me so huge? Why does the woman seem to have a sinister look in her eye? Why did I suddenly feel relieved when I awoke from the dream?

Thinking is the intelligible offspring of the relevant question; but it also relies upon one's capacity to stay with the question until it has yielded an answer. I have always been inclined to regard my dreams and to think about them. But there are many people who prefer not to think too closely about their dreams. These people will often paint or draw their fantasies, or perhaps model them in clay. By this means they feel they get nearer to the pith and meaning of the unconscious than by standing back from the experience in order to interpret its meaning intellectually. It is as though some people understand best with their hearts, while others have to explain everything with their heads. Perhaps we can best understand the primordial, natural mind when we learn to think with the heart and to feel with the head.

This, then, is what analysis means. Speaking as broadly as possible, so as to include every method that attempts to deal radically with the unconscious, analysis is the work of coming to terms with the unconscious. For when you acknowledge that the root of your problem is in the unconscious, and you begin to study your dreams with the idea of trying to find out how the problem looks from below, you therewith acknowledge the fact that the standpoint of the natural instinctual mind is different from that of your rational consciousness. When I try to understand what the dream is actually saying, I am also approximating my consciousness to the primordial human mind which speaks in symbols, instead of with concepts. This is the attitude of the antique sciences, as it is also that of uncivilized mankind in general. The primitive, for instance, conceives the *mana* or doctor-dream as the voice of the ancestor spirit talking. In the records and legends of antiquity we constantly find the belief that important or prophetic dreams are communicated by the gods. The idea of paying attention to the unconscious in a quite particular way is, in fact, almost as old as husbandry and, moreover, has much the same end in view, namely, that of cultivating the increase of nature.

The intuitive science of divination and dream-interpretation is found in the oldest cultural traditions. Hence, the handling of dreams is a method that is immediately acceptable to any mind that is not shut and bolted by rational prejudice. Yet it is essential that we do not conceive this work as a purely intellectual adjustment. To understand something we have to stand under it, in other words, to participate in the event. Therefore, in order to understand the unconscious we must first experience it. How, you may ask, can we experience something that is unconscious to us? Well, a dream is first and foremost an experience. The dreamer finds himself in a perfectly unexpected situation. He encounters persons of every description; animals talk to him. Sometimes trees and birds say surprising things to one in a dream. All these denizens of the dream live and move and have their being, are informed with their own independent energy, and frequently seek their ends in a way that has no regard at all either for the dreamer's will or convenience. If you regard these events as your experience, then clearly it behoves you to try to understand what it is you have experienced; and if it was not your experience, then whose was it?

Let me give you an example of the way in which a man whose mind was profoundly prejudiced against any dealing with the unconscious was, none the less, forced to experience it. The subject is a man of forty-eight, a professor of a specialized branch of science, in which he has gained considerable distinction. He is withdrawn and somewhat aloof in his personal dealings, but talks with ease on his special subject. In replying to personal questions he is cautious, weighing his words with great deliberation. But as soon as he enters the non-personal atmosphere of scientific or philosophic ideas he seems to step out with an easy natural stride. In general his attitude to the world of external objects is reserved and defensive, whereas a corresponding freedom marks his relation to the world of ideas. You will be able to recognize in this brief sketch the features of the introverted intellectual type.

On the staff of the institute of which he is head, he has a colleague who, for no reason he can name, irritates him beyond endurance. This colleague is a rather expansive, boisterous individual, whose scientific attainments are, in the professor's eyes, quite negligible. He seems to be more interested in the students and their problems, in the social life of the college, and in his own rather frequent love-affairs, than in the pursuit of knowledge, or in his own academic career. The professor cannot regard this colleague as a rival in the path of his ambition, and he surely does not envy him his love affairs, or his easy camaraderie with the students. Yet the man has so got on his nerves that he can hardly pass him in the passage without feelings of physical nausea. He would like to avoid all contact with his *bête noire*, but evil chance seems to be always throwing him across the professor's path. But what is far worse, the sudden bouts of irritation are no longer directed only towards the extraverted colleague. The behaviour of the students who attend his lectures can rouse in him sudden and uncontrollable fits of anger. His colleagues begin to look at him askance, and even his power of concentration in the privacy of his own study is becoming affected. It should be mentioned that the patient is a very lonely man. His wife died five years ago and he has no intimate friends to whom he can turn. Somehow he has lost touch with the friends of his youth, and none of his colleagues are on intimate terms with him.

From this description it will be quite clear to everyone what is the matter with the patient. But the patient himself was quite convinced that, if it had not been for the insufferable propinquity of his *bête noire*, he could have gone peacefully on his road. But when I ask him to explain why his colleague could have such an effect upon him, he can find no adequate reason. Actually he has nothing against the man, except that his mere presence infuriates him.

I have selected a case where the one-sidedness of personality is perfectly obvious. It must be equally obvious to you that the blind or shadow side of the patient's personality, i.e. the part that is excluded from life, must be correspondingly maimed and undeveloped. We know, but the patient does not, that the more he builds up on the intellectual side, the more will he be starved and dwarfed in his ordinary human need for relationship. But even if he becomes aware of this fact he cannot just go out and make or find relationship. Because the whole function of emotional expression is inferior, he cannot trust himself in this realm. He is, moreover, quite convinced that no woman could ever be interested in him. Therefore, all our good common-sense advice to him about the possibility of marrying again would fall upon deaf, not to say resistant, ears.

Here, then, is a man who has patiently and of set purpose followed and reached the goal of his ambition. But instead of feeling satisfied and victorious, he finds himself oppressed by a sense of failure, and the idea of suicide already hovers quite near. He has come to the end of his rope.

For a man whose intellect has come to be his greatest enemy, it is worse than useless to rely upon a scientific explanation of his experience. What his soul needs is the spiritual vitamins which can be gained only by immediate emotional participation in a vital experience. His emotional starvation is the primary factor and you cannot cure that by feeding the intellect. You may object that it was just because of his intense emotional disturbance that he realized he was sick. Why then must he remain on that level?

This question brings us to the very threshold of our main problem, namely, the essential character of the analytical experience. It cannot be denied, for example, that the apparition of snakes and frogs and other loathly shapes is a terribly real experience to the patient with delirium tremens. And, inasmuch as the forms that affect the man with delirium are imponderable, intangible psychic images, delirium must be counted as a spiritual experience. Yet delirium tremens has never been regarded as a state of grace. What then is to be our criterion of judgment in respect to psychic experience? It is useless to bring the overworked concept of normality into this realm: because the normal man is precisely the one who asserts with pride that he is not troubled with such things.

I think the best way to answer our question is to tell you one of the first dreams brought by the patient after he had begun the analytical talks. He dreamed he was in a garden which he felt belonged to him, though it was unfamiliar. He noticed that the borders were neglected and that a lot of dead boughs and brambles were choking the fruit trees in the orchard. He was consulting with his gardener (who closely resembled the objectionable extraverted colleague) about clearing a piece of ground, with the idea of sowing vegetables, particularly beetroot and tomatoes. Then he was in the house, and there were workmen about. He had the idea that there was scaffolding being erected, and that a new wing was to be added to the house. The doctor called to see him. Apparently the dreamer had been very ill, for there was an attractive, rather oriental-looking nurse in attendance. The doctor came and counted his pulse, looked at him straight in the eyes and told him he was going to cure him. The doctor was quite clearly the same extraverted colleague. When the doctor had gone, the nurse told the dreamer that the doctor had paid £5,000 into his account at the bank, as a 'nest-egg'.

The point in this dream which immediately holds our interest is the astonishing transformation which the extraverted colleague has undergone in the dreamer's mind. Can we regard this merely as an attempt on the part of the dreaming mind to compensate the sinister impression of consciousness? Or is there a deep psychological purpose behind it? Why, for instance, if the dream is merely compensating the disparaging conscious attitude, does the colleague appear as the gardener? Taking this statement objectively, it means nothing at all—the colleague has no particular interest in gardening nor is he in any sense of the word a doctor. But as an inner experience the dream is immediately relevant. It is full of associations which the patient recognizes with almost boyish eagerness. He had always wanted to have a house in the country where he could grow the things he used to love in the home of his boyhood. Of these, plums, tomatoes and beetroots crowded for first place. He remembered he was on especially good terms with the gardener. They even went poaching together occasionally. He picked up odds and ends of nature-lore from this man, learned how to handle snakes, and how to make a reed pipe with the skin of birch-bark. They had a kind of tacit understanding between them which both respected.

Then suddenly his mother died. They left the beautiful home and went to live in the city. Sometimes he had to stay at his school during the holidays, because his father had often to go abroad on business. Thus, with the fatalism of youth, he assumed that paradise was finished, and all that remained for him was work, ambition, success.

The oriental-looking nurse reminded him of a beautiful Indian girl student who had once attended his lectures, and with whom he had felt the same kind of tacit understanding as he had had as a boy with his friend the gardener; although actually he had hardly even spoken to her.

The episode with the doctor was associated with myself, and with the fact that he had recently been worrying about his health. From time to time he had caught himself feeling his own pulse. He said that all virtue had gone out of him: no energy, no purpose, no meaning in life.

With these associations in mind we must conclude, when the doctor looks him straight in the eyes and tells him he can cure him, that either the dream is making a categorical prognosis which must be accepted as truth, or it is a singularly cruel and pointless mockery.

The whole crux of the dream-experience rests, of course, upon the correct interpretation of the dream gardener and doctor. If we make the mistake of identifying these figures with the actual colleague whom he abhors, the result will be fatal. Such mistakes are irretrievable, because instead of curing the patient's blindness, they intensify it. Now is the time to show him that the reason his colleague got under his skin was because, of all the people in his academic milieu, this particular individual symbolized the neglected other half of his personality. We call this latent, unaccepted aspect of the personality the *shadow*, because it is the part that is repressed and kept in the shade by the one-sided development of the conscious attitude.

As we see in the present case, it is by no means always the least valuable part that is excluded from life. That natural, rather primitive boy, who went poaching with the gardener, is, of course, the nucleus of this shadow personality. As a matter of fact, the boy kept his secret paradise as much as possible from the knowledge of his parents. The paradisiac character clung to those adventurous evenings, just because the renegade, primordial man ran invisibly beside them. At any moment they might have to hide like a hunted fox. Yet the patient was nearer the counsels of nature, and nearer to the secret heart of life itself in those dark woods with his loyal poaching friend, than in the safeguarded, straight-ruled and properly ordered precincts of his accepted personality.

These contradictory aspects of himself were never reconciled, and eventually the free primitive side became wholly repressed, while the frustrated natural instincts were forced into servitude by his tyrannical ambition.

At this point in the interpretation the patient must be informed of the fundamental principle of self-realization, namely, that every part or aspect of oneself that is unconscious will be found projected outwards upon an object. What he has to recover then, from the extraverted colleague, is the projection of his shadow-side. This is essentially a work of salvage. When the shadow is projected, it means that his frustrated, unlived desires, which have remained caged and impotent, observe the uninhibited colleague with envious resentment. But when he realizes the projection, and accepts the shadow as an indispensable, though neglected, part of his own being, he recovers his birthright. Thus he finds himself in the neglected garden which, with the help of the friendly shadow-figure, he can make fruitful again and at the same time he finds his soul, who appears to him under the guise of the Indian girl with whom he once shared the feeling of primordial recognition. The potential value of this redemptive insight is symbolized as a round sum of money. The dream was worth far more to him than £5,000 because, without any question, it promised him the opportunity of a completed life. The dream describes the money specifically as a 'nest-egg', which implies that it is only intended as the nucleus for a fund of an indefinite amount, in other words, an incalculable pyschic potentiality.

An interesting sequel to this dream must be told. The patient discovered, to his amazement, that he began to seek out the company of the once abhorred colleague. He even caught himself imitating him, and eventually he asked him to be his sole companion on a walking tour.

I have selected this case as an example of the analytical experience because, for one reason, everyone suffers to some extent from the same civilized one-sidedness. But also because it demonstrates perfectly the kind of experience which serves the goal of individuation. The kind of emotional experience which disrupts and undermines one's peace of mind is usually the offspring of projection. In the case we are considering, it was a symptom of frustration, due to the fact that the professor had renounced an essential part of his personality which should, in any case, be lived.

His emotions tormented him because they were really symptoms of his own frustrated instincts. You may say they had to be renounced, since a professor of forty-eight cannot go back to his boyhood and start poaching again. This was, in fact, the very objection the patient himself raised to the idea of accepting his shadow-side. The dream answers this objection by representing the accomplice of his boyhood's escapades, not as the poacher, but as the gardener. The same instinctive cunning which knew how to tickle a trout or snare a rabbit, also made him an excellent gardener.

The figure that is selected to represent the shadow is always ambiguous; for if the shadow-side were without blemish it would not have been repressed. But the dream makes no reference to the anti-social aspect of the shadow. Respectability and the whole collective façade of the patient's life plays no part in the dream. Its sole concern is the cultivation of the neglected garden, with an especial eye on those fondly relished delights (plums, tomatoes and beetroot) which symbolize the vitamins of the soul. The idea of adding a new wing to the house and of being cured of his sickness is the logical consequence of this new attitude of acceptance. The house is the mind, the place in which one lives. Therefore when you expand the conception of yourself to include an aspect that has been hitherto repressed, it is like building a new wing to your house. But when you create a new and more truthful view of yourself, you also create a new view of the world. You have, in a word, a more comprehensive standpoint. Hence your psychological house also represents your individual standpoint; your confession or statement of faith. Therefore people with a very restricted knowledge of themselves can only experience a small fraction of reality. To accept oneself as a variegated totality of general human elements, and to exclude nothing that is real and effective, means to be whole. To become whole is to be healed. Hence, the shadow-doctor is speaking the naked truth when he categorically asserts that he can cure the patient.

I wish I had the power to tell you what the appearance of the anima or soul-image (i.e. oriental-looking nurse in the dream) can mean to a man who has reached the end of his tether. It is a significant fact, which has been verified times without number, that the figure of the anima as a rather mysterious, desirable woman tends to appear just at this juncture. That is to say, when a man can go no further along the path of the heroic superior function and, therefore, has to turn back and come to terms with his own shadow. Usually the anima and the shadow appear together in the same dream, as in the present instance.

We use the term superior function to denote the one that you live by, the one that is adapted to the collective task and expectation, the effective one that everybody can see and respect. This hero-function in the present case is, of course, the intellect. You will remember how the shadow-effect had finally succeeded in laming the patient's intellect, so that he could no longer shepherd his thoughts. This is analogous to the betrayal of the hero in the hero-myth. Siegfried was slain from behind by Hagen, whose spear found the vulnerable spot in the back which had been covered by a maple-leaf when the hero bathed himself in the blood of the dragon. The heel of Achilles was the vulnerable place which the snake discovered, to the hero's undoing. In his passionate search for the superman Nietzsche's Zarathustra finds the Ugliest Man right in his path.

The killing of the hero by the shadow represents the preparation of the basic attitude for the problems of the second part of life. It means the sacrifice of the absolute supremacy of the dictator function of the mind, in order that the claims of the repressed functions can be seriously taken up. For no integration of the whole is possible so long as any one function plays the role of absolute ruler.

The present situation of the world provides an excellent example of this truth. It is not the existence of several great powers, all demanding the right to expand, which imperils the peace of the world. The whole future of civilization depends on one single eventuality: namely, whether the conception of the sovereign state is to be absolute or relative. If certain nations cling to the heroic absolute, and refuse in the last resort to submit their national claims to a supra-national tribunal, then it means the collapse of civilization. But if the approach of suicide quickens a response that can shake the civilized world to its foundations, it is possible that the idea of a supra-national symbol of authority, whom all must obey, will bind the nations together, not from choice, but from necessity.

This, as you see, is the critical point in the life of the individual, just as it is in the life of a nation. It actually corresponds to the birth of the soul. A dictator, or an absolute function, is inevitably vulnerable, because his power is established by repressing every other element which could challenge his supremacy. Hence the absolute ruler is always haunted by his own shadow. The attempt to extirpate this haunting fear involves the finding of a scapegoat, because no dictator is allowed to believe that the shadow exists in himself.

It is self-evident that this autocracy of the conscious attitude must lead to an ever-increasing tension which either culminates in a suicidal explosion or brings the individual, or the nation, to his senses. When I spoke of this moment as the birth of the soul, I meant quite simply the advent of realization. As a psychic factor we regard the soul as the symbolical vehicle of purpose, not the plans and schemes of conscious ambition, but the inherent life-purpose which expresses the total purposive momentum of vital-energy in an individual psychology. If a man is completely blind to the deep inherent purpose of his life, the soul remains as a mere unconscious driving force which may eventually overwhelm conscious volition. Thus it frequently forces a man into a catastrophe, where he is either destroyed beyond remedy, or through which he is at last able to realize that the deeper purpose of his life was not the attaining of success, or fame, or wealth, or any other collective goal, but rather in the fulfilment of his individual being. With this realization the soul is transformed from an unconscious, autonomous driving force into a conscious relationship to the inner purpose of life.

The birth of the soul coincides, then, with the genuine attempt to come to terms with the roots of one's being in the unconscious. This transformation of the soul from a compulsive natural force into a ministering function, is beautifully illustrated in the figure of Kundry in Wagner's *Parsifal*. In the beginning of the drama she appears as a witch, an enchantress, an elemental force of nature. She can be released from her daemonic state only by the knight who can resist her enchantment. Parsifal believes in himself and his own purpose, which is to recover the Holy Spear from the evil magician, Klingsor. Kundry, being essentially feminine, submits to the power of a conscious purpose which all her arts of seduction fail to deflect. Thus she is redeemed from her doom and becomes a ministering function.

You will observe how beautifully the anima figure in our patient's dream corresponds with the redeemed Kundry. Until now she has been a blind, unconscious *dynamis*, driving the subject inflexibly along the road of his ambition. By thus increasing the momentum of his repressive ambition, the breakdown is assured which will lead either to suicide or to realization.

Breakdown is inevitable, because the patient has reached and passed the zenith of his sun's course. The vital curve ascends during the first half of a man's life. This corresponds to the main biological activities, in which career, marriage, family responsibilities and collective claims of all kinds have to be satisfied. But when the zenith of the curve is passed, at about forty-five, the descent begins and a certain diminution of the sphere of external activity must be faced.

The interests of the first half of life are expressive of the animal nature, whereas the purpose of the second half corresponds more with the character of the tree. It is concerned with realizing the meaning of life, with integration, and with spiritual, rather than biological, productivity. In the first half of life a man tends to identify himself with his collectively adapted personality. He wants to be in the swim, in the running, to be publicly acknowledged as somebody. He wants to press on, to get to the front of the stage, to achieve something valid in the eyes of men. Thus he also gets infected by the restlessness, the desirousness, the unsatisfied gnawing hunger of the vast collective swarm.

Many men become neurotic at the change of life. They gradually become aware that they are different. Interest fades away from the well-known paths. Perhaps they begin to see themselves as mere items of the human locust-swarm which devours the beauty of nature. They prefer to go off by themselves and ruminate. They even find that old and trusted friends are apt to get on their nerves. Through fear of isolation they may cling all the more tenaciously to their habitual loyalties and interests. But beneath the joviality there is the chill of death.

In order to cross this difficult watershed without loss of soul, it is absolutely vital that a man allow a new conception of himself to develop. The recession of interest away from the goals of the first part of life is like the sap of a tree returning to the roots. To come to terms with one's roots, to reach downwards to the source and origin of one's being in the unconscious, is an essential part of the programme of the second half of life. The illusion of progress which controls the vast movements of civilized mankind urges a man to climb, to strive, to reach ever forwards on the millennial switch-back. But if he is straining to climb onwards and upwards, how can he at the same time go downwards and make peace with his primordial, original nature? Accordingly, the conception of the second half of life is not framed in terms of movement, direction, progress; but rather in terms of growth.

The tree can extend its roots deep into the dark recesses of the earth, and at the same time spread its leaves indefinitely into the light-world above. Thus the individual symbol of the tree, which is the natural expression of man's spiritual development, solves the problem which the swarm of locusts can never even comprehend.

Voltaire's maxim, 'il faut cultiver notre jardin', is, therefore, entirely appropriate to the actual situation of the patient. The return to the garden, the renewed relish in the sun-warmed fruits of the earth, the resurrection of the cunning, friendly gardener, are not a mere regression into second childhood, but rather the return of the prodigal to his father's house, where the fulfilment of his life can be achieved.

But here again the whole issue rests upon the way the dream is interpreted. To a man who is still in the blind, larval state, the very idea of taking a dream symbolically seems like the mere renunciation of desire. But for the man who has passed the zenith, and therefore has a genuine spiritual need, a symbol can become the most vital expression of his deepest longing. So that the further course of his life is guided, nourished and fulfilled by living out the meaning of the symbols which arise spontaneously out of his own depths.

I hope in this very brief demonstration of the inner meaning of the analytical experience that I have been able to clear away some of the fog that gathers in the mind as soon as the word psychology is breathed. I gave myself an almost impossible task, because to condense the problem of a complex individual life into the framework of a practical demonstration calls for a simplicity of thought that I know I do not possess. I can only trust that it has been possible to read between the lines, and to glean some inkling of that vision of the deeps of the human soul which arrested me in my first talk with Dr. Jung on a summer evening by the lake of Zürich, and which everyone who has had the privilege of learning from him cannot choose but serve.

D

Analytical Psychology and the English Mind[1]

I

To the Englishman there seems to be no particular difficulty in knowing his own mind. And yet this is something he very rarely achieves; not because he is inordinately given to psychological masquerade, but rather on account of the persuasive extraverted mental habit of representing reality in terms of self-evident goals instead of inquiring into motives.

Although it can scarcely be argued that the English people are peculiar in possessing an undisputably extraverted psychology, yet no discussion of the English mind and character could profitably omit this fundamental consideration. The goal which the Englishman erects and the path that he follows, have for him the character of self-evident validity, not because they are the product of profound reflection, but because they emerge as the obvious, practical, commonsense things to be done. When called upon to provide a philosophy to explain his actions, he naturally falls back upon an idealistic presentation of general human motives which, to his surprise and indignation, is all too frequently derided by his more discerning critics.[2] The opprobrium contained in the epithet 'perfidious Albion' is put down to the not unnatural spleen of envious Continental rivals. And yet this criticism rankles; for there has always existed in the English bosom a recessive, introverted minority voice that pleads for honesty and sincerity of motive despite the general prejudice which assumes the innate rightness of every national objective.

Many factors have contributed to the consolidation of this collective, extraverted attitude. English philosophy, for example, has always been practical in its outlook, and ethical problems con-

[1] From *Die Kulturelle Bedeutung der Komplexen Psychologie*, Berlin, Verlag von Julius Springer.

[2] A writer in the *New Statesman and Nation* describes this as 'the practical instinct amounting to genius, by which English rulers prefer to face problems in terms of power rather than in terms of philosophy'.

cerning the right conduct of life and behaviour have tended to overshadow the introverted inquiry into the inner psychic cause. Moreover, the identification of the Church with the state has tended to reinforce the innate presupposition that our energetic imperialistic undertakings were in some way guaranteed by the ordinance of heaven. But, above all, what has protected the Englishman so long and so effectively from knowing the 'secret places' of his own mind has been the underlying potency of the national myth.

The *idea of the gentleman* is much more than a convenient collective style: it is a living branch of the cultural tree. The original source of this idea in European society is as obscure as the source of knighthood. But its psychological significance as a tradition gathering honour and desire in its descent from father to son, represents a psychic potential of untold efficacy.

The word itself derives from the Latin *gentilis* = of the same gens or race, and in ancient Rome this word already had the special meaning of belonging to a good family or stock. We can also trace the idea of value or quality as a family inheritance in the word generous, Latin *generosus* (from *genus* = stock or race), meaning: of noble lineage, high-born. The idea, therefore, seems to be rooted in the aristocratic ideal which, in one form or another, has ruled every human society as far back as the historical eye can travel. But the special character with which the English temperament has invested the idea of the gentleman comes without doubt from that body of romantic legends which clustered around Arthur and his knights.

The Arthurian mythology is of course no more English than was the Homeric mythology Greek. Both traditions belonged to an earlier culture that was eventually superseded by a better organized or more enterprising race,[1] which transformed the virtue of the alien traditional relic into a glowing, commanding myth very much as the oyster transforms a piece of grit into a pearl. The preservation of *mana* or power of the earlier race would seem to be a compelling instigation from which the loveliest songs and the noblest achievements of poetic genius have sprung. Indeed, in the case of such works as those of Homer and Malory, we see that the virtue of the earlier culture has been not merely preserved but transformed. It is

[1] This fact might explain the curious contrast between the reserved and rather sceptical attitude of the English people to Glastonbury, the mystical home of Arthur and the Grail, and the popular veneration of Westminster Abbey, the tomb of the English kings. Glastonbury belongs to the esoteric, aristocratic interior, while Westminster belongs to everyman.

as though the poet's visionary art had released the spirit of the more primitive culture from the concrete particularity of local history into the imperishable realm of heroic myth. Though the historian and the archaeologist may lament the magnificent inaccuracy of these bardic chronicles, they are none the less the living vessels from which the spirit of a past culture is poured into the blood-stream of succeeding generations. The enduring vitality of the Christian faith was surely nourished more by the legendary songs and stories concerning Christ, the Virgin and the Saints, which clustered around every mediaeval fireside than by the formidable power of the Church. The myth that lives in the heart of men is like a 'deep pool that never dries'.

Although it can hardly be doubted that the idea of the gentleman is rooted in an aristocratic tradition of noble family or caste, it also contains another root which goes even deeper. This is the mystical feeling of belongingness. The common derivation of the words *kind* and *kin*, of *gentle* and *gens*, is more convincing of the deeper feeling content of this idea than any elaborate historical reconstruction could achieve. We may suppose that the original biological connection of kinship was the sole basis upon which kindly treatment might be anticipated. Kindness, in fact, could be legitimately associated only with those of one's own 'kind'. When a gentle feeling was aroused by an alien being it was as though he belonged to the gens. Thus the idea of a mystical brotherhood or spiritual family evolved side by side with the biological family. This feeling of a larger mystical fraternity developed a power which eventually contradicted, or rather superseded, the primal family-association. The development of corporate feeling thus engendered has been, perhaps, the most powerful implement of culture. Every form of initiation, whether into the tribal hierarchy, or into religious mystery-cults, depends for its efficacy upon a conscious development of this feeling of mystical participation.

The value of Lévy-Brühl's concept *participation mystique*, denoting the condition of psychic merging or unconscious identification with the animate or inanimate environment, rests upon a fundamental psychic necessity. In the civilized mind, as in the savage, emotional integrity demands this sense of belongingness or acceptance as a primal condition of life. We may say that the instinctive state of *participation mystique* is a biological necessity which developing culture gradually transformed into the idea of a mystical order or brotherhood. The former condition pertains to that state of primal unity before the dawn of consciousness. As soon as consciousness appears a sense of discord or contradiction begins to sunder the biological from the spiritual belongingness. But, since this sense of inner division between opposing loyalties forces a man away from his kind and breeds all the desperate ills of unrelatedness, every symbol which could bridge the chasm and unite the opposing strains of heaven and earth has been held in wonder and awe.

The Chinese concept of Tao is such a symbol, for it reconciles the ten thousand things of conscious distinctiveness with the emotional state of primal unity. In Chapter IV of the Tao Te King[1] it is said:

> The Way is like an empty vessel
> That yet may be drawn from
> Without ever needing to be filled.
> It is bottomless; the very progenitor of all things in the world.
> In it all sharpness is blunted,
> All tangles untied,
> All glare tempered,
> All dust smoothed.[2]
> It is like a deep pool that never dries.
> Was it too the child of something else? We cannot tell.
> But as a substanceless image it existed before the Ancestor.

Mr. Waley informs us in a footnote that 'the Ancestor in question is almost certainly the Yellow Ancestor who separated Earth from Heaven and so destroyed the Primal Unity, for which he is frequently censured in Chuang Tzu'. The Yellow Ancestor, then, is the Chinese equivalent for the Serpent in the myth of Genesis, who, for the same reason, has incurred the censure of Adam's posterity.

The power of the concept of Tao lies in its embracing, unifying authority. It reaches from earth to heaven and from heaven to earth: it unites the many and the one, the strong and the weak, the clear and the muddy. It creates a feeling of totality and relatedness that includes and overrules every intellectual antinomy. And this feeling 'existed before the Ancestor'; in other words, the state or attitude of Tao is a remembered experience. It is a visionary recognition of the truth that the state of primal unity exists eternally

[1] Arthur Waley, *The Way and Its Power* (George Allen & Unwin, 1934).
[2] Dust is the Taoist symbol for the noise and fuss of everyday life.

in the unconscious and that, when conscious striving and fuss are abandoned, the separateness of individuality is one with complete relatedness.

However presumptuous it may appear for a sophisticated Englishman to set the idea of the gentleman side by side with the concept of Tao, I must nevertheless expose myself to the reader's amazement. For the power of the gentleman-idea as a symbolic unifier is derived from the same primordial spring.

We have seen that the words 'kind' and 'gentle' are rooted etymologically in the primal guarantee provided by the family or kin as the biological container. This sense of primal guarantee is what is meant by the term *participation mystique* which is the psychic equivalent of the state of primal unity. It represents the original passive state in which one is merely contained, and the original character of the feelings described by 'kind' and 'gentle' pertained, as in childhood, to a passive, will-less state. One of the most striking features of youth is that life fills one with happiness or plunges one into despair. Fate is peremptory and absolute; nothing can be done about it.

Now, the kernel of the gentleman-idea as a cultural symbol is the converse of this passive guarantee of kinship. A gentleman who is only gentle towards his own gens is no gentleman. To be worthy of the spiritual lineage of this aristocratic idea a man must actively create an attitude that extends service and gentleness to all, as though everyone and every creature were his kin. Thus the gentleman-idea in what may be termed the aristocratic interior of the myth is, like Tao, a cultural re-establishment of the biological state of primal unity of feeling in which all living creatures are contained.

The concept of Tao is the expression of the introverted vision of the East that is based upon the ultimate fact of being. The concept of the gentleman is the expression of the extraverted vision of the West that is based upon the ultimate fact of relatedness. The effectiveness of both lies in their embracing authority which combines the highest distinctiveness of individual consciousness with the undifferentiated totality of the unconscious primal state.

Another interesting point of similarity of these ideas is to be found in the manner of their appearance. The Tao Te King was the product of an extraordinary awakening of spiritual vitality in China out of the darkest night of materialistic realism in which everything that was intangible and invisible was derided. The symbol of the gentleman, as we know, was fashioned in the womb of the darkest period of European history, when predatory lusts and unmitigated savagery had wellnigh extinguished the light of Christendom. Just as the idea of a mystical company of knightly men vowed to the service of a spiritual quest emerged out of the age of darkness, so the idea of a legendary ancestor-sage revealing the fullness of ancient wisdom emerged out of China's blackest night.

The parallelism in the lives of the two concepts also extends to the relative deterioration both have undergone through a process of dissemination and formularization. Deterioration in the value of a symbolical idea, however, affects its exoteric tradition only. So long as a symbol is an effective power in the unconscious its esoteric life, as the creative source of feeling, is revealed uncontaminated by counterfeit usage and undimmed by time, in the aristocratic interior of the individual myth.

If we now turn to the exoteric or historical aspect of the gentleman-idea we shall see how it became incorporated in the national character. First we must see that the conversion of the gentleman-idea from its limited biological connotation as the prerogative of noble birth, or caste, to its universal acceptance as an ethical ideal was achieved mainly on the field of arms, where it became abundantly clear that, as soon as necessity provided the opportunity, men of humble stock, like Sir Robert Knolles and Oliver Cromwell, bore themselves with the greatest valour and distinction, often outshining those of the princely caste. The conservatism of an aristocratic caste-system can be maintained, as we see in India, for very long periods so long as peaceful conditions prevail. But under the challenge of war the paramount need for outstanding quality tends to dissolve caste prerogative, thus delivering the concept of human quality from its traditional bed.

The history of the development of the English character reveals the opposing strains of two powerful tendencies: on the one hand a collective conservatism which, venerating traditional forms and ideals, abates no jot of ancient privilege. On the other hand, a vigorous, individual, revolutionary tendency, rooted in the idea of freedom of opportunity and opinion, that jealously safeguards individual quality and right from the pretensions of a favoured class. It has been well said that revolution is endemic in the English soul.

The clash between Royalists and Roundheads in the time of

Charles I symbolized the inevitable issue between these opposing strains. Up to that time the king had been chief of the nobility that was ranged over against the common people as a separate order. The Civil War was not merely the issue of a tyrannous king against an oppressed people; it was the moment of emergence of an unconquerable national spirit in which the ideas of individual right and common weal were felt to have a superior authority even to the divinity of the king.

This national spirit was embodied in Oliver Cromwell whom Carlyle calls 'Nature's own lion-hearted son', and who, more than any other single man, personified the greatness and the weaknesses of the national character. In every crucial moment we observe the decisive, practical eye. He has immediate insight into what is fact, and always he drives towards the practical and the practicable. Seldom does he reveal any criticism or insight into his motives. The course he has to take is manifestly the will of God, and the power of his own ambition, which is all too plain to the observer, escapes his masterful, extraverted vision. Of a simple, humble stock, he maintained his personal simplicity and dignity, even when he wielded more power than any king in Europe. He was able to unite the passion of uncompromising fanaticism with a large and tolerant wisdom in practical dealings. Though a commoner, and proud of it, he was more kingly than a king in the essential qualities of heart and head.

After this emergence of the national spirit, embodied in a truly great commoner, the absolute power of monarchy was gone for ever. But it may truly be said that the influence of the sovereign was enormously enhanced, as a symbol of stable authority, by the very fact that the crown was reduced from an absolute to a relative function of the constitution.

The trial and execution of King Charles by the revolutionary tribunal—which politically was an almost insane blunder, since it gave to a weak and double-faced oppressor whose life had been a series of attacks on the liberties of England, the aspect of a martyr dying in the cause of these liberties—was, in its complete adherence to a single-minded purpose, an extraordinary manifestation of the spiritual revolution that was being enacted. It was as though the opposing strains of the national character, namely, veneration for the constitution with its established tradition and the passion for individual freedom vested in the inalienable virtue of the commoner, had blended together in an irresistible affirmation of the national spirit, under the authority of which even regicide, the unpardonable crime, could be done before the eyes of the whole world. It was as though the king had been judged by the symbol royal of the national myth which enjoins universal relatedness as the essence of the king-gentleman. Hence the fatal verdict had an almost religious sanction: he was 'weighed and found wanting'.

Symbolically, this killing of the king, the first gentleman in the land, can be viewed as a decisive blow levelled by the developing national spirit at the ancient feudal prejudice which tended to vest the idea of special human quality in a privileged, aristocratic caste. For it was very largely the unlimited and unprincipled power of Buckingham, the king's favourite, that excited the impassioned resistance of parliament. The king identified himself with his favourites and officers over against the commons; and parliament could not redress the incompetence and tyranny of his officers except by refusing grants to the king. Thus for many years before the civil war broke out there had existed an impasse between the two forces in the state which generated an ever-increasing tension. At the trial of the Earl of Strafford, who was charged with high treason for the usurpation of arbitrary powers on the king's behalf, Pym[1] magnificently voiced the uprising national spirit when he proclaimed that treason against the people was treason against the throne and intimated that the sovereign who abetted such treason was not himself safe from a 'miserable end'.

This conception of 'treason against the people' was the first clear affirmation in European history of the principle that the liberties and rights of the people were as sacred as the divine prerogative of the Crown. Pym's indictment of Strafford was the expression of patriotic feeling in its purest and most intense flame. He said:

> It is God alone who subsists by himself; all other things subsist in mutual dependence and relation. If you take away the protection of the king, the vigour and cheerfulness of allegiance will be taken away, though the obligation remains. The law is the boundary, the measure, betwixt the king's prerogative and the people's liberty. While these move in their own orbs, they are a support and a security to one another—the preroga-

[1] John Pym was the founder of party government in England. During the life of many parliaments he was the acknowledged leader, and as long as he lived was the soul of the parliamentary resistance to the king. In the covenants and associations he brought into existence he made a vital and permanent contribution to English political development.

tive a cover and defence to the liberty of the people, and the people by their liberty enabled to be a foundation to the prerogative. But if these bounds be so removed that they enter into contestation and conflict, one of these mischiefs must ensue: if the prerogative of the king overwhelm the people it will be turned into tyranny: if liberty undermine the prerogative it will grow into anarchy. Arbitrary power is dangerous to the king's person and dangerous to his crown. It is apt to cherish ambition, usurpation and oppression in great men and to beget sedition and discontent in the people; and both these have been, and in reason must ever be, causes of great trouble and alteration to princes and states. If the histories of those Eastern countries be perused, where princes order their affairs according to the mischievous principles of the Earl of Strafford, loose and absolved from all rules of government, they will be found to be frequent in combustions, full of massacres, and of the tragical ends of princes.

The dignity and passion of this indictment are inspired by the feeling that the king belongs to the nation. He is a function and guarantee of the people's freedom. He is not something beyond and alien to the people he governs. He symbolizes the centre and kernel of the national myth, under whose aegis the solidarity of the people as a whole, as well as the dignity of individual freedom, had been won. Just as Arthur, the ideal king, was the royal centre of the mystical fraternity of the Table Round, so the living king must be the centre of the mystical brotherhood of the whole nation. They are interdependent and interrelated powers like the centre and circumference of a circle. For the king, therefore, to regress back to the barbarian condition, in which the conception of power and quality were held exclusively within the bounds of a privileged caste, alien to that of the people, was not only a crime against the people, but a crime against God.

The spirit of patriotism which broke through in the parliamentary discussions in the days of Charles I breathed a burning intensity and a disciplined restraint which seemed to be supported by the whole authority of the ancestors. It came from the same mythic spring from which Shakespeare and the great Elizabethans drew their inspiration. For the idea of the king as the royal centre constellating the motions and emotions of the human scene, like a sun with its attendant worlds, also governs the triumphant field of Elizabethan drama.

Thus we see that the evolution of the gentleman-idea, from its original seed-bed of aristocratic virtue and privilege into the ruling symbol of the national myth, had an immense social significance. The expanding influence of the idea disseminated the royal *mana*, which thus became an individual quality as well as a prerogative of birth. In this way the esoteric or psychological value of the symbol within the aristocratic interior effected a profound change in the morale of the whole people.

The ethical principle of *fair-play*, so essentially British, demonstrates very clearly the comprehensive effect of this psychological value on the national character. This Arthurian principle has become the generally accepted criterion, whether in the realm of politics, law, business, or sport. In fact, the gentleman's code of the public schools and universities is based solely on this idea. An appeal to the sense of fair-play touches a very deep chord in the Englishman's mind, and no political objective has the faintest chance of success, however intrinsically valuable it may be, if it is advanced in a way that offends this principle.

That it is an effective attribute of the national character is borne out by the fact that the 'pax Britannica', with its principle of impartial justice, is recognized by peoples of widely varying culture all over the globe.

There are, however, certain unfavourable results of the widespread dissemination of the gentleman-idea that are only too apparent to everyone who is not an Englishman. Observe the insular and often insolent air of superiority, the leisured gait of self-assurance, the complacent expression that leans on the inner conviction that a gentleman is present. This sense of being socially guaranteed is liable to fortify a perfectly hatted and spatted *persona* at the cost of a partial or total eclipse of the mind. With regard to numbers of Englishmen it would be hard to say whether they would be more disturbed by the presence of any but second-rate ideas in their heads than by any but the most expensive boots on their feet.

This exaggeration of the *persona* fosters a continual striving for respectability with the cliques and prejudices and exclusiveness that invariably follow in its wake; as though the acceptance by a certain class or level of society were a substantial order of merit. These unconscious, collective expressions of the national character produce a psychological carapace or crust, against which the feelings of the sensitive, discerning foreigner beat in bewilderment. In despair he is liable to assume that any people who live thus incarcerated in a stereotyped style can be scarcely human. The truth is, of course, just the reverse. For in those levels and localities where the original clan-psychology appears unmasked, where the cult of the gentleman has not yet disturbed the pattern of patriarchal feudalism, the rugged and often boorish exterior, the complete absence of any civilized graces reveal the true reason why the Englishman's *persona* is maintained with this all-too-human tenacity.

From this point of view we cannot ascribe the negative aspects of the English character wholly to the widespread cult of the gentleman. Even if early English history did not provide eloquent testimony to the deep-rooted savagery of the indigenous clan-spirit, clan-psychology can still be observed to-day in all its primeval obstinacy among the exclusive county families, particularly in Scotland, in the northern counties of England or on the Welsh border. The passionate exclusiveness of the clan- and caste-psychology is of course a relic of the original local patriotism of barbarian England. It is probably a psychological expression of the reciprocal repugnance and prohibition between different orders which nature employs to preserve the integrity of the biological species. Moreover, we have to remember that Britain, in company with other northern lands, was ravaged time and time again by inter-clan feuds and forays, and that this constant internal blood-letting made England peculiarly vulnerable to foreign marauders. Unless, therefore, a symbol of incontestable authority had emerged that had the power of binding mutually hostile elements into a united nation, England would have remained prostrate before every predatory invader. Shakespeare portrays this situation at the end of *Macbeth*, where the youthful Malcolm is entreated to come back to Scotland as the king whom all the warring clans would agree to serve.

Submission to the king thus became the supreme duty because it arose out of direst need; and the paramount need of the symbol of the knight-gentleman, as the one idea that could cut through the thorny barriers of clan and caste, thus uniting hitherto sworn enemies in a common service, will be equally manifest to anyone familiar with the existing conditions of rural England. For the deep-rooted tenacity of the clan-spirit still permeates the whole body politic. The cultivated *esprit de corps* so proudly cherished by the public schools, the various arms of the services, the political organizations, even by the clubs of Pall Mall, although highly tempered by the cult of the gentleman, bears still the stamp of the original clan-solidarity.

It is, I believe, this effective survival of the exclusive clan-spirit beneath the cultivated mask of the gentleman that the foreign observer finds so baffling. As a Dutch lady once wittily expressed it: 'The Englishman feels no need to boast that he is English. He is above even that.'

Barbarian though the clan-spirit may be, it none the less acts as a vitalizing force and, because it is rooted in the distinctiveness of the primordial group, it works as a complement to the unifying and civilizing form of the gentleman. To the age-old discipline of the clan human society owes its dearest possession: the principle of loyalty. It is not too much to say that the stability and vitality of every society, from the lowest to the highest, depends upon the integrity of this principle. The tribesman is loyal to his clan, the guildsman to his guild, and the knight is loyal to his feudal lord and to the king. But with the gentleman we find the inner, esoteric meaning of loyalty in his adherence to ideas and moral principles. His attitude is ruled by complete, undeviating loyalty to the moral and spiritual code of his cultural form; even though he may be ignorant of the historical determinants by which this form has come into effect. Hence this form is not merely a convention; it is also a very real leading force that acts as a regulating, objective principle forming the character and directing the actions of men.

As an objective, social principle it naturally has the effect of suppressing the tentative, subjective, psychic reactions. Over against a universally guaranteed cultural form elements like feelings, for instance, are a mere personal weakness, only fit for ridicule and contempt. This attitude is fostered by a thorough-going educational discipline which is begun in the nursery and is carried through, sometimes with traditional brutality, in the public schools. This form of collective initiation, by which a boy is gradually alienated from his own personal life of feeling and imagination and is moulded into an adapted social unit, has not, however, remained unaffected by modern criticism, and many schools are springing up which in their fundamental standpoint are a direct challenge to the older tradition.

The idea of 'breeding' has become practically synonymous with this stringent form of social discipline; and among the 'people who count', to have 'breeding' is the sole qualification of the gentleman. The term implies two distinct attributes. To come of aristocratic family is of course the first consideration; but it also means to have absolute control over one's personal emotions. The accepted social form is based upon these two desiderata. The genial discussion of the weather at a social gathering, or the avoidance of all topics of a problematical nature does not necessarily come from assuming the probable brainlessness of one's neighbour, but rather from the guiding sense that anything which could provoke emotions or touch a sensitive spot is taboo. Any word or action that might excite emotions is simply a departure from 'good form'.

English humour with its typical ironical flavour derives from the same source. The Englishman's early drilling has taught him the necessity of seeing certain aspects of his nature in a ludicrous light. Instead of reactions of personal sensitiveness he must learn to join in when the laugh is directed against himself. Thus he will not readily admit that he has certain distinctive abilities or qualities. He prefers to keep up the pretence of being just an ordinary being with no outstanding characteristics. If an Englishman is burdened with brains he is inclined to ridicule his ideas as 'brain-waves', as though they were afflictions, like a migraine or a stomach-ache, for which he cannot be held responsible. Whereas men of other nations feel no particular shame about their intellectual capacities.

With regard to fear and other daemonic disturbances, it is much the same. No gentleman can agree with the fact that he is afraid. It is questionable whether he can even feel fear, so drastically are his emotions disciplined. A Frenchman, on the contrary, would extend his common-sense realism to reflections about his person and would not dream of excluding a feeling so obviously justified by common human nature.

Courage, again, is a quality to which no Englishman lays claim, though his whole tradition venerates the hero *sans peur et sans reproche*. But no man however courageous may ever deem himself a hero. Acts of courage therefore are alluded to in the same ironical way as are mental capacities or deep feelings.

To sum up: I believe it is possible to trace the power of the gentleman-idea:

1. esoterically, as the ruling symbol of the aristocratic interior, and
2. exoterically, as a social or cultural form which has certain of its roots in the basic clan-spirit of the British nation.

Under the latter aspect it is a force that not only compensates the primitive clan-psychology, but raises the fundamental values of clan discipline and loyalty to a higher cultural level.

II

It will readily be grasped that this underlying clan psychology, although invaluable as a social cement, is not altogether favourable to new psychological ideas. Fortunately, however, there exists an introverted interior, wherein the spirit of detachment from the contagion of the group-mind has been ardently cultivated. Here English culture is not merely tolerant, it is generously appreciative of ideas that belong to the main stream of European culture; though it can hardly be said that the English mind shows a native fertility in the realm of psychological pioneering, except in a certain realm of imaginative literature.

England was the first country in Europe to offer a warm hospitality to Jung, and this acceptance was of an entirely different character from the polite excitement caused by a distinguished foreign visitor. Those who received his ideas were deeply moved. It was the cultured mind (in contrast to the merely educated) that warmed to his ideas, and his psychological critique of types, his concepts of the autonomous complex and the collective unconscious, gradually became included within the thinker's horizon. But this acceptance of Jung's fundamental conceptions concerned only the aristocratic interior of the English mind. It was a guarded, not an open acceptance.

Considering the nature of their subject-matter Jung's writings are widely read in England, yet nowhere does one find an inclination to overt discussion of his ideas. They are seldom quoted or openly alluded to, though one frequently finds evidence in quite unexpected quarters that a writer has read and pondered them.

In contrast to this deep and widespread infiltration of Jung's introverted standpoint, the immediate, overt reaction to the ideas of Freud and Adler is significant. Although presented on a relatively limited stage the reaction of the English audience was in both cases of the nature of a collective, extraverted appraisal. To a certain number of doctors and educationists these ideas offered new and practical methods for the pursuit of their calling and their response was open and enthusiastic. But, beyond these specialized fields, the ideas excited very little positive interest, though in the case of some of Freud's later writings a deep repugnance has not been lacking.

In the specialized technical field of *psycho-analysis*, however, there has been a great deal of painstaking research, some of which will doubtless be found to have general scientific value when it is eventually separated away from the one-sided Freudian mode of thinking and presentation.

Though the ideas of Freud and Adler have each won a certain place in the medical world, the Freudian school is represented by men of superior intellectual calibre and power: a fact which appeals forcibly to those who are looking towards medical psychology as a career. The Freudian school has, moreover, a consistent scheme of explanation for mental morbidity, as well as an easily intelligible method. The Adlerian psychology, on the other hand, practically denies the existence of the unconscious and, as a method, it relies on restoring the morale of the patient by instilling the ideas of co-operation and personal utility

The methods of both schools appeal to the extraverted habit of mind that inclines to reduce a problem at once to a convenient, practicable form by the use of a convenient and practicable formula. The Freudian method of analytical reduction and antiseptic ventilation of the infantile unconscious is a more or less self-evident application of common-sense, hygienic principles to the psychic sphere, while the Adlerian method of hortation and encouragement is an equally common-sense application of extraverted educational principles.[1] Both methods rest upon orthodox medical postulates, namely, the obvious morbidity of the patient and the equally obvious soundness of adapted normality. It is therefore not only superfluous, but even somewhat 'mystical' and 'perverse' of Jung to cast his introverted doubts upon these self-evident truisms. To bring in the concept of the soul and the whole perplexing field of religion is quite irrelevant to the sphere of a medical discipline.

Now, this is a hard-headed, practical viewpoint which agrees perfectly with the established extraverted philosophy. It is neither seemly nor practical to introduce religious problems into a purely secular sphere of activity. These things are 'not done', and the collectively adapted extraverted mentality, relying upon its corporate strength, prefers not to discuss anything that has always been taken for granted. The attitude of English psychologists to Jung can only be described, therefore, as that of gentlemanly exclusion. This does not mean, for example, that his early contributions to the under-

[1] The abreaction school should not be omitted from this survey; since the method, although theoretically somewhat obsolete, has several eminent adherents in this country. Its physical analogue would be the practice of removing buried or carious stumps in dentistry.

standing of dementia praecox, or his classic work on the types, are not recognized and appreciated. But in alluding to this aspect of Jung's work there is a distinctly retrospective flavour which would be appropriate only to an author who has since died.

If I have dared to portray the English psychological arena with a somewhat ironical pen it is because I am convinced that this spiritual obscurantism is obsolete and in no sense represents the true quality of English culture: albeit there is a certain filial piety in this inflexible unwillingness to question the inherent rightness of tried, practical methods. For, as I have already shown, the reductive, the educational and the abreactionist methods are merely psychological variants of long-established therapeutic principles.

From psychological premisses such as these the problems of the widening or extension of consciousness, of the understanding and acceptance of the psychic totality of the meaning of individuation —the whole world, in fact, which Jung's ideas inhabit—simply do not arise. Indeed, to an extraverted mentality, that has been schooled by tough necessity to regard social adaptation as the first rule of life, a philosophy that ascribes paramount importance to the idea of the Self seems to be the voice of treason.

Thus the obscurantism of the medical psychologists, who decline even to consider a psychology with a soul, can be comprehended and in some measure excused, when it is realized that it arises very largely from an inherent loyalty to known and tried principles of medical and social hygiene. But although these are the priests of medical psychology in England, they do not represent the feelings of the congregation, as a recent example will illustrate.

A learned medical society had somewhat injudiciously elected a Freudian analyst as its president and his presidential address, which consisted of a thoroughgoing reduction of religious ideas and experience to the realm of infantile illusion, was reported at some length in *The Times*. The chorus of protest that was instantly aroused, culminated in the voice of a distinguished literary critic who wondered on what grounds medical psychology was filled with this 'adolescent presumption'. This is by no means an isolated instance, for whenever and wherever the voice of lay criticism becomes audible one finds this same note of amazement at the singular fact that, of all the branches of science, psychology should remain wedded to the mechanistic, materialistic philosophy which has already proved incompetent to explain either the structure of the material universe or the fundamental problems of biology.

To the outside observer this attitude of psychological obscurantism must appear as a kind of thought-phobia (a symptom to which extraverted psychology is admittedly prone), but when it is seen as an inherent loyalty to established medical principles we can relate it to that deeper historical tendency in the English national character, mentioned above, which gives a single-minded veneration to traditional forms and usages.

There is another feature of this extraverted tough-mindedness of which I can scarcely trust myself to speak, lest a spate of resentful words should be irrevocably loosed. It is the deplorable habit of all men who refuse, or seem to refuse, the labours of independent thought and self-criticism, always to cling together in groups and circles for mutual support. If the spiritual *dynamis* were the accredited scientific counterpole of the primordial energy of sex we might be tempted to describe these circles of pooled thinking as 'homospiritual' congregations. For just as the purposive energy of sex is shorn of its penetrating, effective will in the tepid homosexual underworld, so the creative power of the spirit seems, in these groups, to have become congealed into habitual mental agglutinations. The indescribable dullness of these so-called psychological groups is, moreover, strongly reminiscent of the characteristic atmosphere of homosexual frustration.

When I ask myself why this group atmosphere of intellectual complacency fills me with fury, I find that my anger leads me to the brink of the known, familiar world and, there beyond, I see spiritual forms emerging from the dark, the limited and the contained, into the winged freedom of the world of light. Then somewhat wearily I turn again to the psychological class-room and I see men catching these free denizens of the light-world in order to confine them in glass coffins or test-tubes and pass them from one to the other for microscopical examination.

This vision brings me back to what I have described as the aristocratic interior where the living symbols of the national myth still rule in immortal beauty and power. Even though rudely worked counterfeit images are passed from hand to hand in the streets, the living originals are not betrayed, because the river of England's deeper spiritual life still runs from its ancient source.

All the unfavourable, obscurantist, tough-minded features of

English psychology are part and parcel of the extraverted, collective habit which expresses the worship of practical efficiency. And this unfortunately is the side that is most in evidence. One can find an entrance to the aristocratic interior only in moments of genuine individual feeling when the pursuing sense of social necessity is temporarily suspended. In such moments the cultured English mind reveals a generous, open-minded hospitality to new ideas. For example, the idea of accepting and honouring the Self as the impersonal will of the total psychological subject comes into direct succession to the idea of fealty to the king; the idea of accepting and reinstating unconscious functions and elements that have been suppressed by an exclusively social adaptation is seen as a new extension of the principle of fair-play; the gradual unfolding of the process of individuation in the autonomous life of the psyche means a deeper and more intimate realization of the concept of evolution; Jung's integration of living concepts from undirected dream- and fantasy-representations, as, for instance, the shadow, the persona, the anima, the individuality, is recognized as the necessary extension of the empirical principle to the realm of spiritual phenomena.

The list of examples need not be lengthened. Enough have been given to show that the hospitality already accorded to, and waiting for, the fundamental conceptions of Jung in the aristocratic interior of English culture is ensured by the fact that the principles which govern Jung's conceptions are already rooted in the Englishman's basic philosophy, which in its turn is an expression of his racial myth.

The reader will have observed that in every example given above the acceptation of the psychological conception involves a process of *extension* or *expansion* from an existing limited connotation to a field of analogous reference in the psychic world. The history of the evolution of the spirit shows this process of the expansion of meaning to a field of analogous reference as its constant principle. From the evolution of the idea of god to the scientific vision of the universe, the movement of liberation and expansion of *meaning* expresses a consistent development of consciousness.

I have attempted as faithfully as possible to depict the two opposing strains or tendencies in the English character, and my attempt has led to the disclosure of an inherent incompatibility of attitude and behaviour which I must suppose to be fundamental. On the one hand we find an individual, and spiritually aristocratic, interior which welcomes every enlargement of the royal power of the spirit.

In the history and myth of England this is symbolized by the king-gentleman, by King Arthur and the Table Round, and by the Quest of the Grail. On the other hand we find a conservative, collective attitude that holds rigidly to the forms and usages of the past, fighting obstinately against any innovation that could menace its venerated idols. It is symbolized by the clan. The one is free, open, individual; the other is niggardly, shut and collective. The judgment of the former issues from the heart in unison with the head, while the verdict of the latter is conditioned almost exclusively by precedent. The tragedy of these incompatibilities declares itself when a man of heart attempts to translate a truth belonging to the aristocratic interior into practical politics. The attitude of an executive committee to such a challenge resembles that of a highly orthodox oyster being presented with a pearl.

Many individual examples of the existence of this psychic paradox will readily come to the reader's mind. A particularly tragic case came to my notice recently. He was a cultured man of fifty-five, of an aristocratic Scottish clan. Having grown increasingly resistant to the intolerant exclusiveness of his social milieu he began to form relationships of a peculiar intimacy and devotion with pitmen, sailors and, sometimes, with outcasts. Men and ideas that were beyond the pale drew him irresistibly with a sense of adventure and new life. Below the rigid, collective crust a kind of psychic secret society was thus formed which eventually sapped the loyalty to his own caste. But the questing spirit that went down to find the general human kinship that was so much more real and comprehensive than that of the clan also embraced the primeval renegade. For, naturally, when the generally human becomes the bond of kinship, sexuality cannot be excluded, especially that form which society most condemns. Thus homosexuality, of the abandoned, renegade type, began to take a share in the quest, until at last the police were warned and outraged society had its revenge.

I mention this case because the 'secret society' (i.e. a more or less disreputable psychic underworld) is the unenviable subterranean complement of a too rigid social form. If we take the collective norm as our base line, these two secret departures can be represented as the curve of mystical kinship, extending *above* the line in the spiritual quest, and reaching *below* towards the sexual. Frequently, as in the case cited above, the upward and downward curves are emotionally identical, in so far as they are both migrations from the too rigid enclosure of the clan-mind. The prevalence of this renegade psychology seems to be associated especially with extraverted societies, where the tyranny of social expectation is felt by many to go beyond the point of toleration. The renegade *motif* or archetype comes into effect, then, as a definite point of resistance to the existing social pattern. The migration that follows the resistance can be a mere abandonment to the resistant mood, in which case characteristic anti-social *sequelae* must be anticipated; or it can be undertaken as a genuine quest for a new and better hypothesis, when a positive individual achievement may result.

The existence of the British Empire provides ample evidence of the power of the extraverting, migratory tendency in the national psychology. Moreover, the duality of attitude with its ambiguous cultural effects is patent to every eye. The constructive colonizer and pioneer adventurer is the superior twin of the renegade and the beachcomber.

On the introverted plane the migratory tendency has also played an important part in the spiritual life of England, as is shown in the Protestant movement away from Rome and the passionate spirit of reform that flames in the heart of a Shelley, a Wilberforce, or a William Morris.

This spirit of resistance to the existing social and ethical pattern would, from a reductive standpoint, seem to be indistinguishable from the incestuous resistance of the son to the mother; but we must beware of the fallacy, which vitiates much psycho-analytical reasoning, of assuming that analogous phenomena are, *ipso facto*, identical. The analogy with the rebellious son does, however, provide us with a valuable dye-stain which brings into visibility the character of certain social phenomena as an analogous field of reference. For, just as the mother symbolizes the state of primal unity from which individual consciousness detaches itself, so the clan symbolizes the primal social matrix of *participation mystique* from which a new and more conscious social experiment emerges. In either case the point of departure represents a moment of risk in which the attitude of abandonment or of devotion is almost equally possible. The outcome of the departure in either case is directly dependent upon which of these spirits governs the migratory movement. Where the migration is carried out in a spirit of devotion the new social pattern tends to be a reproduction of the maternal society, only on a broader ethical basis.

It is possible, then, to represent the original clan matrix as a closed circle which would reproduce itself in endless repetition unless, at some definite point on the circle, a force of resistance was developed from which the evolutionary movement from the closed circle to the open spiral could take place. The evolution of a society like that of any other differentiated organism must, therefore, embrace the operation of two opposing yet interdependent principles. On the one hand, there exists the mechanism of reproduction embodied in the species, on the other, there is the principle of resistance or mutation, symbolized by individuality.

It can with some justice be contended that what I have described as the two characteristic opposing stresses in the English character merely offer a special case of the introverted-extraverted antithesis, and I think Jung himself would agree with this. But he would also, I think, agree that there is a characteristic peculiarity in the way this duality manifests itself in the English mentality. The extraverted attitude has always been the dominant spirit in our national life, and its peculiar effectiveness in the sphere of practical reality is shown by the steady, reliable grip with which the Englishman handles any situation in which the executive function is needed. It is when we approach English life and character from the introverted angle that we are amazed at the blindness of the tough-minded, collective attitude which seems wholly incompatible with the spirit of a great people.

If this dominant, exterior attitude of England were the whole truth, little indeed could be expected from her in the present critical passage of the world's history. But when we discover the recessive, introverted potentiality which I have described as the 'aristocratic interior', we can there discern a passion of inner feeling that is the dynamic counterpole of the tough-minded, collective inertia. Viewed as an isolated phenomenon, this collective inertia looks like a blank resistance to the realities of the spirit; but, under the historical perspective, the contending stress and embrace of these opposing forces is seen to be the key to the steady growth and development of the English character.

If England to-day is one of the most powerful stabilizing forces in the European situation, it is because the function of the crown is guaranteed by the whole national feeling, and it derives this guarantee from the realization, born of long and bitter conflict between king and commons, that political equilibrium is the expression of reciprocal allegiance.

In the psychological sphere, I believe that the practical poise of the English mind and habit of life is the expression of a reciprocal allegiance, born also of bitter conflict, between the passionate individualism of the aristocratic interior and the indomitable conservatism of the extraverted, collective psyche. The fact that public opinion in England is a free power which may not be tampered with by any governmental prohibition is, I believe, a direct result of this psychic duality. For recognition of the necessity of reciprocal allegiance is the inner guarantee of fair-play.

It will be understandable, given the historical and mythic background of the English psyche, that individuation is not an ideal that would, at once, take root in the English soil. As a result of its formidable, age-long schooling in social discipline, an instant prejudice firmly clamps the English mind against anything that flavours of the 'cult of self'. How then is it possible for the redeeming concept of individuation to gain access?

From anthropological investigation of the transfusion of cultures we know that only those elements of the migrating culture are assimilable which are germane to the indigenous myth. In other words, the indigenous cultural myth exercises a selective influence, receiving into itself those elements which enhance its existing content and rejecting the rest. The symbol which rules and which, therefore, will exercise the principal selective influence in the English myth is the knight-gentleman. It is a symbol of general power because, as we saw in the beginning, it embraces the spirit of relatedness in its highest cultural expression.

Under the aegis of this symbol the realization of the idea of totality of being is open. For example, the idea of relating to the anima and, through the anima, to the denizens of the unconscious is cogent to the English mind under the aspect of the knightly quest. Similarly, the idea of giving fair-play to the repressed functions or of 'consuming one's own smoke' instead of making scapegoats of others is also entirely in harmony with the indigenous myth and character.

Thus, in the work of introducing Jung's conceptions to the English mind, I have found that the open sesame to the aristocratic interior is the principle of relatedness in its widest possible significance. Through this doorway the meaning of individuation can find its dwelling-place in the closely guarded heart of the Englishman.

III

So far I have dealt only with the conscious psychological appreciation of Jung's ideas. As a psychologist I am naturally confronted with this problem. But, putting the conscious acknowledgment of psychical facts on one side, I should myself be lacking in psychological appreciation of facts if I did not mention one realm of British culture where psychological intuition and experience have long been cultivated and expressed in a relatively unconscious way. It does not strictly belong to my theme, and a thorough examination of it would be a considerable work, but I would be guilty of an important omission if I made no allusion to it.

Continental observers have often delighted in the fact that the tough-minded common sense of the Englishman is dogged by a very dubious shadow. For in no other civilized country are so many haunted houses to be found; no 'family cupboard' is without its 'skeleton', and the host of spiritual nomads who go wandering after 'strange gods' is legion. It is, indeed, almost a proof of genteel descent to harbour a ghost in the family. A society of respectable scientific standing has actually been formed to investigate these, euphemistically styled, supernormal phenomena.

Without attempting to explain the presence of these denizens of the ghost-world in our midst, their very existence points to a remarkable psychological fact: namely, that side by side with the English practicality and common sense there exists a sensitive intuitiveness of certain unconscious psychic events. And this sensibility is by no means limited to a more or less primitive mediumship in respect to banal family ghosts and their psychic spawn. It also extends to deeper and more meaningful realms of the unconscious, illuminating the unseen forces that govern human destiny.

There is a certain sphere of English literature which can truly be called psychological creation. It is indeed all the more valuable as evidence, because the respective authors make no sort of claim to produce 'psychological stuff'. Inasmuch as the facts they reveal are incidental, and not the authors' main purpose, they are intrinsically valid as psychological evidence. In many cases the writers cannot even be considered good authors from the strictly literary standpoint. They may merely be writing adventure stories, and their style is often redundant and amateurish. Yet these writers are moved by something deeper than their conscious literary motives. Often one gets the impression of an experience, lying at the root of their creative need, which is hard for them to understand and express, but which nevertheless grips the readers' interest as by the presence of a genuine psychological imperative.

Many of these authors began to write their stories long before anything was generally known about the psychology of the unconscious,[1] and even to-day they tend to show an antipathy towards any scientific exploration of their special realm.

Perhaps the most widely read of these unconscious psychologists is Sir Rider Haggard, who has written a copious anima-saga centring in the figure of 'She-who-must-be-obeyed'. Another beautiful portrait of the anima by a writer who is also a great literary artist is found in W. H. Hudson's *Green Mansions.* In both these stories the anima is conceived as dwelling remote in the heart of a distant continent, and imbued with a magical power and wisdom which she derives from an ancient, extinct culture. The anima-figure is usually accompanied by the renegade, a liaison that is not surprising when we reflect that only those who are driven by inner necessity far from the collective highways could ever hope to discover the queen of a distant and inaccessible fastness.

There is another type of anima story in which the anima is identified with the renegade motive, while respectability looks on askance. From these stories no positive solution is ever forthcoming and usually, as in David Garnett's *Lady into Fox*, the story ends in violent death or bitter frustration. In others of Garnett's stories, notably in *The Sailor's Return* and *Pocahontas*, we find the recurrent theme of the returning prodigal or renegade attempting to bring back a primitive princess into civilized English life; an attempt that always ends in disaster. It is as though the writer feels that the task of uniting the deeper primordial strata of the unconscious with respectable conformity is, in the last resort, an insoluble problem.

D. H. Lawrence was also impaled on this problem. And he too was inclined to identify the renegade tendency with the anima-figure, as, for instance, in *Lady Chatterley's Lover*. Only at the very end of his life did he realize that the renegade motive, as such,

[1] The conception of a dissociated personality was, for instance, graphically portrayed by R. L. Stevenson in *Dr. Jekyll and Mr. Hyde* before the idea was generally accepted by science. And *Dracula* by Bram Stoker, portraying a most ghoulish embodiment of neurosis as a vampire denizen of the ghost-world who escapes by night from the ancestral vault in order to suck the blood of one's nearest and dearest, was written towards the end of last century.

could never establish, though it might initiate, a new departure. In *The Man who Died* he was able to create an anima-figure who symbolizes a surviving spirit of devotion to Osiris, the original dying-and-resurgent god, and his story anticipates the birth of the new Christ from this symbol of devotion.

Portrayals of the animus by women writers are also to be found, but these are more elusive and never quite as objective as the corresponding anima-creations of men. There is, for instance, *The Evil Vineyard* by Mary Hay—a bad book, it is true, from a literary standpoint but alarmingly good in the presentation of a certain negative aspect of unconscious feminine influence on a husband. In *Lolly Willowes*, an exquisite literary jewel by Sylvia Townsend Warner, a typical, refined, elderly spinster breaks away from her tribal destiny, as a mere lady and family-aunt of general usefulness, and encounters her animus in the form of a gentle devil. Through this departure she eventually becomes a real human being; in other words, achieves individuation in her own inimitable way.

Among a number of works in which the unconscious is more or less clearly evoked one should mention Ronald Frazer's *Flying Draper*. Here the author, through, seemingly, a mediumistic identity with a woman's unconscious, has drawn an amazing animus-figure who discovers the power of spontaneous flight through the air in answer to the heroine's unconscious love-summons, and, thereafter, becomes a progidious disturber both of domestic and of public peace.

Another book, written ostensibly by a woman and with profound psychological insight, is *A Man Named Luke*, by March Cost. And then, there is that astounding work by John Cowper Powys—*A Glastonbury Romance*.

This work belongs to a different order, since it occupies a place of its own in English literature. The author combines the most sensitive mediumship to the unconscious with a deeply religious attitude. Glastonbury is the home of the Grail. The Christian legends settled here because, long before the sacred chalice of Christendom was brought to England, the magical cauldron, or the inexhaustible font, had been venerated on this sacred earth. Because of the concentration of faith in this living symbol for untold centuries, it has acquired an intrinsic power, or *mana*, that finds now a spontaneous and highly ambiguous expression in the lives of all who come within its spell. But although the characters suffer, in their various ways, the enchantment of this spiritually charged atmosphere, the visionary passion of the author has invested them with an integrity of individual life which stands in vigorous contrast to the idea of blind psychic determinism. Although *dramatis personae* of an unconscious drama of unimaginable potency in which they re-enact their archetypal roles, they are no mere puppets in a cosmic marionette theatre. They are also tremendously themselves. Their individual destinies are intensified by the unconscious energizing forces, not as by an alien power, but rather as an impersonal or cosmic reinforcement of their original nature.

The impression left by this prodigious book—there are twelve hundred pages, each with its own surprising flavour—is as though one had been granted a vision of human life with the fourth dimension made visible and actual. The criminal, the perverted, the ascetic, the magician and the fanatic—all the elements and ingredients of the human soul are stirred and mixed within the magic cauldron of the racial myth; and there issues forth an impersonal conception of human personality, in which immortal symbol and mortal deed are resolved as in a single chord.

The author must surely have Welsh blood in his veins, and he is deeply versed in the legendary background of his race. It is not improbable that the existence of this mediumistic penumbra in the field of British literature may be concerned with the intermingling of the mystical Celtic and the hard-headed Anglo-Saxon strains in the British mentality. It might well be that the peculiar vitality of the race is the result of the inherent oppositions, within the national psyche, of the older indigenous spirits of the land with the gods of the Roman and Saxon invaders.

With this very brief survey I have merely indicated the existence of a relatively large field of English letters in which the dimension of the unconscious becomes more or less clearly operative. It is not too much to say that all these authors have expressed, in one way or another, an inner, esoteric knowledge of the reality of the psyche. They testify, in the particular idiom of their craft, to the reality of the deeper regions of the soul and present it to the English public. The popular taste for these books seems to show that, therewith, something is expressed which the average individual could not put into words, but is eager to touch.

What is this imperative, commanding something that shimmers beyond the threshold of the known, familiar world and compels men to tasks beyond their comprehension? In the attempt to answer the riddle I should like to quote some lines written by Sir Rider Haggard as a kind of epilogue to *She*:

> Not in the waste beyond the swamps and sand,
> The fever-haunted forest and lagoon,
> Mysterious Kôr, thy walls forsaken stand,
> Thy lonely towers beneath the lonely moon.
> Not there does Ayesha linger, rune by rune
> Spelling strange scriptures of a people banned.
> The world is disenchanted; over soon
> Shall Europe send her spies through all the land.
>
> Nay, not in Kôr, but in whatever spot,
> In town or field, or by the insatiate sea,
> Men brood on buried loves, and unforgot,
> Or break themselves on some Divine decree,
> Or would o'erleap the limits of their lot—
> There, in the tombs and deathless, dwelleth She.

The Provisional Life[1]

The title I have chosen is a descriptive epithet borrowed from Jung, which captures a characteristic phenomenon of the modern world in a phrase that cannot be bettered. It denotes an attitude that is innocent of responsibility towards the circumstantial facts of reality as though these facts were being provided for, either by the parents, or the state, or at least by Providence. If we regard the concept of Providence as expressing a childlike attitude of trust in a benevolent deity, we may regard the provisional attitude as its shadow, namely a state of childish irresponsibility and dependence.

The case I am submitting as an example is that of a young American woman of thirty-two who had recently married a young man of considerable promise in the world of the theatre. The salient feature in the history was an ambitious, dependent, highly nervous mother who, having divorced her husband, the patient's father, when the patient was two years old, sought both her solace and her vocation in a continual emotional stir around and about her only child. An atmosphere of romantic expectation, rooted in the unfulfilled youthful ambitions of the mother, produced in the developing child a nervously exaggerated personality and at the same time a burden of hysterical fears. Every attempt she had made to launch her individual life had been undermined by fear suggested to her by the mother. She had an exceptional histrionic talent and trained enthusiastically in a classic French theatre. But no sooner was she given a role in which there lay promise of distinction and success than her nerve gave way, whereupon her mother urged her to abandon her career. Her erotic life consisted of a series of highly romantic affairs in which childish projection completely falsified the nature of the object. Stage heroes and operatic tenors monopolized her interest to the exclusion of all men of mortal stature.

Although fear and self-distrust had aborted every attempt to launch her separate life, yet her peace of mind was singularly unaffected by her failures. Nothing apparently went deep, and a childish zest for enjoyment and pleasure was the keynote to her conscious personality, notwithstanding the facts that she had to

[1] *Zentralblatt für Psychotherapie und ihre Grenzebieta*, Bd. viii, H. 2 S. Hirzel, Leipzig).

undergo an operation on account of obscure abdominal seizures, was frequently compelled to take rest-cures for nervous breakdown, and that nearly every organ of her body became occasionally eloquent with symptomatic fury. Of these the most irritating symptom was frequency of micturition which amounted at times almost to incontinence.

When one contrasted the cloudless gaiety and childish expansiveness of the conscious personality with this distressful physical state one could not resist the impression that the conscious was claiming exemption from problems at the expense of the body. It was as though a localized storm of fear gathered, for example, in the region of the bladder; but, apart from the annoyance caused by the frequent retirements, the serenity of consciousness was never seriously disturbed, a plausible physical explanation being always at hand.

There was, however, a symptom which produced a certain clouding of the conscious horizon. This was a persistent sleepy lethargy, against which she had to fight to maintain even the minimum of attention demanded of a gifted child. She described it as a kind of heavy mist behind the eyes, which first became manifest at the time of puberty and had persisted ever since. She often felt as though she were being forced to sleep in spite of herself. The sleepiness never interfered, however, with her pleasures, upon which all her disposable energy was directed.

The husband was an ambitious, gifted artist with an ironic flavour that was not altogether free of the suspicion of frustration. He was the only son of his mother. She, too, had divorced her husband, but had married again. In relation to his work he was competent, painstaking and aware. Concerning almost everything else he was absent-minded; although socially he was considerate, loyal and generous. His attitude to the frequent illnesses and hysterical incompetence of his wife was above reproach. He was attentive, solicitous and endlessly patient. In fact his virtue was so apparently effortless in this respect that one could almost believe that his wife's frequent indispositions were not wholly unwelcome. Marital relations had long since lapsed; in the beginning because of his wife's illness and operation (curettage), but latterly from absence of erotic initiative on the husband's side, aided by the unconscious *noli me tangere* attitude of the wife. The attitude of the respective mothers oscillated between that of anxious concern and unrequited expectation.

Both the husband and wife wished to consult me about their

marriage problem and I recommended independent analysis of both partners. The dream I have selected for discussion was contributed by the wife and ran as follows:

My husband and myself are in our bedroom at our hotel. He wants a bottle of my mineral water and an electric iron to press his trousers. In the drawing-room next door are our two mothers and Aunt Matilda. The door between the rooms is open. In the evening we are all going to a 'Heroic Concert'. The words 'Napoleon', 'Waterloo', and 'Heroic' go through my mind in connection with the concert. Henry disappears and I am hurrying to get dressed. I notice that Henry has left the iron under the dressing-table. It is red-hot. I notice that the dressing-table is on the opposite side of the room from where it usually is. I see the shoes and bottles of mineral water under it and am furious with Henry for leaving the red-hot iron there. It is unbelievably careless of him to do such a dangerous thing. I rush over and put the iron on some newspapers and they become scorched. Also the sheets from the bed have their ends trailing on the floor too near the iron and I move them away. I don't remember if I put the iron out, but anyhow it passes out of the picture.

In the room where the mothers are I can hear little Vasha (a charming child who lives in the same hotel as ourselves) telling them a fairy-tale. The grown-ups are fascinated and hang on her lightest word. I hear Vasha say, 'and whenever I get to that place I am scared stiff'. I have a feeling she alludes to some place that is haunted by fairies. After a while mother comes in to me and shows me a book of Vasha's, a book of fairy-tales. I open it and see a charming picture, a host of red squirrels hanging by their tails from the branches of a tree. Each squirrel has a single taut string like a violin string and is fiddling hard upon it. I exclaim with delight at the picture, but mother says there is a much nicer picture further on. I open the book at the picture she likes, but it is not half as nice as the squirrel picture. It shows an old spinster-like woman with her head turned, looking with a rather furtive, sly expression at a funny little animal that follows her. This animal is one whose photograph I saw in a newspaper. It was supposed to look as though it were laughing but actually it was yawning. The little animal in the book obviously belongs to the old witch woman. Mother calls this animal a 'battledore and shuttlecock.'[1]

The opening statement of a dream, like the first bars of a symphonic movement, contains, as a general rule, the principal theme with which the dream is concerned. We know, then, from these opening bars, that the intimate relationship of the husband and wife

[1] An old-fashioned game in which the shuttlecock, a half-sphere with feathers stuck into the flat surface, was hit backwards and forwards over a net by players armed with a tambour on a stick, the battledore.

is under review and, from the fact that the *mise en scène* is an hotel bedroom (a collective and transitory situation), that its provisional character is about to be criticized.

The mineral water is associated with the aura of fuss which the patient has secreted around herself as part of her neurotic alibi. Since her operation she has had to drink a special kind of mineral water instead of natural fluids. There is an electric iron which she uses, but the husband has never in fact used it, nor does he valet his own clothes. We can infer, therefore, that the dream-mind has improvised this scene from familiar elements for a psychological purpose. The one element 'mineral water' is fluid, cold and fussy with effervescence. It is connected with the wife's neurotic attitude of fear. The other element is solid, hot, metallic and active with electrical current. Clearly these represent a sophisticated expression of a natural pair of opposites that are being pressed into service for sartorial purposes. The airy waters seem to allude to the effervescence of neurotic fuss and narcissistic fantasies which the patient indulges in, whereas the iron is a tough earthy substance which at certain times is ardent with heat conducted from a general power supply. In plain English, then, it is the passional heat of sexuality that is being adapted for 'Heroic' social ends. The trousers are the clothing of the nether or instinctual man, and the more ambitious one is for social success the more conspicuous becomes the crease in one's trousers. It is almost a public affirmation of the encased discipline, the tramline orderliness of one's primitive instincts.

Thus when we examine the elements of this sartorial exercise of the husband we are able to read plainly enough the famous word 'sublimation'. Hot iron and cold water in their natural state would symbolize a primordial masculine and feminine antithesis. They are elemental opposites. But here both the water and the iron are represented in an altered, adapted form. They are the original elements with a difference, and the difference is the expression of a certain sophisticated inhibition. Both elements have been to some extent denaturalized and the association of the mineral water with the wife's neurotic habit of life supplies a causal connection between the wife's neurotic fears and the husband's attempt to sublimate the passional element of sexuality into extraverted social channels.

It is important to observe that the failure of the husband's attempt is due primarily to the mistaken collective prejudice that sublimation is a possible substitute for the creative process which not only changes the superficial aspect of things, but effects a radical transformation. On the basis of their associations we can, for example, identify the two opposite elements of the dream-picture with the basic psychical constituents, fear and love. Thus, on a deeper level of association the dream alludes to that primordial conception of human psychology symbolized in a very early cosmogonic myth of Greece. The myth states that before the world existed there was a vast cosmic egg which divided into two halves. The one half was Eros; the other Phobos. These coupled together as male and female and out of this mating the world was born.

This myth is the archetype of the creative process in the psyche which, in the absence of prejudice and rational interference, ever and again creates or re-creates the basic individual attitude. Clearly, therefore, the elements of the creation of a new world are present in the dream but the creative process is, as it were, broken into by the sublimating zeal of the husband.

We can assume, therefore, that there exists an *a prioristic* idea in the husband's mind which prompts him to disbelieve in the possibility of a spontaneous psychic evolution and which, therefore, forces him to the heroic attempt of diverting the primal forces of the unconscious into safe and accepted channels. Jung, with perfect justice, has described this attempt as a psychological swindle; since it denies equal validity to the elemental opposites of human nature and, therefore, can only be achieved at the cost of bitterness and frustration.

Inasmuch as the sublimating impulse is necessarily something that estranges the human being from his original nature it is always represented in dreams as coming from an alien source. Like syphilis or scarlet fever, it is acquired from the environment and must not be conceived as belonging to the primary psychic constitution.

The dream tells us that the sublimating impulse is active in the husband's psychology but the *vis a tergo* which impels the impulse is represented in the immediate proximity of the two mothers and Aunt Matilda. In dream-analysis we have learnt from experience that the relation of synchronism or juxtaposition between symbolic figures in a dream expresses a causal connection existing between them on the psychological plane.

It should here be explained that Aunt Matilda is an old lady of the New England Puritan mentality whose devotion to her niece has a certain morbid intensity that savours unpleasantly of the vampire. These three old women have been collected by the dream-mind from the ends of the earth (for naturally they are not really living with my patients), and have been placed in the adjoining room, like three old witches 'listening in' on the conjugal intimacies of the young married pair. The sinister allusion to the three witches or the three Fates spinning the unseen web of fate is unmistakable, so that immediately our minds are on the *qui vive* to detect the result of the witches' spell. From the history we have already been warned how the expectations of the child-centred mothers hover, so to say, in the air above the sleeping pair. But there are also grim undertones ringing in the word 'mother-in-law' which belong to the psychology of witchcraft. Why, in primitive societies, is the mother-in-law rigorously tabooed to the son-in-law? It is because the state of unconscious psychic identity or *participation mystique* between mother and child inevitably provokes the mother-in-law to become a disturbing unconscious participator, in other words a passionately interested eavesdropper, in the erotic intimacies of the bride and bridegroom. But this is not the whole story. As a rule, the active sexual life of the mother and mother-in-law respectively is finished, and yet, in very many cases, the unconscious erotic fantasying is by no means done with. And just because this unwanted and unfulfilled sexuality has no effective expression in life it takes on the character of respectable frustration which, as we have already seen, is merely another term for sublimation. Thus it comes about that the effect of the witches' brew is to impel the devoted son-in-law to do likewise: namely, to attempt heroic feats of sublimation out of unconscious sympathy (i.e. identity) with the invisible frustrated participants—the mothers.

The momentum of the dream is now well under way. From the sublimating power-house in the drawing-room next door there issues the idea of spending the evening at a 'Heroic Concert'. This idea again involves the weaning of the libido from the intimate scene of the personal relationship to embrace the notion of a *concerted* activity in which, presumably, all the 'witches' can join. But why is its heroic character so emphasized? It is a singular fact, which analytical pioneers have interpreted in various ways, that the hero is almost invariably cared for by two mothers, his own and a foster-mother. Sometimes the foster-mother is an animal as with Romulus and Remus, sometimes she is a princess or a patrician as with Moses and Leonardo da Vinci. But always we find that situation, drawn with such tragic intensity by Leonardo himself, of the two mothers bending over the child, one holding the child and satisfied, the other yearning and unsatisfied. Thus the two mothers might symbolize the conscious and visible aspect of the mother and her unconscious counterpart. We can scarcely doubt that it is the pressure of the mother's sacrificed possibilities and ambitions, her unrealized hopes, in a word, her unfulfilled libido that is projected into the son; thus laying down the keel of a hero-complex with its heroic ideal, which may subsequently develop into the major impetus of the son's life. But just because he is launched with the power of a will not his own, whose origin is obscure and whose ends are not explicit, the possibility of individual insight into this aspect of his fate is denied him. Very often the resistance against this impelling 'alien' will is projected upon the wife, and since, with her woman's instinct, she often divines the true source of the 'alien' will, the relations between wife and mother-in-law are proverbially difficult.

Thus, with the dream to guide us, we can unravel the skein of fate and follow the line backwards, from the husband's attempt to 'sublimate' his sexuality into the 'Heroic Concert' to the three mothers in the next room. The words 'Napoleon' and 'Waterloo' are intoned in connection with the word 'Heroic'. But Waterloo was where Napoleon's genius forsook him and his Icarus flight ended in defeat.[1] With this warning in our ears, therefore, we are not surprised when the attempt at heroic sublimation ends literally in smoke.

The husband now disappears from the scene and with characteristic absent-mindedness leaves everything for someone else to attend to. This scene is a perfect description of the shadow-effect of the hero-ideal resulting from a mother-complex. The psychological *vis a tergo*, which we described above as an alien will, impels a man always to go beyond himself. The impelling force that is invisible and remote from his own knowledge of himself, is projected and transformed to a goal beyond the horizon. Thus the man with a mother-complex tends to be regardless of the near and immediate, straining his eyes and faculties to the far distance. He is literally absent-minded because his mind is in his distant objective, rather than in the immediate present. I have seen an English mediaeval drawing of a

[1] There is an interesting psychological nuance in the fact that Napoleon, like so many other national leaders who inaugurated a cultural departure in which a new national spirit emerged, was himself an alien.

witchlike woman using her son as an arrow and her husband as the bow. She is aiming to shoot her son over the sun. This launching of the son by the mother as an heroic shaft, energized by her brooding, unfulfilled will towards life, is also excellently portrayed in D. H. Lawrence's autobiographical novel *Sons and Lovers*. Naturally this daemonic magnification of the ordinary biological impetus of life is essentially a shadow-picture. On the one side we see the witchlike effect of the mother upon her son arising from her own unfulfilled ambitions and unsatisfied longings; but on the other we may find endless devotion, a clear-eyed vision of the ideal man and a patient formative love that merges the real and the ideal in a glowing atmosphere of faith. Hence the typical ambitendency of the mother-complex; in one man manifesting itself in the style of the *enfant gâté*, in another appearing as the instigator of heroic visions and enterprises. To a very large extent the determining factor is the mother's attitude. If her overweening devotion is at bottom self-indulgence, though her 'sacrifices' abound beyond measure and her prayers rise in a continuous stream, the answer of heaven is invariably a spoilt child. But the man of real heroic stature cannot be accounted for in terms of the mother's psychology. He comes in his own time whether or no. If the mother has wisdom she will not try to put her own brand upon him. For a great man needs a wise mother.

The dream emphasizes the negative side of the picture, because both husband and wife are so deeply immersed in the *participation mystique* of childhood that they are quite unable to discriminate the vital individual necessities of their marriage relationship, with its orientation towards the future, from the retroactive sentiments which command absolute allegiance to historical family ties.

There is an intimation in the dream that the dreamer has now to view her own psychology from an opposite standpoint. For the dressing-table that carries her mirror, in which she is naturally accustomed to see herself in a certain light, has been moved across to the other side of the room. Such allusions to the fact that the situation is now being viewed from another angle are by no means uncommon in dreams.

Now, in reality, the wife is just as absent-minded as the husband, and they are continually blaming each other for their respective lapses of memory. It is more noticeable in the husband, because in respect of his profession his mind is alert and keen. Hence his forgetfulness in the domestic sphere is particularly galling to his wife. Whereas the wife is vague, unpunctual and regardless of facts, because her mind is applied to nothing, soaring into space on the wings of romantic fantasies that are never intended to become real. Thus both are living the provisional life; but the husband, as in so many American interiors, is cast for the role of the scapegoat. The shoes, the bottles of mineral water, the dressing-table all pertain to the wife, and it is just here that the thunderbolt of unutilized energy is so indiscreetly deposited by the husband.

We must remember that the situation that precipitated this dream was a realization on the part of the husband that something ought to be done about the problem of the marital relationship. He had begun to see that his unconscious attempt to sublimate the sexual libido into terms of ambition and social success was not wholly satisfactory, and had accordingly made certain tentative overtures. Even the question of having a child had come into his mind, although in view of the wife's hysterical dread of pregnancy and physical pain he had dutifully tried to suppress his feeling.

The wife imagines she wants a full sex-relationship, but, actually whenever the husband approaches her, a swarm of contrary reasons and urgent gestures of procrastination fill the air. So that in the end he is made to retire with his need unsatisfied and with the exasperating suspicion of being guilty of lack of feeling and inconsideration towards his afflicted wife. The shoes, the effervescent mineral water and the dressing-table symbolize the wife's narcissistic fortress, her neurotic island of fantasy and self-content which must not be imperilled by the disturbing intrusion of purposeful energy. She has spent her life, under the mother's guidance and example, in carefully excluding from her paradise anything which threatened to become real. This is not because she does not admire real achievement (she even worships it in others), but because to admit reality into one's own life means to take responsibility for something and to serve it unconditionally. And this means to be shaped and, perhaps, even transformed by an unknown power. This is the very core of the neurotic fear of life, the dread lest something should so seize hold of the mind that one might be carried away and delivered over irrevocably to an unknown and unpredictable fate. At bottom, it is the ego's yearning dread of the Self.

Accordingly, although her mind is constantly surrendered to voluptuous fantasies, her body is a virginal citadel against which the husband's decorous onslaughts make no serious challenge. Her citadel is being faithfully protected by the three exponents of 'sublimation' in the next room. But though the ramparts are guarded, the dynamic masculine element of fire gets into the heart of the citadel, and, naturally, the husband is responsible. He ought to be looking after that fiery element, since it was he with his fiery ambition that brought the unruly passional element into her unproblematical paradise.

Lear, the original English word-cartoonist who invented the limerick, has beautifully depicted this provisional attitude of the ineffectual isolationist.

There was an old man who supposed
That the street door was *partially* closed,
But some very large rats
Stole his coats and his hats
While that futile old gentleman dozed.

The rats are, of course, the excluded aspect of the instinctive life which consciousness has repressed. In our patient's psychology it is the fiery element of passionate purpose that has been excluded, and that, now, gets in. Apparently the fiery god resents being relegated to the pressing of trousers and reverts to his original human function, namely, that of creating a domestic fire. Not being offered the hospitality of a hearth he proceeds to make a fire with the materials at hand. The first thing the wife supplies him with is some newspapers. Suitable material one would say from his point of view, but surely not from hers. Why then does she do it? When someone does something which has exactly the opposite result from what was consciously intended we can infer the presence of an unconscious tendency that will decide the event, conscious resistance notwithstanding. But the newspapers are not only combustible material, they also symbolize collective opinion, or the general view. Thus in giving the newspapers to the fire-god the wife is performing a symptomatic act which is a way of saying that she would like to be free in this, her personal interior, of the tyranny of collective opinions and conventional ideas.

But when the sheets of the marriage-bed show a tendency to become compromised by the fiery visitor, the situation must be dealt with firmly, and they are moved out of harm's way. From this we might conclude that although the attempt at the social sublimation of the sexual libido has broken down, the libido thus released is not yet to be given hospitality as a welcome guest. The reason for this refusal is given in the second half of the dream.

The focus of the dream now shifts from the problem with the husband and lights upon the little girl Vasha. All that can be gathered about this child is that she is a charming, expansive girl of ten who often reminds the patient of her own childhood. The significant fact is that this artless little creature with her world of fairies is being idolized by the mothers in the adjoining room. The recoil from the challenging visitor who threatens the hitherto virginal peace of the marriage-bed leads naturally to the little girl who symbolizes the childish immaturity of the conscious attitude. Since the patient is quite unaware of her own childishness, the little girl might represent her shadow, which everyone else can see.

The reader will remember the fact mentioned in the history, namely, that a clinging fog of sleepiness invaded her mind at puberty and has persisted ever since. Puberty is the first decisive watershed where, as Jung has shown in his *Psychology of the Unconscious*, the libido tends to divide against itself; a forward-moving stream being countered by an almost equal regressive tendency. When the major portion of the libido achieves the transit the regressive movement is gradually overcome. But when, as in the present case, the transition from the childhood personality to the developing seriousness of adolescence fails, then those functions which would have emerged to meet the claims and challenge of maturity lie as it were dormant in the unconscious, becoming manifest only in the form of disturbing symptoms. It is by no means uncommon for a person whose best potentialities are not yet hatched out of the unconscious state to be beset by an apparently overpowering desire for sleep. It would seem that the term 'dormant' is more than usually apt, and that we might conceive the dormant unconscious self as exercising a magnetic influence, attracting to itself the libido out of consciousness, thus producing a compulsive, sleepy lethargy.

It is perfectly evident, both from the patient's history and from the dream, that the mother played a determining role in preserving and maintaining the engaging childhood personality. In her uprooted, purposeless life she needed the comfort which the child's dependence upon her supplied. She also needed the illusion that her duty towards the child absolved her from any other serious claim or vocation. The child became her neurotic alibi, and she employed every emotional resource to hold the child within this illusion of absolute mutual dependence. Moreover, were the child to develop into a free woman, creating a full and fruitful life, she would become an insupportable challenge to the mother's barren field. The unconscious neurotic art of a frustrated woman is immeasurably cunning and often completely ruthless in the pursuit of its negative goal. There can, therefore, be little doubt that the main responsibility for the unachieved transition from childhood to adolescence must lie at the mother's door, aided and abetted by Aunt Matilda whose doting affection demanded the same dependent, childish attitude in return.

Vasha, then, is borrowed by the dream-mind from the immediate milieu in order to personify the drama of the witches' spell which has to be broken if life is to be victorious in this individual experiment.

An important association was given to that part of Vasha's recital where she says, 'and whenever I get to that place I'm scared stiff'. The association was with Mary Rose, Sir James Barrie's psychological masterpiece, in which the heroine is enthralled and captured by the non-human aspect of the unconscious. Mary Rose, when still a child, had accompanied her father to a small island in the Hebrides, and, while he was fishing, she followed enchanting music and was caught and hidden by the fairies. No trace of her could be found, and the anxious search had to be abandoned. But, at last, after thirty days, her father saw her again on the island and rowed across to fetch her. She had no memory or knowledge of the intervening days, but when she came back into civilization she seemed different and showed a disinclination to grow up. Some part of herself had become 'fey' and stayed behind on 'the island that wants to be visited'. She eventually marries without being told of the disturbing incident of her childhood and is again drawn to visit the island with her husband. Again she hears the enchanting music and, again, disappears; but this time for twenty-five years, and when she returns like Rip Van Winkle she carries no trace of the intervening years. They have aged her no more than a night's sleep would have done. There is one detail that is especially interesting from its similarity with our dream. While talking to her lover one day Mary Rose suddenly hallucinates the figure of a little old woman whom she describes as 'a queer one'.

This association of the dreamer throws, therefore, a revealing ray of light on the nature of the fear that besets this too-childish personality. It is the expression of the hidden danger that lurks within the folds of the enchanted state. The magical childish mentality is easily enthralled. Mary Rose follows the enchanting music in a timeless paradisal condition, abandoned wholly to the dream or fantasy state. This abandonment means the annihilation or suspension of every disciplined function. It is a negation of every other factor and consideration; hence a kind of suicide.

The book of fairy-tales which the mother shows the dreamer goes to the heart of the danger by revealing the fact that to become enchanted means to be caught and held by a spell. The picture of the squirrels hanging by their tails and playing on taut strings suggests the enchantment of airy fantasy, the squirrels symbolizing the libido that is lured away, like that of a child, into unrealizable day-dreams. But the second picture reveals this state of enchantment as a creature in the toils of a witch. The little animal of the dream was associated with the picture of a kitten she had seen in a newspaper. The creature was actually yawning, but the words beneath the picture had read, 'the cat laughs'. This association came rather too near, because the patient herself has cultivated a particularly expansive smile which she uses for all occasions and with which she disguises her inert and wandering attention. The lethargic, yawning cat symbolizes, therefore, the vacuity of consciousness from which all independent purpose has been subtracted. The state of the libido is like that of a hypnotized subject, suspended and without volition. Hence the mother's allusion to 'battledore and shuttlecock', a child's game in which the monotonous batting of the shuttlecock between two persons is its sole charm.

The 'old spinster-like woman' does not resemble the mother, and yet is clearly intended to symbolize the sinister influence which has become characteristic of the relation between the mother and daughter. This is due to the state of unconscious identity whereby the frustrated and repressed condition of the mother's unconscious holds the daughter's libido in thrall. The witch might be described as the symbol of negation.

This dream provides us with a complete psychological diagnosis of the marriage problem from the angle of the wife's psychology. The husband's heroic attempt at sublimation of the passion of sex into asexual social channels is necessitated by the virginal, neurotic immaturity of the dreamer's attitude, which is again determined by her unconscious *participation mystique* with the neurotic mother.

How can this vicious circle be broken and the spell-bound libido released?

That is the problem which the analytical method brought into focus and for which a solution had to be found or created. I cannot attempt, in the space allotted to me, to follow out the development of the solution that actually took place. The discerning reader will already have observed that the passional element, represented in the dream in the electrically heated iron, passed out of the orbit of the dream without being dealt with. It was this element which became the pivotal factor of the subsequent phase of the analysis. The dynamic symbolism eventually detached itself from the inadequate forms of sublimation and descended as a storm-wind from the mountains to shatter the house of the spell-binding mother. From this point the patient began to feel herself as the possible mother of a future child, instead of being merely the child of her mother. At the same time her relationship to the actual mother became less complicated and more human.

My object in writing this brief study was to demonstrate the immediate practical bearing of dream-analysis in the re-creating of the general attitude. The attitude is the form or vehicle of individual adaptation both in relation to oneself and to the world. But just because, as we see in the dream, it is composed of factors that lie to a large extent outside the range of conscious insight, it is almost impossible to make one's basic attitude an object of consciousness without the aid of the dream-mirror.

When we consider the fact that the possibility of an effective connection with reality in either sphere depends upon this vital subjective factor, it is clearly of the greatest practical moment that we should find a reliable means by which we can bring it into harmony with the richest meaning of life.

That this end cannot be achieved by relegating to fate all responsibility for the essential needs of body and soul is the burden of this dream. To live provisionally means to depute to the unconscious just those functions of realization and responsibility that are needed for navigating an intelligent and effective course. The place which these functions should occupy in consciousness is filled, instead, by fuss and self-justification. For when a function that should be conscious is repressed into unconsciousness a sense of inferiority and self-accusation necessarily results. Hence people who are living the provisional life are constantly impelled to explain to anyone who will listen how the circumstances of their life, their ill-health, their intense sympathy for the suffering of others, their extreme sensitiveness to noise, light, heat, cold, psychic atmosphere, climate, constipation, insomnia and the rest, all conspire to prevent them from living a normal responsible existence.

The only possible cure for this condition is by the slow and painful realization of just those factors and functions which have been consistently pushed out of sight. To obtain this result the analyst needs to cultivate a binocular vision whereby the actually existing problem is viewed in the light of its psychological aetiology.

If I have dealt too exclusively with the negative aspect of the dreamer's psychology it is because the dream threw into relief the neurotic influences which had estranged her from her own proper being. It is necessarily, therefore, a somewhat one-sided picture for which I hope the very attractive lady who inhabits the other half of the house will forgive me, if ever her eye should happen to light on this somewhat critical study of her shadow.

The Psychological Background of the Parent-Child Relation[1]

I wish to thank you for the honour you have done me in inviting me to inaugurate this Symposium on Mental Health in Childhood and Adolescence. It will be interesting to see how differently this problem can be viewed from varying standpoints, and even more so, to see whether these differing views can be reconciled.

The fact that there are many ways of approaching the problem is not, in my view, a matter for regret. It only means that the field we are exploring is a complex one containing many different aspects, and, therefore, can be approached from many different sides. It is almost certainly a subjective illusion to suppose that the avenue which one has oneself selected is the only fruitful approach. But in order to reduce confusion to a minimum, it is, I think, a sound practice to state at the outset one's point of view.

It is, as you know, perfectly possible to study the mechanisms of the mind. They can be abstracted by the intellect, and can easily be handled as material for scientific research. This abstract of the mental mechanisms can be explained, for instance, according to the mechanistic hypothesis, and many valuable observations have been grounded on this basis.

I propose to leave this aspect to other contributors to this symposium, who are better equipped to present the biological environment of the child. What interests me in particular is the problem of the child-soul; in a word, values in preference to mechanisms. But the spiritual values which nourish the soul of a child, and which become the directive factor throughout his development, are not susceptible to a purely intellectual treatment, because values are judged by feeling rather than by the intellect. Yet what are called human values are as integral a part of the psychological inheritance as are the great biological machines, sexuality and the will-to-power. In general, it is a fair distinction to say that the psychology

[1] A paper read before the Medical Society of Individual Psychology, London, on 8 October 1936.

of Freud is based upon the concept of mechanism, whereas the psychology of Jung is based upon the concept of value. Being a general distinction, this is not intended to be precise; but it is sufficiently true to provide us with a means of orientation.

Let me use a theoretical illustration which provides at once the distinction between mechanism and value. Suppose a given man to be attracted sexually to a given woman. It is open to him, at least theoretically, to approach her on the assumption that he is acting in accordance with a general biological mechanism, for which he cannot be held accountable. His voice, his expression, his whole manner of approach will accord with the fundamental assumption that he is a mere pawn moved in this way by fate. The same man might approach the same woman from the standpoint of value. That is to say, his feeling would be in it. Because he values his instinct, he also values the woman to whom he offers it. His offer would, therefore, be backed by his personality. Again, his face and voice and gesture, his whole attitude, would be eloquent of the value he is trying to express. It is undeniable that sexuality is the activating motive-power in both cases. It is equally clear that what determines the psychological resultant is not mere instinct, but rather the individual attitude to the instinct.

When we speak of values, therefore, we necessarily have to employ this borderline concept of attitude. For the individual soul the problem is not, at bottom, a question of sexuality or any other urge; but rather the way in which the libido is honoured as the manifestation of life. We have, therefore, to bring into our psychological equipment the concept of *basic attitude*, inasmuch as this factor decides how the instinctive mechanism is individually determined.

The instincts are common to all mankind, not to mention the rest of the animal kingdom. They belong indifferently to the primordial, natural man, as well as to the cultural. But values belong to the cultural inheritance, and manifest just as great a variety as there are differentiated cultural organizations. Instinct is the everlasting 'I am'; neither good nor evil. But values are the expression of the historical continuity of the cultural process, and are, therefore, an essential aspect of the time-dimension: not the past alone, but also the future. For the stream of history does not end in the present moment as in a cul-de-sac. There is also a forward extension which, in our psychology, is represented by the determining effect of unborn future potentialities on the present moment.

Individual feeling is based in the main on these historical values. They are the *a priori*, or ancestral, elements in our psychic structure, and are represented in our dreams, as in Chinese culture, by living ancestral figures.

This dynamic time-dimension pervades the whole fabric of the parent-child relation, for the symbolic value of the child is due to its being the forward extension of the parent's individuality into the future.

The importance of this conception is by no means confined to psychology. Leading biologists, such as the late Professor Haldane, Professor Coghill of Philadelphia, and Dr. E. S. Russell of London, have long since realized the necessity of introducing the time dimension into our conception of the living creature. Dr. E. S. Russell, for example, expresses himself as follows:

> Time then enters as an essential element into our definition of organism. The living thing, at any one moment of its history, must be regarded as merely a phase of a life-cycle. It is the whole cycle that is the life of the individual, and this cycle is indissolubly linked with previous life-cycles —those of its ancestors right back to the dawn of life. And the activities of the organism at any stage of its career can be understood, only if they are reintegrated both in the individual and the evolutionary life-cycles.[1]

This citation from Dr. Russell's writings presents, to my mind, the only biological standpoint from which the problem of the child-mind can be approached. It confirms our view that before we can properly understand the mechanisms of the child-psyche, we must first form a picture of the psychological background; the actual soil in which the child-soul is rooted.

When we consider this problem of background we can distinguish two distinct levels. The first and most obvious matrix is, of course, the parental psychology. I shall call this the *personal background*, since it consists of those personal factors which affect the child through its continuity, or state of emotional identity, with one or other of the parents, and also by the character of the relationship existing between the parents.

The second, and far more elusive, background consists of the impersonal, mythological contents of the collective unconscious. We can discern this impersonal psychic matrix in two ways: (*a*) by observing the child's behaviour when it is entirely alone and solely

[1] E. S. Russell, *Interpretation of Development and Heredity*.

preoccupied in fantasy-play; and (*b*) through a study of the dreams of children.

Everybody who has had the opportunity of observing children in their own environment must have recognized the remarkable difference in a child's character when trying to adapt to the persons of his *milieu*, and when he is entirely alone, absorbed in the world of fantasy, or experimenting freely with objects. In the former character he is obviously conditioned by the expectations, the attitude, the demands, and often the interference of the persons upon whom he depends. In the latter, he seems to float upon a timeless and tranquil stream which is unruffled by insistence or blame or approval. Many children seem to be able to drop through into this realm of impersonal fantasy, as an escape from their all-too-competent supervisors. In this state, they seem to be caught up in a dream, or else they incorporate the things around them into a waking dream-content. The dream then becomes expressed through certain magically endowed objects.

I propose to deal first with the personal background, or at least attempt an outline of certain elements of the parental constellation. In a later section I shall present a few dreams of children which afford a glimpse of the impersonal background.

The psychical matrix in which the individuality of the child gradually forms is, as we have said, the parental psychology. In the average case, the infant's dependence upon the mother, at first absolute, then gradually lessening, results in a state of psychic continuity amounting almost to identity, between the child and the mother. The security of the infant-mind depends upon this state of contained identification with the mother.

We know, from the analysis of so-called adult people, that the state of emotional identification with one or other of the parents very often lasts throughout life. As a rule it is only completely broken in the individual who is singled out by fate to realize the solitariness of his individual soul. This extraordinary persistence of an infantile state of dependence cannot be explained by any theory which comprehends only the conditions and events of the present life-cycle. It is not due to a fantastic prejudice in the minds of the great pioneers of modern psychology that both Freud and Jung had to base their fundamental conceptions upon mythological patterns. When Freud, for instance, explains a certain aspect of the parent-child constellation as a rehearsal of the Oedipus myth, he really implies that he is using a very ancient idiom for a very archaic, emotional state. And when Jung speaks of the mother as the devouring monster, and the experience of the unconscious, during the analytical process, as the night-journey under the sea, these are not mere figures of speech. To use Dr. Russell's phraseology, there are certain events occurring in the depths of our psychology which 'can be understood only, if they are reintegrated both in the individual and the evolutionary (or ancestral) life-cycles'.

The identification of this child with this mother is only one item in a chain of indefinite duration. It is merely the case in point. But really to understand its meaning, we need the historical vista that will embrace the innumerable antecedents to this contained state, namely, those similar states and events which have been regularly repeated in the biological life-cycles ever since the dawn of life on this planet.

We find, for instance, a very interesting analogy to this infantile condition in the beginnings of civilization. In his valuable work, *Human History*, Sir Grafton Elliott-Smith presents a picture of certain indigenous food-gathering people still existing on the outskirts of civilization. He mentions the Eskimos, the Australian Aborigines, certain tribes of North American Indians, the Bushmen of Africa, the Punan of Borneo, the Andamanese, etc. These people, though far apart as the poles, share a remarkable similarity, both in character and social organization, and they show a remarkable difference from the so-called cultural races and tribes. They have no kings, no gods, no cultural heroes. They have a natural family-communism, and their virtues are not named and cultivated, nor are their vices deplored. They will not grow grain, nor provide against future adversity. As a rule, their houses are the merest shelters, made of boughs and, with the exception of the Eskimos and Indians, they wear no clothes. In fact, they resolutely decline to leave behind their contained natural state. They are contained within the law of their species, in the same way as the animals. Their natural dignity and piety seem to be due solely to the fact that they have maintained the primordial state of man, as though still contained, psychologically, in the womb of Nature; not remote as we are from the primordial source of life. They do not resent adversity, because they have no other hope, and no other basic premiss, than that of the son wholly obedient to the law of the original Mother. The type of initiation among these people, when it exists at all, is individual rather than collective, and has the effect of enhancing the youth's natural courage and mettle. Hence these people cannot be enslaved.

In relatively primitive societies, which are no longer in this pristine state, tribal organization, with a corresponding hierarchy, tends to take the place of the original familial basis. Accordingly, the individual members live in a state of psychic continuity, or identity, with their tribe and tribal environment. But the form of tribal initiation, existing among these collectivized peoples, has the effect of alienating the adolescent youths from their original, natural state. Having passed through the initiatory ordeal, the youth is contained wholly by his tribal organization. In a certain sense, therefore, initiation serves the purpose of substituting the law of the tribe for the original unconscious law of the species. This state of emotional identity with, or participation in, a collective matrix is found also among civilized people as a background psychological condition. Jung's experiments in word-association tests, for example, show that mother and daughter, or husband and wife, tend to have identical word-associations, even up to 30 per cent or 40 per cent. In savage psychology Lévy-Brühl has described this state as *participation mystique*.

This unconscious state of identity is a background condition. It does not appear on the surface. Personality is a positive formation which calls attention to itself. But identity is a passive state, wherein the individual is merged with his cultural background or psychical container. We become aware of it only by certain defects or omissions in the personality-picture. Take, for instance, the case of Hamlet: a good soldier and man of action; a worthy prince, except that he is given to melancholy soliloquies. He loves Ophelia, he desires her as his mate; yet he cannot take her. His love-will is not there. Psychically he is impotent. But if he does not possess his love-will, who does? Where has it been left behind, or deposited? No essential function or element can be conceived as absent from any given psychic constitution. What is lacking in the conscious personality will be found either dormant in the unconscious, or projected into an object. It is because certain functions remain, split off, or isolated from consciousness, that they become manifest in the form of projections upon objects. The scene in the bed-chamber with his mother, where Hamlet stabs the invisible eavesdropper behind the arras, is Shakespeare's symbolical answer to our question.

Hamlet is impaled upon his mother's sexual treachery, because of his unconscious identification with her. It is as though, emotionally, he was anchored in the mother's unconscious, and therefore, although the wind of desire ruffles his sails, he cannot get under way.

Yes, you may call this Hamlet's incest-problem. And so it is. But since no man actually wants to sleep with his mother, or fears to be castrated by his father, is it not better to regard incest and castration as idiomatic expressions of the archaic backward-drawn state of the libido, whereby the will that should belong to the son remains passively contained in the mother?

This recession of the libido backwards to its source is not confined to human psychology. We share this tendency with all living creatures; for what we call regression is nothing but the instinct to recoil from the next evolutionary phase. Creatures that undergo metamorphosis, as for instance, certain insects, afford excellent examples of this tendency. In the larval stage of lepidoptera there is a certain mortality at every change of skin; there is a certain percentage of unhatched eggs, and a still greater percentage of individuals fail to survive the histolysis of the pupal stage. We can observe the liability of domesticated animals, such as hens and dogs, to fatal disease between adolescence and maturity. These facts correspond with the incidence of neurosis in man, at the nodal points of transition in the life-curve. Wherever we look we find evidence of the fact that evolution imposes an increasing strain upon the developing organism, and that certain individuals, in face of this strain, find it more plausible to recoil than to go forward. Civilization is merely an accelerated process of evolution and, because of its formidable momentum, the various evolutionary phases of the individual life-curve entail a degree of tension and strain which certain individuals cannot tolerate. The vital energy either flows forward to its evolutionary objective, or backward to its source. In the human family, this backward stream of libido is necessarily motherwards, seeking, apparently, the original state of contained security. The father represents the cultural symbol of masculine authority and progression. Hence, the infantile libido is liable to collide with the accusing authority of the father in its regression towards the mother. Thus the drama of the unconscious, namely, evolution versus regression, which is the one supreme conflict of civilizing man, finds an excellent symbolical expression in the familial pattern of incest.

If, from the proud realization of our own normality, we exclaim 'but there ought to be no regression', we merely interpose an artificial postulate between our intelligence and reality. The actual facts of experience assert and reassert the fact that at every critical juncture, or transition point, the vital stream tends to divide against itself, exactly as though an obstacle, or watershed, had been reached. In this crisis the backward-flowing stream of energy tends to resist the impulse that rises to take the onward leap.

Because this is a regular phenomenon of life, all our ideas as to what ought to take place can only prejudice the issue. Our progressive assumptions merely serve to estrange our minds from a true understanding of the case. In the presence of a retrogressive recoil, it is better to ask, 'What value could this backward movement have, in the long run, for this particular subject?'

Herein is to be found the great dividing line between Freud and Jung. For Freud, psychology is primarily the study of psychic mechanisms. For Jung it is the understanding of psychic values. Knowledge of the characteristic, or typical mechanisms, is necessary and fundamental. No one could question it. But the understanding and appraisal of psychic values is surely of greater importance; because, without it, we are quite unable to do justice either to the evolutionary or to the creative urgency in man.

When, therefore, from the standpoint of value, we ask the question, 'Why does this individual turn backward at a particular juncture, instead of going forward?' we find, in nearly every case, a positive ground, which can be briefly stated as the need to retrieve something that has not been lived out in the previous phase.

The case of a patient of mine illustrates this. He was a young Irishman of twenty-six who could not face any of the responsibilities of adult life. He had been to an English public school and university, yet remained a complete anonymity. School and college made no mark on him, and he no mark on them. He was scarcely visible. By flowing with the surface stream, he was just able to do what was required of him. But education failed to educate him: it just flowed over his head. At the university his whole interest was in boys, whom he watched with a passionate, absorbed interest. He was so spellbound by certain boys, that, although it was his dearest wish, he was quite unable to make any approach to them. Naturally, he had a tremendous problem relating to his mother, upon whom his adoration and his criticism fell in equal measure. The father, a retired officer, was a good deal older than the mother, and had tried to win the son's affection by identifying himself with his hobbies on the same level as the boy. Both parents had, in fact, competed for the boy's interest out of a secret hostility to each other.

The real problem with this lad was that, being somewhat frail and small, and, therefore, somewhat lacking in masculine vitality, he had remained too long identified with the mother. Instead of seeking its own goal, his instinct was caught up and preoccupied with the love-problem of his young and attractive mother, a problem which galled him like Hamlet's wound, and which eventually shattered his faith, breeding bitterness instead. The mother had ceased to love her husband and was involved in a subterranean affair with a younger man; although good form and respectability were never openly violated. The boy's instinct was sucked down into this erotic situation, as in a vortex; so that he was not free to go out and live his own boyhood with other boys. He told me he had never really played as a child. Always his activities had a rather precocious adult tinge, as though he were reflecting his mother's or his father's interest, rather than following his own. He was aloof and distant with other children, and at school and college he never felt he was among his own peers. This aloofness was a symptom of the deep emotional entanglement in a problem, belonging to the generation above his own. He felt and behaved to other boys as though he were already on a level of experience that was far above theirs. In reality this was an illusion, a false premiss, a disguise to cover the fact that he was even more inexperienced than boys of his age. Emotional identification with an older person is one of the most frequent causes of neurotic failure in the young. For it means that the libido is diverted from the problems and tasks belonging to the adolescent phase, and becomes precociously invested in adult tangles from which the youth has no means to extricate himself.

This case of obsessional neurosis is relevant to our theme, because it shows how the roots of the neurotic tendency are fed by the marriage problem of the parents. And when I say this, please do not misunderstand me. It is not because the marriage was unsatisfactory and problematical that the child became a neurotic victim; but simply because the family situation was rotten underneath, while apparently respectable on top. It pretended to be a fair example of the human trinity, in which the basis of reciprocal loyalties affords security to the child-soul, whereas, actually, there was resentment, frustration, and fundamental disloyalty to the human pact. If everything had been ventilated in a spirit of candour, the child would not have become fatally involved. He would perhaps have been upset that the parents had to blow up occasionally, but he would not have been drawn into their problem. But because of the presence of a basic disloyalty, the mother tried to pull the boy over to her side, in order to use him as a weapon against the husband. Also, and this was psychologically more unpardonable, she attempted to win the boy's sympathy and support, in order to assuage her private sense of guilt in respect to the lover.

It was most interesting to observe how the lad poured his most bitter scorn on anybody, or anything, which had the flavour of insincerity. It was the one thing he hated most. And this was because his boy's soul had been ravaged by an atmosphere of emotional insincerity.

It has been my experience that the worst injuries we have to deal with in psychotherapeutic practice are not caused by direct traumata, or even by brutal acts, but rather through constantly breathing an atmosphere in which the ideal, professed on the surface, is betrayed behind the scenes. Unreality and moral contradictions in the parents' love-life sow the seeds of hell in the child-soul.

Another frequent ground of spiritual disturbance is caused by parents whose lives are ostensibly controlled by a traditional code of values which, in fact, has lost all relation to existing reality. The discrepancy between the parental code and the generally accepted values and ideas in the world outside the home, often produces a tragic isolation of the child-soul and a complete inability to adapt to a self-contradictory universe. Franz Werfel has portrayed this tragedy with great insight in his novel *The Pascarella Family*.

Here again it is the factor of sincerity rather than divergence which counts. If the parents' ideas are rooted in genuine conviction, the child respects the attitude even though he may eventually criticize the content. The confusion is worst where forms and values are insisted upon for sentimental reasons, while at the same time the parents conduct their lives in a way which is a betrayal of the ancestral virtue. In such cases the child is invariably contaminated by the air of spiritual unreality, and hard-boiled, worldly cynicism is often the result.

So far we have dealt with the harmful effect of spiritual inertia, whereby the child is presented with an ambiguous, distorted view of reality which often covers up a dangerous rift between the parents.

Let us now consider another case, in which the distance between husband and wife is, in a way, natural and inevitable. Where, for instance, a too great difference in age, or an insoluble difference of caste and race creates a psychological distance which nature cannot span. As an example of this latter type, we are given a remarkable picture in D. H. Lawrence's *Sons and Lovers*. The superiority of the mother in relation to the father, both in regard to character and social level, is shown as the origin of the morbid mother-son constellation. This superiority breeds a certain feeling of contempt and scorn for the father. All the mother's passionateness is turned away from the father, and falls in a fateful concentration upon the favoured son. All her sacrificed ambition, her will and desire for a fuller life, is projected upon the son in an intense and, apparently, selfless, formative love. The son becomes her desire for life, the pattern into which the deepest desires of her nature are interwoven. Psychologically, the boy is more than a lover even: he is her creation, her vessel which she launches into life with an impetus that takes on the character of a ghostly daemonic influence. Lawrence was a daemonic personality, driven by the force of some alien will which, throughout his whole life, impelled him to create a new heaven and a new earth. The passion which consumed him, and which often blazed out in irrational volcanic outbursts against his wife, his friends, and his environment, becomes intelligible when we read *Sons and Lovers*.

I know of another case in which a young American wife, growing up beside an aged husband, projected her passional nature into her only son. From the time he was conceived she was determined to make a genius of him. In a way she succeeded, but at a tremendous cost. For his almost superhuman concentration on his career as an artist, rooted in the emotional identification with the mother, made him unscrupulous and irresponsible towards every other human tie. Marriage, friendships and social loyalties were all burnt up in the one intense flame.

A second son had been adopted, who was naturally overshadowed by the elder brother's genius. The mother's creative idea covered him also, but without the passionate flame. He became an introverted, somewhat mystical painter, who longed to emulate the elder brother's genius. But his vitality had always the character of the ebb-tide; so that he felt completely isolated in the extraverted American scene, and all his achievements were chilled by the atmosphere of frustration. Like his brother, he too could not create a home, because no warmth of loyalty and affection had been cultivated for the service of the human hearth. The younger children, who were all girls, were even more depleted, and entirely failed to maintain a foothold in the world outside the orbit of the mother's power. Her power had become absolute in her own orbit; not because she was an exceptionally gifted personality, but because the husband, being already rigid with age and conservatism, had no means of withstanding her energetic masculine will.

It is important to note than in this latter case, as in that of D. H. Lawrence, the effect of the mother-complex was entirely different in character from the obsessional case mentioned earlier. The flame of genius may entail very considerable sacrifices of other functions, which is shown in the fact that most men of genius have a neurotic shadow-side. But genius is an affirmation of value, and its flame is sincerity. The mother of the man of genius has a real passional goal, which she usually follows with intense and single-minded sincerity. Whereas in our obsessional case, the mother served no gods other than her own egotism. Being at bottom cold-hearted and easy-going, she simply attempted to steer an egotistical course without causing scandal.

In both cases there was the problem of disparity of age between husband and wife. But this fact does not afford us a true key to the psychological background. It is only a contingent factor. In the obsessional case the father had reached his zenith in the pre-war epoch. All his associations, feelings, and prejudices belonged entirely to that period. He identified himself with his youthful success in athletics and in the army, and failed completely either to understand, or adapt to, the modern world. Psychologically he was a relic of the past, and all his values were out of key, continually jangling, like the notes of a cracked bell, in the world of to-day. In the other case the aged husband, an old-fashioned American Puritan, made no attempt to inhabit the same world as his wife. He was a patriarch without potency, and his relation to his children was apparently limited to a silent participation in the family meals. None the less, the wife was always loyal to him and never, in any way, undermined the children's instinctive respect for their distinguished father. Accordingly, although the family atmosphere was restrained by the presence of the patriarchal figure, it was not vitiated by underlying insincerity, as in the former case.

In cases where the parents belong to different races, thus bequeathing to the child two distinct and perhaps mutually antipathetic cultural traditions, the resulting mixture is usually somewhat unstable. This precarious psychic organization is, frequently, made even more unfavourable by the effect of social prejudice, which always anticipates the worse from every cultural *mésalliance.*

The viewpoint which I have tried to present to you to-night is based, fundamentally, on the psychology of values. From this point of view we must regard the individual as a mixture of general human elements. These elements are constellated in a certain unique, molecular grouping by the cultural valuations they receive from parental and environmental influence. Individuality is like an experiment of nature, in which a unique and distinctive grouping of psychic elements is being tried out. Where the mixture contains cultural elements of a too great disparity, the resultant individuality will show signs of instability and a tendency to disintegration. When a somewhat doubtful mixture is not too heavily conditioned by adverse influences, individuality may succeed in producing an integrated combination of a highly original character. A completely harmonious mixture, in which the cultural values are handed down to the children from both sides with complete conviction, usually results in well-adapted children, who tend rather to reproduce than to make history.

I have laid great stress on the factor of sincerity in the parental attitude, because children are influenced only by the way in which the parents actually live. If their precepts and teaching are at variance with their lives, it is the latter which impress the children, not the former. No camouflage is effective in masking the truth from the child-soul, and I have found again and again that the child's reactions are constellated by the unconscious rather than by the conscious motivations of the parents.

I remember a case in which two boys had a persistent fever, and were actually sent to a sanatorium at Davos, diagnosed as incipient tuberculosis. The mother then came to be analysed, and a fierce resistance against the husband was gradually pulled into the light. This state of resistance had been rigorously repressed in order to preserve her ideal of domestic harmony.

On the very day that the actual state of affairs was realized by the mother the temperature-curve of both boys fell to normal and the fever never again returned.

Such facts need to be generally recognized, because the almost complete defencelessness of young children is a very serious problem in mental hygiene. Jung tells of the case of a man who came to him for analysis, and declared he never dreamed. During the early days of his analysis he brought some dreams of his boy, aged ten. It was at once apparent to Jung, by the character of the dreams, that the boy was dreaming not his own dreams, but his father's. The father, who was psychologically opaque, had realized nothing of what was happening to him. Therefore, his little son had to become a kind of medium to the events taking place in the father's unconscious. The child-psyche is highly suggestible, and can very easily assume a mediumistic function; but it is an imposition upon the individuality of the child which may have destructive effects.

It is through such observations as these that we are able to understand the vulnerability of the child-soul to atmospheric conditions. Just because the psychological state of infancy and childhood is based upon unconscious identification with one or other of the parents, the parent who insists on remaining unaware of his problems necessarily makes his child the scapegoat of his sophisticated obtuseness. Our psychological knowledge is still very limited: but it has at least originated a new moral feeling which in the course of time is liable to change the whole character of human relationship.

For this reason, the view I bring before you to-night is not likely to be popular, especially among those who, of necessity, have to deal with the problematic child under institutional conditions. Few parents are fully responsible in relation to their children, and very few indeed are willing to accept the view that they may be responsible for their child's sickness.

Scarcely ever are we in a position to analyse the whole parental situation. But the more that doctors, educators and parents are informed of the real facts of human psychology, the more is it possible to regard the child as the potential indicator of his parents' unconscious problems. Many workers in child clinics are already attempting to handle the parental aspect of the child-neurosis. Indeed, everyone who has the practical handling of children must, to some extent, be aware of the psychical interdependence existing between all members of a familial group; but we have a long way to go before public opinion will allow the all-too-personal sanctity of the home to be invaded by impersonal psychological principles.

I am, of course, aware that the cases I have cited to-night could be envisaged from the standpoint of the Oedipus pattern. But I do not find this explanation sufficiently comprehensive, since it tends to place the onus of guilt upon the child who has the incestuous longings, and, because it is merely a mechanism, it allows for no individual distinctions between the mother who makes use of the incestuous constellation for her own personal ends, and the one who infuses into the mother-son relation an impersonal goal which transcends her own personal interests. The Oedipus pattern helps to make visible a certain psychic mechanism, but it leaves the spiritual problem of value out of account. Notwithstanding this criticism, we owe an enormous debt to Freud for the invaluable light he has shed upon the darkest areas of the human mind.

DREAMS

The dreams of children very often provide valuable information about the background influences which are causing the neurotic disturbance. But there are also those other dreams of children which are as impersonal and profound as the stars: dreams which confound our understanding when viewed as the products of an immature child-mind.

By the courtesy of Dr. Michael Fordham, I should like to cite a case that came under his observation at the Child Guidance Clinic at Islington.

The subject is a boy of eight, who was sent to the clinic with a history of constantly playing truant from school. The boy was timorous and frightened of other boys. He was always trying to get away from the conditions of his life. On one occasion he actually ran away from home and got engaged as a page boy in an hotel.

The father is a weak, dependent creature, whose infantile tie to the mother precludes all interest in other women. His wife is merely a modified edition of the mother. His negative emotional attitude also shows itself in hysterical, violent moods and in truculent drinking bouts. He is, in a word, possessed by an archaic anima-daemon, namely, an inverted emotional complex, which colours his inner attitude with the character of frustration. Because his original emotional potential never became detached from the mother, his emotional capacity is terribly restricted and ineffectual in character, giving rise to irrational suspicions and paranoidal projections. This inverted emotional complex of the father terrorizes the domestic scene with inexplicable moods and tyrannical behaviour. Because he himself is a victim to the anima, he projects the devil that possesses him upon his next-door neighbour, and also upon the Jews. He asserted, for instance, in the presence of his family, that his neighbour was an unscrupulous bounder who owed money to his (the father's) firm, and who was not even married to the woman who passed as his wife.

One day the little timid boy invaded the neighbour's house when no one was at home. He upset the furniture and stole a bottle of scent for his mother, to whom, by the way, he was deeply attached. Because of this escapade the boy was brought to court. When the father appeared in court he burst out in a violent attack upon the neighbour, as though he were the devil himself.

The son's emotional identification with the father became evident on another occasion when he absolutely refused to make friends with, or even speak to, a certain boy who wanted to be friends with him, because the boy was a Jew.

These facts are enough to sketch in the outline of the psychological background. This boy had the following recurrent dream. There was another woman in the house besides his mother. She would come and seize him, and either lock him up in a room, or else try to put him in his father's trouser-press and squash him flat. He tries to call to his mother and, sometimes, she is able to rescue him.

The boy's dream accurately personifies the influence, caused by the father's emotional inversion, as a woman. This sinister figure represents the father's undisciplined emotional state. The father, when in his right mind, is just an ordinary human creature. But when possessed by the unbridled anima-complex, he is like a dangerous wild beast, infecting his environment with despotic moods. The boy sees both a father and a daemon; but the father himself does not see the daemon. The boy is, therefore, paralysed by inward fear which isolates and shuts him up in a subjective dungeon, where everything seems unsure and the gentle human forms he loves become inaccessible. The idea of the trouser-press is converted into a symbol of torture. In dream-language the lower part of the body is the unconscious, instinctive side of a man. Hence the trousers symbolize the father's instinctive problem. The son should not be entangled and crushed by this problem of the father. The boy is naturally tormented by the opposition, the irreconcilable contradictions, in his father's nature, which no one alludes to and no one explains. The trouser-press refers, then, to the father's need of self-discipline, and, therefore, the dream is a direct criticism of the father's unconsciousness.

In this case the mother remains constant, and offers security, while the father manifests the problem of duality. The boy's relation to the mother, therefore, offers him a haven against the irrational storms that break without warning from the father's unconscious.

The force emanating from the undisciplined complex is the most dynamic, as well as the most disruptive factor in the boy's environment. It is this force which makes so deep an impression on the child-soul, and which hypnotizes him to act as a kind of medium to the father's complex. As a result of the father's daemonic projections, the boy becomes his scapegoat. He is estranged from his own nature, and is even exposed to public disgrace by the background constellation; while the father remains entirely unconscious of how he is destroying his own child. In such a case drastic remedies are needed. Either the father must be analysed, and taught how to take responsibility for his own psychology, or the child should be removed for a time from the dangerous area of contamination.

This dream is clearly concerned with the morbid influences of the personal background. Let us contrast this with a dream of the impersonal background.

The following case is mentioned by Frances Wickes in her book *The Inner World of Childhood.* It illustrates, very beautifully, the immediate nearness of the child-psyche to the background of the collective unconscious. The adult mind has a more or less dense layer of unconscious and semi-conscious experience-deposits between the conscious function and the collective unconscious. Jung calls this layer the personal unconscious. But the child-soul has little, or none, of this intervening layer and, therefore, can be regarded as immersed in the collective unconscious. It is like an excerpt, or an opacity forming in the unconscious, somewhat analogous to a nebula forming in space. The child-soul is, therefore, in immediate relation to the fantastic imagery, to the primitive or mythological figures of the collective unconscious.

The dreams of young children can simply amaze one by their uncanny depth. The most profound ideas are represented in a child's dream, ideas which can be understood in their right perspective only when the mature individual looks back and remembers the dream that impressed itself upon his childhood's memory.

Mrs. Wickes describes the little girl as being rather fearful. She was afraid of people and new situations. She was also very afraid of the dark. She lived too much in the world of fantasy. By good fortune, she went to a school, when she was seven, in which a sympathetic teacher was very quick at sensing the problems of her pupils. This teacher was often able to respond to and elaborate the queer symbolical content of the little girl's mind. The dream is as follows:

I was at my desk. The floor opened and there was a big hole. The desk went down, and I went too. Then the desk stopped, and I went on. There was a passage that was underground. There was a snake, black with yellow spots. I walked right down his mouth. I walked all around inside him, and then I walked out again, and I came right out into bright sunlight.

This dream represents the impersonal, or general, background of the child-soul. Just below the floor of the child's consciousness we find the characteristic archetypal images of the general human unconscious. The snake is the symbol of the living archaism of the unconscious, in a word, primordial instinct, conceived of as non-human, maternal source. The combination of black and yellow is perhaps an impression of the original dualism of night and day. It is as though the child entered a primordial state in which there is, as yet, no conflict of the opposites. The underground passage probably refers to the birth channel, the transition from the darkness of embryonic existence into the light of day. This child-soul, having only recently emerged from the darkness of unconsciousness into a conscious human world, finds it still perfectly feasible to drop through the floor and re-enter that other realm of symbolic images, leaving the world of things and people behind her. For an integrated adult-mind this is practically impossible, because one gets involved in the labyrinth of one's personal past. The adult-mind is contained in the stream of history. Whereas the child-mind is fundamentally unhistorical, like the primitive, and therefore easily drops through into the timeless realm of the general unconscious.

My last example is a dream, remembered by a woman of thirty, who places the occurrence of the dream in her early childhood. The dream made a deep impression upon her, and this is how she remembered it:

I was in my parent's garden, and in front of me was a golden staircase, stretching from heaven above down to the earth. At the top of the golden stairway was a golden throne which was empty, whilst at the foot of the stairway was a stone, and on it was sitting the dejected figure of Christ. The whole scene was brilliantly illuminated against a dark sky, and up and down the stairway went angels. I went forward and kissed Christ, feeling very sorry for him, but he made no response.

The dream was so vivid and beautiful that she remembered praying every night that it might come again. She told it to her parents, omitting, however, the important facts that the throne was empty, and that Christ did not respond to her spontaneous advance.

I am again indebted to Dr. Michael Fordham for this beautiful example of a prophetic dream. In his paper on the Collective Dreams of Children, he informs us about the subsequent history of this child.

She began, somewhat precociously, to criticize the Church teaching, and would hold discussions with visiting clergymen about the apostolic succession and such matters. Later, at her confirmation, she did everything that was possible to get herself into the right frame of mind for the divine revelation that she expected. But when the day came she could think only of the prettiness of her dress, and there was no other experience at all. As she grew up, she became so miserable at home that she was allowed to go to Paris, where she became an atheist.

She also began to experiment pretty freely in the manifold possibilities of modern life.

At the time the child dreamed this dream, there can have been no real understanding of its meaning. But the fact that the little girl withheld from her parents any reference to the empty throne in heaven, and to the lack of response of the dethroned Christian deity, seems to imply a warning sense that the dream might give pain to her parents

Although, from the subsequent history of the subject, we can see how this dream predicted the individual problem, yet it can also be regarded as a statement of the general conflict that besets the modern soul. The god-value that was enthroned as an ideal image, absolute in power, in the remote spaces of the heavens, has indeed descended again to the human level. As an incalculable *dynamis*, it even creates a terrible unrest. Men are driven, they know not why, to achieve something, they know not what. This regressive metamorphosis of the ideal image was envisaged by Luther, who called it the *deus absconditus*—the concealed god.

The lack of response of the seated figure of Christ is, therefore, a symbolical rendering of the fact that this modern soul was unable to make the traditional response to Christ. She had to part company with the authority of tradition in order to discover again the original guide of instinct. Christ uttered his revelation two thousand years ago. In the meantime, civilized man has moved from the age of faith, and is led by his desire for knowledge. At bottom, the modern soul believes only what it knows. Beyond this knowledge of his own experience, man is inclined to be agnostic. But when we reject our childhood's shield of trusting faith, we have to learn to take responsibility for those functions which, before, were delegated to God. Thus the vacant throne in heaven actually synchronizes with the beginnings of a science of the unconscious on the earth. Whether this is for good or for evil we do not yet know. The angels on the golden stairway seem to suggest that the traditional guardians of the Christian values are still active, and vigilant, even though the throne of authority is vacant.

The first part of my paper is concerned with the personal psychological background of the child-soul, namely, the parental relationship. The second part is intended to give a glimpse of the general, or impersonal, background which, for want of a better term, we must call the collective unconscious. It is of the greatest practical importance to distinguish these two elements of the child's psychical make-up; because we only breed confusion in the mind, if we assume that the mythological images of the racial unconscious are only figures of the parents in disguise, or if we mistake a symptomatic criticism of the parental attitude for a phylogenetic reproduction of the Oedipus pattern. In either case the character of the product provides the clue

It is impossible to discuss the problem of the child-mind to-day without also embracing the question of the human relationship of which the child is a product. A scientific contribution is assuredly not the place for moral soliloquies concerning the meaning of marriage. But science is interested in discovering the conditions which have a determining effect upon the psychological health of the child; and when these conditions become generally known, it can scarcely be doubted that a new and penetrating light will be cast upon the marriage relationship. It is even possible that a new commandment, 'Thou shalt not make thy son thy scapegoat', will eventually be added to the decalogue. For as soon as the truth, that a child has to live the unlived libido of his parents, enters the moral consciousness of a generation, it is bound to add an immense educational and evolutionary impulse to the marriage relationship.

Marriage has already become problematical. The 'ideally happy marriage' seems to belong to a misty, bygone age. But even if we no longer believe it to be ordained by heaven for man's happiness, we must surely confess that marriage is an indispensable educational opportunity.

Freud versus Jung

AN ELABORATION OF A RECENT DEBATE CONCERNING BASIC PSYCHOLOGICAL CONCEPTIONS[1]

Freud discovered a new technique for the investigation and treatment of neurotic conditions. He also elaborated a theoretical viewpoint which, in conjunction with the technique, is called the Freudian method.

The method of obtaining free-associations by which the mental context of the dream constellations can be reached is an invaluable technical asset, but the whole theoretical system that Freud appended to his discovery is not merely open to question, but belongs in my opinion to a sophisticated metaphysic which is foreign to the spirit of science. The claim which this system makes to be a scientific psychology needs to be scrutinized and its inherent sophistication of attitude exhibited in its true colours. What, then, do we mean when we speak of science?

Science is knowledge gained by systematic observation, experiment and reasoning. Philosophy as a branch of science is defined as 'the examination and logical analysis of the general body of fact—a science which both in reason and in history precedes successful dealing with special elements of the universe.'[2] Psychology is defined as the science of the phenomena of the mind. I shall have occasion to refer to all of these definitions in the course of my argument.

I have said that the Freudian theory belongs to a sophisticated metaphysic. For the sake of experiment let us permit ourselves momentarily to be transported into a sophisticated logic-light system. If we can find a way out of the model, it may help us to see over the wall of the more formidable labyrinth of Freud.

The model I have selected is the classic sophism of Achilles and the tortoise. In this unequal contest the tortoise is allowed a start, and we are asked merely to concede that Achilles by virtue of his superior

[1] A debate on the standpoints of Freud and Jung, held at the British Institute of Philosophical Studies on 11 October 1927, by H. G. Baynes and John Rickman.

[2] *Century Dictionary.*

speed is able constantly to diminish the distance between himself and the tortoise. This seems reasonable, and we acquiesce. At this point a fine ear could almost detect the click of the sophist's gate behind us, for we are now in the system. The race has begun, Achilles starts at *A*, the tortoise at *B*. When Achilles reaches *B*, the tortoise is at *C*, *B–C* being less than *A–B*. When Achilles gets to *C*, the tortoise is at *D*, and so on *ad infinitum*. Although our common sense will rage at the impotence of the hero in his ignominious struggle, we are none the less contained by the premisses we ourselves conceded. Where is the trick? Something must have been overlooked. We failed to examine the hypothesis with which the ingenious sophist baited his trap. Too lightly was it assumed that it represented all the essential factors involved. If the *whole* situation had been taken into account, logic would have produced a truth instead of a tricky sophism. For logic, like mathematics, is only a machine; it can neither increase nor diminish; it brings out nothing but what we first put in.

In the present instance, by limiting the speed of the hero to the bare function of diminishing the interval between himself and the tortoise, we allowed it to be assumed that the receding tortoise was the hero's goal, and by this limitation we made even that goal unattainable.

Now when we mention the word 'goal', we have chanced upon a real bugbear of the sophisticated mentality. If we release the hero from the toils of the pusillanimous premiss he will of course go springing over the tortoise. But now we have to assume another goal for the hero above and beyond the reptilian one; for with this spring he also leaps out of the sophist's system into the problematic realm of teleology.

This word seems to have the power of evoking superstitious terrors from the dark ages which can apparently pinion the mind from behind and instil into it the dangerous notion of some hypothetical goal of divinity. At heart the scientific sophist is, like Frankenstein, terrified of his own spiritual possibilities. He dare not entertain the notion of any goal at all because his own logic would not allow him to remain with a relative or programmatic goal, but would goad him pitilessly down into his own particular hell, i.e. the Absolute.

If I were asked to put the case against Freud in a nutshell, I would say that he consistently views the heroic or divine element in human achievement in terms of a 'reptilian' formula. The 'reptilian' derivation is regarded as a scientific truth, while the heroic spirit is regarded not even as a problematical possibility, but as a mere sublimation product of checked reptilian tendencies. My aim is to show that this way of regarding man is not scientific.

In a recent discussion of the relative standpoints of Freud and Jung, the opener for the Freudian side, Dr. Rickman, took particular pains to dispel the idea that Freud ever had a viewpoint. According to him Freud had only made discoveries, while Jung had only made a viewpoint. It would scarcely profit us to argue this point, because it is an elementary condition of the mind that no interpretation of any phenomenon can be made without a viewpoint. It would be quite idle to deny that Freud has made interpretations. Therefore he must have had a viewpoint. What interests me especially is not that Dr. Rickman said this, but why did he say it? Is it perhaps because the examination of a certain view is likely to disinter the premisses on which the view rests, and can it be that these premisses will not bear too close a scrutiny?

The labyrinth of Freudian speculation—I use the term advisedly since a large bulk of Freud's later writings is self-confessed speculation—and the labyrinthine complications of his over-subtle kind of thought make a detailed critique almost impossible.

If one attempts to distinguish between the content of empirical fact in Freud's writings and the wealth of assumptions which are almost uncontaminated by fact, one finds oneself inextricably involved. I have therefore preferred to attack the system at its foundation. If the foundations are shown to be unsound it becomes superfluous to demolish the superstructure.

First let us review what Freud in fact discovered. He discovered the mechanism of repression. He discovered that the dreams of neurotic persons exhibited the repressed contents. He discovered that the repressed contents appeared to be exclusively connected with erotic tendencies, usually of an infantile or immoral character. He discovered certain infantile sex-patterns which he described in mythological terms (Oedipus-complex, etc.) and he discovered the technique of free association by which the mental context of the dream-imagery could be brought into consciousness. These discoveries are a very great achievement, and if Freud could have restricted the scope of his work within these empirical boundaries his claim as a pioneer of science could never be impeached. Properly speaking his work is a research into the unconscious sexual components and determinants of the human psyche, a research which any future psychology must take into account. But when Freud goes on to assume that the fact of universal sex-repression has provided him with a formula that adequately explains the immense variety and productivity of the human mind: when, in fact, he erects a psychological system upon a one-sided theory of psychic causality, then reason revolts and challenges his system.

Now the characteristic Freudian attitude to any criticism of the system is to assume that the objector's reaction to the dogma is motivated by his own unrecognized sexual repression. This attitude is frequently accompanied by a smile of intellectual complacency, not to say superiority, which would seem to imply a very unusual degree of sagacity and insight. This smile is an important psychological sign, and it is by no means peculiar to the followers and colleagues of Freud. It is really a 'cult' phenomenon and it appears when the identification with a given formula has excluded the existence of honest doubt from consciousness. The smile seems to say 'we know', 'the deep enigmas of the soul are answered'. It is a symptom of over-compensated doubt. In reality it is a smile that is fathered by faith rather than by knowledge. A mind that could plumb those depths where lie the secrets of the human soul would surely not display its awful knowledge with just that smile. This specific symptom must not be overlooked, because it denotes an attitude that conceals unconscious doubt and therefore excludes the possibility of objective discussion. Even were it always the case that adverse criticism is reinforced by unrecognized sex-repression, this fact does not necessarily invalidate the criticism. But, as a matter of fact, this assumption, that a critical modern mind is still horrified and disgusted at laying bare the 'bones of the ape', is immensely exaggerated. Only a sophisticated mind is shocked at the facts of his own instinctual nature, and only a sophisticated attitude could continue to assume that perfectly real objections to the Freudian dogma are invariably based upon an unwillingness to accept the 'horrible' truth.

But we must remember that for a decade or more Freud fought almost single-handed against a collective attitude which not only refused all recognition of his discovery, but even added personal vilification to its contemptuous refusal. Is it to be wondered at that these wholesale and barbarous projections thrown at a pioneer, just at the time when objective criticism was most needed, should have left him small inclination to accept that meagre quantity of real criticism that was subsequently offered? But this is a retrospective explanation. As pioneers of a new psychological orientation we neither need nor have any right to expect a general acceptance. But we do want a critical hearing. Our science has been starved of sound criticism. Like every other science psychology can never thrive in the seclusion of the laboratory. It needs a more bracing air where the special can meet and grapple with the general. Only in this encounter can the new acquisitions that our science has already won become incorporated in the general mind of our time.

I have enumerated Freud's discoveries and now, before embarking upon a critical survey of his theory, I am conscious of a desire to express our profound indebtedness to the man whose psychological penetration and unflagging devotion found and opened the door to the investigation of the unconscious mental processes.

This has already proved to be an incalculable gain both to science and to general culture, but the need to preserve this acquisition from the paralysing influence of a one-sided theory cannot be gainsaid. Ideas, like children, cannot too long survive in an infantile dependence on their progenitors. They too have to live in the world and only through a thoroughgoing criticism do we learn their actual worth.

The first of Freud's discoveries that I enumerated was the mechanism of repression. (The term 'mechanism' is used, psychologically, to denote a psychical activity or process that works independently of conscious direction.) In his valuable retrospect of the psychoanalytic movement published in Vol. II of *These Eventful Years* (Enc. Brit. Pub. Co.), Freud writes:

From the estimation of the phenomenon of resistance there resulted one of the pillars of the psycho-analytic theory, namely, the theory of repression. . . . The impressions and psychic feelings, for which the symptoms were now substitutes, were not forgotten without reason, or in consequence of a constitutional inability for synthesis, as Janet thinks, but had experienced repression *through the influence of the psychic forces*[1] whose success and distinction lay precisely in keeping them from consciousness and excluding them from memory. . . . As motive for repression and also as cause of every neurotic disease, one must conceive the conflict between two groups of psychic strivings. . . . The repression

[1] The italics are mine.

regularly emanated *from the conscious personality*[1] (from the ego) of the patient and concerned ethical and aesthetic motives. Repression affected the feelings of selfishness and cruelty, which may be generally conceived as evil, but above all the sexual wish-feeling, offer of the most glaring and forbidden kind.

The symptoms of the disease were thus a substitute for forbidden gratification, and the disease seemed to correspond to an imperfect taming of the immoral elements in man.

In this excerpt from Freud's own writings we can find evidence of that deep confusion of psychological ideas which permeates his whole theoretical system. Having observed the phenomenon of resistance he inferred the existence of 'psychic forces whose success and distinction lay precisely in keeping certain contents from consciousness'. That is to say, repression is a mechanism which operates independently of consciousness. In the next paragraph he states: 'The repression regularly emanated from the conscious personality (from the ego) of the patient and concerned ethical and aesthetic motives.'

By thus identifying an unconscious mechanism with the conscious personality (the ego is the '*I*', that which feels, acts and thinks, everything, in fact, which is connected with the self as a conscious being), Freud ignores the first necessity of psychological definition, namely, the necessary distinction between the ego and non-ego.

The conscious personality consists of all those contents and associations organized around the idea of self and throughout which conscious direction prevails. The unconscious comprises everything that is outside this organization. Therefore an unconscious mechanism cannot be described as emanating from the conscious personality. That repression is a fundamental necessity of biological economy is proved by the existence of the rigid sex taboo in primitive peoples. Moreover the repression of sexuality is absolute throughout the whole animal kingdom except for the brief periodic breeding season. How do these facts accord with the statement that repression proceeds from the ego? A repressed content is, as we know, the most inaccessible of all contents to conscious insight. How can this be so if consciousness is the source of the repression? Repression, in fact, is an innate tendency of which the ego is as much the victim as are the instincts.

To ignore the distinctive nature of consciousness means to deprive

[1] The italics are mine.

ourselves of that essential objectivity which is the first desideratum of scientific inquiry. The reader will remember that the function of philosophy was defined as 'the examination and logical analysis of the general body of fact—a science which both in reason and in history precedes *successful* dealing with special elements of the universe'. Now the terms 'conscious' and 'ego' are ideational contents belonging to that general body of fact. In other words they have a perfectly definite meaning. Freud, apparently without examination or analysis of what these terms generally denote, proceeds to make use of them in a way that contradicts their real sense, and we are led to suppose that he himself is indifferent to the problem. The nature and scope of the conscious function apparently does not interest him. We shall return later to this depreciation of consciousness by Freud. It is to my mind part and parcel of his mechanistic view of the psyche which I have likened to the sophism of Achilles and the tortoise and which we shall have to discuss more fully in its proper place. But before passing on to another aspect of the discussion, it must be pointed out that this identification of repression with consciousness had a most disastrous and far-reaching effect upon Freud's theories. He, naturally, had to conceive the repressed and distorted instincts as attempting by every kind of sly disguise to slip past the censorship of the conscious ego. He actually invented a censor—presumably an unconscious deputy of the ego—to guard the gates of consciousness during sleep. The morbid symptoms, dreams, fantasies, everything, in fact, that arises from the unconscious, was regarded as a substitute for forbidden gratification. It will be obvious that such assumptions arise from the mistake mentioned above, and become quite meaningless when repression is seen as a factor of inherited social instinct. Repression does not proceed from the ego; it was required by the needs of race-survival. Hence the almost unbearable power of taboo. Like every other instinct, repression is liable to be taken to excess, which means morbidity.

I shall now discuss Freud's attitude to the dream and shall attempt to show that the complicated dream-machinery invented by Freud is beset with this same confusion of thought.

In the same article from which I have already quoted, Freud writes: 'The formula—the dream is a (disguised) fulfilment of a (repressed) wish—best describes in principle the essence of the dream.' He then adds: 'By studying that process which transforms the latent dream-wish into the manifest dream-content (the dream-work), we have been enabled to discover most of the knowledge that has thus far been acquired on the subject of the nature and functions of the unconscious psychic life.'

It must be said at the outset that the above formula which purports to describe the essence of the dream seems lamentably poor. The fact that from earliest times dreams have impressed the hearts of men as having a fateful significance, that men deeply versed in the wisdom of life have steered their course by the aid of dreams, that at the most critical junctures in life dreams have often come to men as the very voice of heaven speaking to them, that primitive peoples to this day regard dreams as the voices of the spirits of the dead—these facts, which after all belong to the general body of knowledge, do not seem to have had any weight with Freud in his search for an adequate formula. The sense of a profound significance contained in the dream, as also the inner feeling of freedom belonging to the will, are phenomena of the mind and therefore belong to psychology as a science. But Freud takes no account of these things. That is to say, certain quite general facts of our mental life are simply ignored in favour of the deterministic doctrine which puts them out of court from the outset. Perhaps it is the fate of determinism to become so hypnotized by the tortoise that it cannot discern the wings of the heroic spirit of man.

Now I want to draw attention to the term 'wish' in Freud's formula. A wish cannot logically exist without a wishing subject. The ego cannot be that subject *ex hypothesi*. Therefore, either he means that the dream-wish is something that would be wished under more congenial circumstances, i.e. the embryo of a wish so to speak, or Freud has anthropomorphized the unconscious sexuality and the dream-wish is its offspring. This may seem to be a pedantic objection, but it is not so. An inevitable confusion of thought seems to attend Freud's theorizing, because he chooses to ignore the given conditions under which psychological facts must be viewed. In using the term 'wish' in describing unconscious tendencies, he shows us that he is projecting the character of a conscious process into the unconscious motivation, and is thereby lacking in objectivity. Similarly, when he uses the term 'disguise', we are tempted to ask who invents and arranges the disguise. To assume that the dream-content is disguised because its application is not clear reminds us of the Yorkshireman on the Continent, who assumed that the

Parisians were talking gibberish in order to make a fool of him. But what was it that blindfolded Freud to the real meaning of the dream? He had already found a key which had given him access to part of the dream-content. He had recognized the presence of sex-allusions in dreams, and this fact provided him with his hypothesis. I think it is true to say that as soon as Freud had this key in his hand his objective judgment forsook him. He proceeded to apply this formula to the whole content of the dream, and everything that could not be made to agree with it was ignored. This hypothesis with regard to the dream is precisely similar to the sophist's hypothesis with regard to Achilles. They are both true so far as they go. But because neither of them embraces the whole of the facts, they both falsify reality and consequently leave us unsatisfied. The whole machinery of disguised wishes, of manifest and latent content, of distortion effected by a dream-censor, is a complicated network of rationalizations required for the support of the all-too-inadequate formula. It would be hard to find a scientific hypothesis that demanded a more elaborate rationalistic paraphernalia for its justification, or a greater credulity for its acceptance. I make bold to say that the 'dream-work' elaborated by Freud is an ingenious theoretical artifact which reveals nothing about the real nature of the dream, but only the intricacies of the mind that invented it.

During the past twenty years and more Jung has developed a most delicate and penetrating technique of dream-interpretation which has long since dispensed with this cumbersome paraphernalia, and which by honouring the dream as an organized expression of the mind allows its meaning to speak. By this I simply mean that the total value of the dream tells, the values sensed by intuition and feeling as well as those of the intellect. In the making of the Freudian mechanism the dream itself had far too little say. To understand the language of dreams we have to become attuned to the mind of primitive man. What does this involve? Not a mere laying aside of the rational prejudices of the civilized mind, but an attitude of complete receptivity in order to learn what the uncivilized can teach. Living beside him, watching his constant use of metaphor, of crisp dramatizations, of oblique allusions, his complete innocence of abstractions, his plastic unity of expression—thus can we get an insight into the mind of the primitive and thus we can also understand the language of the dream. For it is the same.

The oblique expression is the natural one. No uncivilized man speaks directly to the point. But this natural obliquity is not a disguise. That is a rational interpretation of an essentially irrational fact. If Freud had discovered a potsherd covered with the hieroglyphs of a language still unknown to science, he would not have permitted the assumption that the unknown scribe had employed this figurative language in order to disguise his meaning. He would resort to this hypothesis only if a practical joke were suspected. And yet by identifying the repressive agent with the ego he converts the latter into a grotesque figure of authority, suggestive of an old-time pedagogue whose canings and impositions evoke in his victims only a genius for evasion and practical jokes. In a recent work[1] Freud has introduced the Super-ego—derived from the father—which, by reason of its ancestral connotation, somewhat mitigates the inadequacy of his original conception.

It is a tragic fate that the pioneer who rediscovered the dream, that most enigmatic and energetic expression of the soul, should have failed so cruelly to understand the value of what he had found. In his haste to rob it of its meaning he constructed a machine that macerated the husk, but the living kernel of the dream escaped him.

I must now refer to another vital factor in psychological investigation, which Freud seems to have misconstrued, and which is especially calculated to put a bandage over the eyes. I refer to the peculiar character of the relationship between patient and analyst.

One of the most important of Freud's discoveries was the free-association method by which the patient was encouraged to talk, apparently at random, around the figures presented by his dream. By this means the context of the dream-drama could be spread out in the light and the connections established between the dream and the hidden stream of mental life from which it arose. Now although these associations are apparently free from rational censorship, they are none the less strongly influenced by suggestion. Freud was on the *qui vive* for the subjective determinants that gave rise to the free-associations. But he overlooked one essential thing, and this was the overwhelming influence of his own personality upon the patient. He supposed he had isolated the patient's psyche and had obtained the ideal laboratory conditions in which the patient's mental mechanisms could be studied in complete objectivity. But he could not exclude his own influence from the experiment. And

[1] *The Ego and the Id* (Hogarth Press, 1927).

this he failed to take into account in appraising the dream and the associated material.

This is the more remarkable because Freud had himself emphasized the infantile character of the transference relation. The most outstanding feature of an infant's relation to the parent is a plastic suggestibility—'réagibilité' better describes the character of this relation—to the expectations and views of the parent. Whether the expectations are assumed or real, the child is constantly reacting to them.

Under the influence of the transference the patient becomes profoundly suggestible to the analyst's personality and viewpoint, and the fact that Freud had a certain formula, that meant a very great deal to him, undoubtedly acted like a powerful selective stain, drawing sexual associations to the front, while keeping those that would not tally with the formula invisible. I have myself treated a patient who had previously undergone a Freudian analysis. She confessed that, in order to please her analyst, she had fabricated a circumstantial history of early sexual traumata involving both her brother and her father. Her analyst eagerly availed himself of this material, explaining her neurosis as determined by these entirely imaginary events. Another example of a similar kind was a man whose neurotic troubles were the result of homosexual adaptation which had distorted his whole character. I very soon realized that the association-material he gave me was selected material. When I drew his attention to this fact he explained that, whenever he had any dealings with a hetero-sexual individual, there was an automatic reaction to the hetero-sexual orientation, whereby the normal homosexual associations were repressed. Often, he told me, when going over the dreams afterwards, he was shocked to discover how much material had been unconsciously withheld. It took me several interviews before he was able to counteract this habitual reaction and give me the whole material. These are not exceptions, they represent a perfectly regular occurrence, as regular in fact as the transference. Not only are the 'free' associations affected by the analyst's standpoint, but the character of the dreams undergoes a striking transformation through the influence of a new conscious standpoint. Patients who have previously been analysed under the Freudian method have shown me the dreams they had had during this phase, and I can well understand that the Freudian analyst can find a constant verification of his dogma in these dreams. For they are full of sexual symbolism, although often accompanied by an ironical intonation. Whereas in a new atmosphere, where the sexual dogma no longer prevails, the dream regains an individual freedom of expression.

Jung discovered the unavoidable influence of this personal factor when experimenting with word-association tests. He found that the personality and sex of the experimenter introduced an incalculable factor of variation. On one occasion he was experimenting with a colleague using the electro-galvanometer. He asked his colleague to think of something disagreeable, and a very slight response was elicited. Then Jung asked him if he had had in mind a certain incident that had occurred that morning in the hospital. Immediately there was a vigorous oscillation of the needle. The content in the mind was apparently identical in both cases, since Jung had happened to light upon the thing his colleague had had in mind. But in reality the content had acquired a strong emotional tone through the factor of relationship. Dynamically, therefore, a content that is known or shared by another person has an entirely different energic value from one that is not shared. Furthermore, the particular individual with whom the content is shared forms another specific factor. From such observations Jung realized that it was quite impossible to exclude the personal equation in any psychological work. He accordingly decided to take it fully into account. But this conclusion involved certain consequences. Scientific method has always insisted on the necessity of establishing absolutely rigid conditions in which the observed phenomenon can be verified and reverified. Freud, like all Western scientists, was schooled in the mechanistic causality of the natural sciences. Given certain causes and conditions, certain results will always be obtained. It was the most obvious and natural thing for him to assume that the same scientific method and doctrine would hold good for psychology also.

Here, I think, he made his chief mistake. He assumed he could obtain the necessary constant conditions by which scientific objectivity could be obtained. The incalculable individual factor is incompatible with this condition of constancy and it was consequently suppressed. No analytical method can ever be devised that will satisfy rigid laboratory conditions. The very nature of the investigation makes this impossible. Hence we are merely deluding ourselves when we attempt to force psychological research into a tradition which is essentially unsuited to the nature of its material.

The followers of Freud make great play with the term 'psycho-analytical method'. Freud has actually dropped into the habit of speaking of psycho-analysis as though this abstraction perceived, recorded, made conclusions, and affirmed facts with a pontifical inviolability and regularity. If we are indiscreet enough to investigate why this scientific automaton should be pushed forward so ostentatiously in the writings of the Freudian school, we are struck by a very surprising coincidence. The automaton seems to grow, like Frankenstein's monster, by virtue of a persistent and numbing depreciation of human personality. Even the individuality of the different analysts engaged seems to be engulfed by the automaton. Thus, on the one hand, we find an almost ecclesiastical apotheosis of the method, and, on the other, a constant tendency to reduce human personality to the level of elementary human fractions. These twain are complementary phenomena and, in my view, they form the most damning testimony against the dogma which is responsible for them.

Human personality is a tremendous fact and any psychological dogma that tends to diminish its importance by a fanatical insistence on a particular method is self-condemned. Now in the analytical relationship the interplay of two personalities is the essence of the situation, and the effects produced by this relationship call for the most delicate conscious handling. No patient will react in identically the same way to two different analysts, even though they practise the same method. The material will be different, the reactions will differ, the whole demeanour will respond in the most unmistakable way to every nuance of the personal situation. This change is naturally all the more striking when another psychological viewpoint comes into the arena and new vibrations deeper than the personal are brought into play.

Like every other form of repression, this repression of the personal factor in the Freudian dogma has its teleological aspect. What is the scientific ideal, then, which could operate so powerfully as to exclude from consideration one of the most essential factors in human psychology?—an ideal that was apparently taken over unquestioningly by Freud as a necessary postulate of scientific thinking.

Again we must say it was the mechanistic tradition. In his opening statement of the Freudian position, Dr. Rickman laid especial stress on the rigid determinism of Freud's method, and he left a very distinct impression on my mind that he identified the term 'scientific' with the deterministic hypothesis. This identification is quite commonly assumed, but the grounds for such an assumption are by no means sure. I must here refer to those definitions that I mentioned at the beginning. 'Science is knowledge gained by systematic observation, experiment and reasoning.' Psychology is 'the science of the phenomena of the mind'. Now determinism is a 'doctrine which holds that human actions are uniformly determined by motives acting upon a man's character and that he has not the power to choose to act in one way so long as he prefers on the whole to act in another way'. This doctrine is itself a mental product, a phenomenon of the mind which, by the requirements of science, must be systematically investigated. It is not an *a priori* condition of all minds, since many highly intelligent minds in the West as in the East are equally convinced of the reality of freedom. It is in fact a way of interpreting experience. As a psychological phenomenon the experience of the sense of freedom is universal. It is only the interpretations of this experience which differ; the determinist explaining it as a delusion, the voluntarist as real. It does not lie within the province of science to decide the issue between these two rivals. But it does lie within the scope of psychology to take note of the experience and to inquire into the grounds upon which the different interpretations rest.

I pointed out earlier that no interpretation of any fact was possible or even conceivable without a viewpoint. A manner of interpretation reveals a certain way of viewing things. There is a German word *Weltanschauung* which expresses this basic psychological attitude. As Jung has observed in a recent paper: '*Weltanschauung* is a most distinctive word and can hardly be translated into any other language. For it not only expresses a conception of the world, but at the same time the distinctive manner and form with which a man views the world. Thus there is an aesthetic, religious, romantic, practical *Weltanschauung*, to mention only a few of the possible attitudes.' Having shown the similarity between the concept 'attitude' and *Weltanschauung*, Jung continues: 'What, then, is to be understood by attitude? Attitude is a psychological concept which designates an especial grouping or ordering of the psychic contents that is orientated either by a goal or by a so-called governing idea.' As psychologists, then, we are not so much concerned with determinism as a doctrine, but rather with the deterministic or mechanistic attitude. We have now shifted our point of attack to something behind the doctrine, as it were, something more fundamental.

The deterministic attitude regularly approaches the psyche from the angle of causation. It is governed by the past, by history. It is always seeking behind the present individual moment for its derivations and historical antecedents. It assumes that if all these past determinants could be known the present psychological moment would be completely explained.

At this point I would like to explain why I associate the singular depreciation of human personality, to which I alluded above, with the deterministic attitude. How does the relation between analyst and patient figure in the Freudian schema? It is conceived as an infantile transference of the patient to the analyst, whereby the infantile experiences, attitudes, and memory-contents of the patient can be brought to light. That is to say, it is a purely historical or retrospective interpretation of the relation, which omits to take into account the active influence of the analyst's personality and basic attitude upon the selection and presentation of these infantile contents. In focusing exclusively upon the past determinants, we exclude not only the present but also the future determinants.

The rigid determinism of Freud will not allow the existence of future determinants. Theoretically Freud has conceived libido as purposive in character, but he is apparently satisfied with this purely general conception. Nowhere in his writings does he envisage the problem of any specific goal, or function, or aim of the libido beyond that of direct or vicarious gratification. The picture he throws upon the screen is only focused and clear on the historical plane. It either becomes vague or else abruptly stops at the point where history flows into the actual present and on into the future. The causalist viewpoint always tends to assume that, because the present psychic situation can theoretically be explained from discoverable historical determinants, the future in like manner is absolutely determined. But the will provides a point of departure, a new beginning, which is not determined historically. Thus a deterministic attitude will necessarily be blind to the whole horizon of future possibilities in its effect upon the psyche. The future possibilities are so to speak already contained in the undeveloped capacities of the individual. They are germinal realities; and nothing, as we know, is more potent than an embryo. It compels devotion with all the authority of the future race. But to admit the force and reality of future possibilities means to allow a final or purposive conception of psychic processes. The vital importance of Jung's conceptions in handling the real problems of life is that they embrace this purposive orientation of the libido.

It will be seen then that the historical interpretation of the relation to the physician, as a repetition of the infantile situation, is only a partial view of the case. The patient's actual situation is an impasse; the libido is seeking a goal, a way out. The impasse is broken only through a gradual weaning process, by which the growing power of a future determinant attracts libido away from the historical determinants. The physician is the way towards that goal. The libido can be released from the neurotic past for the purposes of the future personality *by way of the analyst*. That this is a true reading of the case is shown by the nature of the images that are projected upon him. He becomes the father, the medicine-man, the priest, the initiator, the deity, etc., that is to say, the one who knows the way, expressed in varying mythological terms.

These images would be rather meaningless unless viewed in the light of the expectations aroused by the analytical process. These expectations appear very exaggerated if taken literally, but when we remember that the analyst is the guide into the world of the unconscious, where the major portion of the patient's values and possibilities lie wrapt in the mummy wrappings of the past, it is not difficult to understand why the transference expectations should be expressed in mythological images. These expectations are aroused not because the analyst represents a certain method, nor on account of this or that personal distinction, but because he represents the gateway to that understanding of the unconscious where the 'buried treasure' lies hidden. The retrospective viewpoint only sees the repetition of an infantile position *vis-à-vis* the father, a daily confirmation of the Oedipus-complex or some other sexual pattern. But why? What is the purpose and function of the transference?

The attitude peculiar to the transference is perfectly appropriate and necessary when viewed, not merely historically, but also from the viewpoint of the future and the present. A man who sets out to climb a dangerous and unfamiliar mountain, or to penetrate unexplored territory, or to fly over the Himalayas, would show an attitude to his guide or pilot not at all unlike the transference-attitude met with in analysis. There is, of course, this difference that the neurotic patient is sick and, therefore, displays a relatively greater dependence. It can be objected that a sufficient aim is admitted in the hope of a cure. But the neurosis is itself the result of the lack of a positive goal or value in life. Thus a permanent cure depends upon the possibility of the way being discovered, by which that positive value can be realized.

Another character of the deterministic attitude is to dwell upon the structure and topography of the psychic apparatus rather than upon its function. Freud has invented a most elaborate apparatus with a quite speculative topography, but his conception of psychic functioning is entirely inadequate. One cannot escape the impression that his interest is confined to the problem of causal derivation and does not concern itself with the problem of teleology. This absence of curiosity as to why the psyche functions in specific ways would be unaccountable were it not for the deterministic prejudice which ignores such questions as superfluous.

I have said enough, I think, to demonstrate that the deterministic or exclusively historical attitude is not scientific, since science cannot afford to exclude any factors whatsoever which determine the nature of the living process. A temporary exclusion of vital determinants both in the present and in the future may be necessary in order to confirm or verify a particular formula, but a total exclusion is not scientific; it is merely fanaticism. In this connection I would like to repeat some observations made by Dr. J. S. Haldane in a lecture on the Fundamental Conceptions of Biology. He says: 'Structure depends on environment and environment on structure, and if we attempt to separate living structure from its active environment we simply fail. Form, composition, activity and environment are inseparably bound up together.' In another place he says:

> If we attempt to resolve the life of an organism into a number of separate processes we reach no intelligible result. . . . The wholeness in the phenomena of life is not merely externally imposed, as in the case of a machine; and if we neglect the inherent element of wholeness we are also neglecting life itself. . . . By studying the responses of renal excretion, of respiration, of circulation, of blood composition, of the nervous system, and of every other organ and tissue in the body, to changes in environment, we can discover how each organ or tissue plays its part in life as a whole, but if we leave out of account *life as a whole* because this consideration savours of teleology we reach nothing but an unintelligible jumble of unconnected observations.

I quote Dr. Haldane at some length because he is attacking the same mechanistic laboratory attitude that I am criticizing in Freud. He says that if we take a living organism out of its natural environment and study it under rigid laboratory conditions—such as we are told are essential to the psycho-analytic method—in order to obtain exact data, we are no longer dealing with the organism as a whole, but only with its structure. This is a perfectly sound procedure, so long as there is no danger of confounding the structure thus observed with the total individuality of the living organism.

Science being empirical must always avail itself of hypotheses that limit the field of the problem to be investigated. The danger, however, is a very real one that the hypothesis, whose chief service lies in circumscribing the field of inquiry, begins to assume the air and dignity of an independent science, denying any validity to those other hypotheses that are required to complement its inherent limitations.

As an example of this process we can name the organic or physical hypothesis in medicine. Man having a body, disease will be traceable to a bodily cause. This hypothesis circumscribes the field of research and therein lies its immense fruitfulness. But when this hypothesis is identified with the science of medicine so that any other possible hypothesis comes to be regarded as unscientific, it becomes a creed. Many other hypotheses could serve equally well to limit the field of research, such as: Man is a moral being, or a spiritual being, or an emotional being, and therefore disease will have a moral, or spiritual, or emotional cause.

Science in the real sense as 'knowledge gained by systematic observation, experiment and reasoning' aims at complete knowledge, and does not exclude any hypothesis that is systematically followed out. Therefore I must repeat my indictment against the deterministic Freudian dogma. In so far as this dogma is regarded as alone being 'scientific', whereby any other possible hypothesis comes to be regarded as 'unscientific', we must expose this pretension as an attempt to create a vested interest, or a cult. For such a pretension is entirely foreign to the true spirit of science, which is never bigoted, arrogant, or partial. It is a product of culture, and shares the devotion and freedom of culture. Science is an instrument, not an end in itself. When it assumes an inquisitorial mien and forces the irrational nature of the living being into an arbitrary and rigid formula, it is no longer science, but a crude spirit of barbarism. Science will not tolerate a theory that crushes the individual psyche with its winged powers into a procrustean bed of sophisticated assumptions. The psychology which is inspired by the spirit of science has to be as plastic, as manifold, and as comprehensive as the psyche itself. It can never be a simple, rule-of-thumb, formularized method. The scientific method developed by the exigencies of the natural sciences has failed to provide a basis sufficiently wide and elastic to embrace the essential facts of psychic experience. A realization of this fact would be the foundation stone of the pyschology of the future, which by including every aspect of the human mind will deserve to be called the servant of man.

While at work on this paper I chanced to read a very able editorial article, entitled 'Science and Philosophy', in *Nature* (22nd October, 1927). The author has expressed much the same ideas, and has stated the general problem far more ably than I could do. He writes:

> The last twenty years have seen the foundations of physics torn up and rebuilt, and the change has come about not only by the press of new knowledge, but also to a great degree through keen, hard thinking about the fundamental conceptions of the science, through true philosophical criticism, carried out by the physicists and mathematicians themselves. We can no longer rest content with the simple materialistic schema which satisfied Descartes and Laplace.

Further on he says:

> The mechanistic method, however, is itself an interpretation of Nature. It is, to use Dr. Chalmers Mitchell's own words about vitalism, 'a proclamation of a belief and not an inference from observation'. Its sole justification is the practical one, that it does up to a point help us to understand the activities of living things. But there are other methods of explanation possible, and it is unwise to rule them out as unscientific. Since physics has found a revolution in its fundamental concepts necessary, it seems dangerous for biology to cling to the cast-off beliefs of the nineteenth-century physicists. . . . The time is indeed ripe for a critical revision of biological concepts. We need not fear that this will lead us into mystical by-ways. It is probable that there will always be something left unexplained—even Dr. Mitchell doubts the possibility of the part interpreting the whole—but clear thinking not only about the facts of observation, but also, more important still, about our own methods of interpretation, will help to reduce and render manageable the mysteries of organic life and evolution. . . . Let clear thinking and logical scrutiny be applied not merely to the generalizations resulting from observation and experiment, but also to the underlying conceptions, the basal philo-

sophies, in accordance with which these generalizations are formed. Let us scrutinize everything—even our most cherished scientific principles.

These are wise words, and they are the product of a new epoch of scientific thinking which has already dawned. Our quarrel with Freud must not be misconstrued as a polemic of rival methods of psychological therapy. It goes far deeper than that. It arises from a need for a fundamental restatement of psychological conceptions. It may be objected that this is the province of philosophy. I would reply that it is precisely the divorce of science from philosophy that makes Freud's whole theoretical position so inadequate. Let me quote again from the article mentioned above:

> Shall we call this criticism of conceptions science or philosophy? This brings us to the heart of the matter, and to our tentative conclusion, which is that the nineteenth-century divorce of science from philosophy is good for neither side, and that co-operation should now be the order of the day. The benefit will be mutual. . . . In the recent discoveries both in physical and in biological science, there is ample material to keep the philosopher busy for years. The man of science for his part can learn much from philosophy. He can learn how biased and provisional his views of Nature may be, how difficult it is to get rid of irrational presuppositions which may colour all his thought.

The writer of this article has biology chiefly in mind when he urges the need of a fuller collaboration between science and philosophy, but if he were to turn to psychology, he would surely find that 'need' imperative. Yet however valuable it would be to achieve the desired co-operation between the scientists on the one side and the philosophers on the other, the synthesis that is needed most of all in psychology is that between science and philosophy in the individual psychologist.

Philosophical deliberation is not as a rule an outstanding factor in the equipment of the extraverted scientific investigator, and, therefore, it was hardly to be wondered at that Freud should have taken over the mechanistic hypothesis from the scientific inheritance of the nineteenth century. Furthermore, the isolation which bias and prejudice forced upon him in the first decade of his research was most unfavourable for that co-operation with a deeply philosophical mind which he most needed. In spite of this isolation, however, the possibility for such a co-operation actually came across his path. For Jung has by nature a philosophical temperament, the shoot of a tree that for generations produced philosophers and physicians in regular succession. But the disparity of mind and basic standpoint proved to be too great and the possibility never ripened. Freud became increasingly isolated from every viewpoint and scientific labour other than his own, while Jung went on to lay the foundations of the new science in broad psychological conceptions which were commensurate with the emerging culture of a new epoch.

As an example of this difference of attitude, I must refer to Jung's fundamental conception of the general or collective unconscious. Freud at first, just as much as Jung, was struck by the inexplicable depth and power of the influence of the parental image operating as a fate throughout the individual's whole life. 'Reason', said Jung, 'does not allow us to attribute this fateful effect solely to the influence of infantile memories of the actual parent.' Behind the personal memories he inferred the existence of a racial factor, an inherited function-complex arising from general human experience in the age-long past. The significance of the father-principle is concerned not merely with the image of the father in the personal past, but with the father-imago, a racial engramme, the power and authority of which is the expression of its untold antiquity.

Freud agreed that this inference was born out by empirical observation, but he argued that such a concept was not scientific. He might have said that a concept of such range went beyond the limitations of the mechanistic hypothesis to which he was wedded.

Jung, as we know, could not confine his mind within a nineteenth-century strait-waistcoat, and with real regret he parted from Freud. He elaborated the concept of the collective unconscious to embrace the whole sphere of inherited function-complexes, which he termed 'archetypes', by means of which the historical continuity of all human experience exists as specific psychic tendencies or ways of functioning in the individual psychology. The validity of this concept is based upon an immense variety of empirical observation and clinical experience, and its value is shown by the fact that it is being assimilated by the progressive scientific and philosophic thinking of the new epoch.

As an example of Freud's amazing detachment from the thought and work of other minds, I must quote a passage from one of his later works, in which almost furtively he opens the door himself that Jung had invited him to open over twenty years ago. He writes:[1]

[1] *The Ego and the Id*, p. 82.

All the experiences of life that originate from without enrich the ego; the id, however, is another outer world to it, which it strives to bring into subjection to itself. It withdraws libido from the id and transforms the object-cathexes of the id into ego-constructions. With the aid of the super-ego, though in a manner that is still obscure to us, *it draws upon the experiences of past ages stored in the id.*[1]

This is a good example of the labyrinthine thinking I alluded to earlier, but I have selected it for another reason. It is inconceivable that Freud was unaware of the fact that another worker in the field of psychology had already elaborated a comprehensive concept of the 'stored experience of past ages', but his habit of aloof detachment is now so strong that Freud does not even mention the fact, that at this point his speculation comes into agreement with the conclusions of another worker in the same field.

Again I must repeat this exclusiveness is not scientific. We shall find that this same attitude has hindered Freud from gaining a full appreciation of the significance of dreams. It is quite impossible, for instance, to believe that he was unaware that in the most ancient cultures, as well as among primitive peoples to-day, dreams are regarded as bearing a prophetic light upon coming events. Wise men of all ages have regarded dreams as intuitions concerning things not immediately accessible to consciousness, and particularly in relation to future happenings. In contenting himself with his formula, 'the dream is a (disguised) fulfilment of a (repressed) wish', Freud either excludes or ignores this whole weight of human feeling and reflection as though it were mere idle supserstition and childish fantasy. That is to say, the *consensus gentium* has no weight with him. He shuts it out as of no account. As has been shown by Jung, the *consensus gentium* is a valid proof concerning the actuality of certain profound facts of our psychic life, as, for instance, the experience of God, of freedom, of love, or such ideas as immortality, fate, etc., which are based not upon empirical evidence, but on the *consensus gentium*. Hence a psychology that excludes the latter can deal with only a very partial field of human experience.

The *consensus gentium* in all times and among all unsophisticated peoples has maintained that impressive (*mana*) dreams proceed from the soul or that they are the voices of the spirits speaking to men. But deterministic science has no place for the concept of the soul. Freud's apparatus includes a pre-conscious, an unconscious, an ego,

[1] The italics are mine.

a super-ego, a censor, and an id, but nowhere is there a place for the human soul. Is it altogether surprising then that the human soul has no place for this incomprehensible apparatus of Freud?

To round up my argument I propose to introduce a living human witness. The woman, whose dream I give below, is by no means a merely pathological case. She is a married woman, with fine mental power and rich imagination. She had had matrimonial difficulties and when she came to analysis she was suffering from considerable mental disturbance, which showed itself in anxiety states and a morbid guilt-complex. When she had this dream she was a year or two over forty, and had submitted herself to a Freudian analysis with real earnestness. Her analyst was a woman assistant of an American analyst of some standing.

She dreamed that she was in the woods and came to a pool of slime. She picked up some of it and said to the man following her: 'Isn't it beautiful?' There were other people following along, but she went first. The path became narrow and went along the side of a brook that ran in a narrow ravine. Suddenly there appeared a beautiful pheasant to the left of the path, but when she looked closer she saw that it had a newspaper tail. She was disappointed, but went on, and then another pheasant came out from behind a tree. This one had a perfect tail. She walked on, and, suddenly, blocking the end of the defile was a huge lion. She was terribly frightened, but when she stood a moment the lion spoke, and then his head changed into that of Socrates. Socrates now said to her: 'You must always worship God in the sun.'

The critical associations to the dream are as follows:

Slime was associated with botany. She had just recently discovered the world which the microscope reveals. It was an entirely new dimension in her experience and conception of Nature.

The pheasant was associated with one she had seen some years before in a wood when walking with a man who was 'over-sensitive to Nature in the abstract, and blind to human realities and responsibilities'. The pheasant had impressed her as strikingly beautiful.

The newspaper tail was associated with newspaper in an ill-kept water-closet.

Socrates was perhaps the most important figure in her mental world. He represented a light-bringer, a piercing sun-like mind, a supreme representative of the logos-principle.

The dream impressed her so deeply that she took it to the analyst with a keen anticipation of learning its meaning. Anyone at all versed in the Freudian method will observe that the dream-material lends itself in some respects to a reductive interpretation. In the treatment of the dream her analyst interpreted the slime as faeces, and even went so far as to explain the patient's new world of botanical interest as a disguised indulgence in anal-erotic fantasies. The pheasant with the newspaper tail gave her another opening for the anal-erotic explanation. But her *tour de force* was reserved for Socrates. This figure she interpreted as a symbol of the analyst under whom she (the assistant) was working, and around whom, out of deference to the theory, the patient's anal-erotic fantasy begins to play in its search for a father-surrogate.

The whole dream, in short, was an anal-erotic fantasy. No attempt was made to deal with the dream as an impressive experience, or to explain why a dream that is concerned with repressed infantile fantasies should express these desires in such impressive, even religious images, or why deep feelings should be aroused by them. Dreams of this character have real power. This one, for example, was powerful enough to end her interest in the whole Freudian schema, and eventually to send her across the Atlantic to find out whether Jung could understand her dream and help her to find her way.

I would like to point out that, although this dream contains obviously morbid allusions, the purely reductive approach does not do justice to the kernel of the dream. Now let us be simple enough to forget about 'dream-distortion' and 'censorship' and 'disguised wish-fulfilment', and ask ourselves at each step: What does this mean? What can we learn from this image or that association? Remember that the dream language is the primitive language of metaphor, and that every part of the dream is referred not to outer objects, but to the dreamer's own psychology. Now let us see if we can discover what the dream is saying.

The defile is an analogous situation to the birth-channel; that is to say, the dream states that the psychic situation is a fateful one. When once the birth-process has begun and the defile is entered, there is no turning back. The stream, of course, represents the direction of the libido which she is constrained to follow.

The essence of the dream is a process, a movement. The dream proceeds from the wood, suggesting the possibility of lost direction, and the pool emphasizes the idea of stagnation. The neurosis is a condition of stasis. Thus the stream running through the defile suggests a prospective way out of a neurotic stagnation. On the human plane there is also a procession headed by the dreamer. She is followed by a man—a characteristic opposite-sex representative of the unconscious—and many others. This means that the dream has a collective or general as well as a personal reference. All the elements of the psyche are taking part in the process.

Now what has happened just recently that relates the dream to the actual present? She has taken the plunge into this new world of unconscious life and meaning which analysis has begun to bring into focus. It is a crucial step, because the analytical goal to know and to understand the morbid side of her psychology does not necessarily stop there—Achilles can also leap over the tortoise. All the dormant, unlived possibilities of her nature—the chained and buried titans under Olympus—may begin to rouse from their long slumbers and seek a new gateway into the light of day. This new dimension of understanding and self-knowledge is indicated by her attitude of interest in the pool with its vegetation.[1] The dream uses this metaphor because, in reality, the microscope has just revealed to her the unsuspected marvels of the vegetational underworld. Analysis can easily figure in a dream as a microscope or a telescope; that is to say, an apparatus that has the power of making, what was before invisible, visible. Her delight in the new discovery is clearly expressed when she shows the slime to the man.

This seems to me a most important point in her self-realization. She needs to apprehend the facts of her own nature and her strong neurotic tendency with a microscopic exactness and objectivity, and this the reductive technique can achieve; but at the same time she has to say good-bye for ever to the sophisticated, two-dimensional valuation of the slime as just slime. The knowledge of the contents of the personal unconscious is rightly and necessarily repressed, unless one is prepared to see the unpleasant facts of one's own nature in a new perspective. This perspective is obtained by a new insight both into nature and into one's own inner workings, whereby a new relation is won between the isolated, auto-erotic world of the personal unconscious (symbolized by the pool) and the world of the impersonal and general, towards which the stream is leading her, beyond the defile whose exit is guarded by the lion.

[1] N.B.—Collections of water symbolize the unconscious, *i.e.* the element whose content is hidden.

The incident of the pheasant is important, but it can be understood only when referred to a particularity of the woman's psychology. It alludes to a vivid moment of sensation, as though she had then for the first time really seen the splendours of a cock pheasant. This moment occurred when she was walking with a man, whom she described as being 'over-sensitive to Nature in the abstract, and blind to human realities and responsibilities'. Thus a vivid contrast was presented to her mind, of the especial beauty with which nature's largesse invests the erotic *motif* in certain birds, and the highbrow detachment of her companion. Now what is the pheasant saying to her? Here it must be interpolated that the patient herself is an introverted intuitive type, and is therefore liable to undervalue that whole aspect of reality for which the function of sensation holds the key. There was also in her, as in most women, a tendency to mistake intellectuality for intelligence, just as most men are liable to mistake the meretricious for the genuine in the sphere of the erotic. This inferiority on the side of objectivity would mean a liability to prefer an opinion, an assumption, or a rationalistic explanation to the labour of independent observation and keen, balanced thinking. Dreams reveal the fact that woman has an inferior masculine figure in her unconscious (a compensatory figure to the image of the divine or perfected man), which manufactures assumptions and opinions of a collective type. The quality of these *a priori* assumptions has been described by Jung as accredited or mass views. He has applied the term 'animus' to this ambivalent masculine representative of the feminine unconscious; while the corresponding feminine figure in man's unconscious he calls the 'anima'. I have introduced these considerations because the pheasant utters a very salient warning, if the ear is attuned to the dream language. The especial grace and magnificence of the erotic *motif* in such birds as the pheasant is manifested in the tail, and it is just this splendour that in the first bird is changed to a newspaper. We have observed the fact that the erotic libido in woman, when checked of its natural expression, is very liable to go into a kind of compulsive intellectuality described above as animus opinionating. It is a kind of specious collective thinking, which can completely shut out objective reality, particularly, therefore, sensation. The man she was walking with in the wood represented just this dangerous aloofness from immediate and human realities.

The psychological result of such an auto-erotic regression of the libido would be a depreciation of eros, the true principle of woman. This cheapening of eros is beautifully shown by substituting an old newspaper—collective opinionating *par excellence*—for the pheasant's tail. Moreover, the association with the water-closet underlines the comment on her auto-erotic inclination.

The pheasant, therefore, represents a real psychological danger she has got to encounter, since this sophisticated kind of thinking can completely extinguish a true appreciation of life and can rationalize away value and wonder and greatness with the 'nothing but' method of depreciation. This poison kills the spirit, and it is the presence of this possibility in her psychology that explains the intense resistance she felt to the 'nothing but' interpretations of her analyst.

There is a very definite positive indication that she can overcome this most subtle danger in the fact that she sees the pheasant again, and this time with a perfect tail. Nothing less than an erotic renewal or rebirth is symbolized here. Now let us follow the movement of the dream further.

Her new objective interest in the slime (product of the neurotic stagnation) and the warning about the danger of auto-erotic animus-thinking lead up to the terrifying lion at the exit of the defile. These symbols are preparing her, as in a kind of initiation, for an altogether new horizon. Just as the child emerges at birth from a secure contained state into a world where it is exposed to perils, risks, and experiences of an absolutely new order, so the emergence from the contained and little world of the personal into the vast horizons of the impersonal or racial unconscious is fraught with very real danger. To plunge unprepared and without understanding into the primitive levels of the collective unconscious means to go right over into insanity. Therefore the exit is guarded by a lion, a racial archetype of supreme and terrifying power, mythologically identified with the sun.[1] The lion is the dynamic, while Socrates is the ideal, aspect of the symbol. Hence they belong together. The lion represents the overwhelming energy and power contained in the universal primordial image, power which can seize hold of the reason with the grip of an *idée fixe* or a paranoidal delusion, or inspire the greatest poems and deeds of heroism. It is, as Jung has shown in his *Psychology of the Unconscious*, a sun-symbol, containing a supreme intensity of libido, i.e. psychic value.

[1] The Zodiacal sign Leo stands in the month of July, the zenith of the sun's power in the Northern Hemisphere.

Socrates symbolizes the principle of logos, the objectivity of a poised and vigorous mind, which can cut and clarify and express in broad and comprehensive concepts things that, to a darker and more primitive reason, are vague and monstrous and unseizable. The Socratic mind is like the sun. It brings things out of vague and shadowy darkness into the clear definition of light. It is the sun of consciousness.

If panic should seize her now and she turns to flee from this new world of mental experience, she will probably become insane. The lion will devour her. But if she goes on faithful to the principle of consciousness, she can gain the Socratic spirit and become a 'child of the sun', the source of energy and light.

The central meaning of the dream is contained in the final message spoken by Socrates. Socrates speaks from that world in which Christianity had not yet dawned. He calls her back to an earlier conception of God before the Christian vine had spread over the earth, and had shut man away from a direct and pristine contact with Nature. He calls her to behold the earliest symbol of God, back to the beginning of thought, in order to bring to light a more comprehensive conception of God than that of traditional Christianity. Her neurotic stagnation meant a world without God in the sense of a supreme psychological value.

It is self-evident that the dream is concerned with the religious problem. Accordingly, it more accords with the spirit of science to say that the lion represents the dynamic aspect of God,[1] than to say that her interest in the slime is a disguised wish to play with faeces.

For a time this woman was wellnigh overwhelmed by the unconscious, but she held on, and with the help of Jung's amazing insight and understanding she is now in full and imaginative possession of a keenly balanced mind.

There is, of course, a great deal more in the dream that I have not touched upon—a dream of this impressive character is really inexhaustible, and every attempt to interpret its meaning only leaves its essential mystery the more unfathomable—but I have sketched in enough of the general psychological portrait to show that such a dream would be grossly misunderstood if subjected to an exclusively reductive treatment.

The dream is a kind of portrait in which invisible traits and

[1] Psychologically, the idea of God represents a supreme psychic value.

tendencies are thrown in figurative guise upon the screen. The work of interpretation is, of course, an art more than a science, though like every art it rests upon certain general principles which are the province of science. The best practical test of a dream-interpretation is the same that we apply to a portrait, namely: does the interpretation give a truthful and balanced likeness of the patient as a whole?

The riddle of the dream has puzzled the wisest heads of every age, and although we may be somewhat nearer the solution to-day, the riddle still remains. Why is it that nearly all the investigators who have grappled with this enigma have proclaimed, in equally confident tones, an answer that is at variance with all the rest? I need not enumerate these various and manifold solutions. Psychoanalytical literature abounds with them. If the dream were an objective phenomenon we could prove that one of these solutions was true empirically, and that the falsity of the rest depended upon inaccurate observation. But the dream is a subjective product, and consequently certain important elements go to the making of it which are invisible to a purely empirical eye. If, for instance, I am regarding my own dreams, there is one essential factor which my training in natural science has not prepared me to observe. And this is my own conscious attitude, or—to use the more expressive German word—*Weltanschauung*. Jung was the first psychologist to realize the essential importance of this factor in the investigation of the unconscious mental processes. He observed the fact that a thoroughgoing examination and revaluation of the conscious attitude exercised a profound influence upon the dreams. He was also the first to realize that a deep and unprejudiced study of one's own dreams produced an essential alteration and renewal of the conscious attitude.

May I remind the reader that the gravamen of my criticism of Freud is that by consistently undervaluing the importance and meaning of consciousness his psychological conceptions are alien to the spirit of science?

Not only did he fail to see that the interpretation of the dream was conditioned by the attitude with which his consciousness viewed the dream, but also that the individual intensity and range of the conscious function is a paramount factor in the actual construction and quality of the dream-material.

Just as he failed to realize the constant and intimate reciprocity existing between the personality of patient and analyst, so he also failed to realize the intimate reciprocity between the nature of the unconscious activity and the moral consciousness of the subject. I use the term 'moral' advisedly in this connection, because valuation is the essence of consciousness, and morality, in the truest sense of the word, is wholly concerned with values.

Naturally if we were able to regard a neurosis as a localized psychological disorder, we would also be justified in regarding the analytical method as a purely medical technique, for which the problem of consciousness or of *Weltanschauung* would be altogether superfluous. But no scientist to-day with any real knowledge of neurosis could conceivably regard it as a localized disorder. It is, as we know by bitter experience, a wrong way, and therefore a wrong view of life. We are not allowed to rest with a medical technique that excludes the broader and deeper issues with which the problems of our neurotic patients challenge us.

There is none the less a disposition in medical circles to try to limit the terrain of psycho-therapy to a specialized technical procedure. I should like to quote some remarks of Jung in a recent paper[1] upon this disposition.

There are many scientists [he writes] who avoid a *Weltanschauung*, because this is supposed not to be scientific. But it is manifestly not clear to these people what it is they do. What actually occurs is that they purposely leave themselves in the dark as to their guiding ideas; in other words, they remain on a deeper, more primitive level of consciousness than that which would correspond to their full conscious capacities. A certain criticism and scepticism is by no means always the expression of intelligence, rather the opposite; especially when a person uses scepticism as a screen to cloak his lack of *Weltanschauung*. Not infrequently it is a deficiency in moral value, rather than intelligence. For one cannot form a view of the world without viewing oneself, and therefore in the same way as one views the world, one also views oneself. No small courage is demanded for this task. Hence it is always fatal to have no *Weltanschauung*. To have a *Weltanschauung* means to make an image of the world and of myself, to know what the world is, and who I am. Literally this is impossible but *cum grano salis*, it means the best possible knowledge. . . . If the image we make of the world does not reflect back upon ourselves, we can be content with any sort of beautiful or diverting sham. But such self-deception has the effect of making us unreal, foolish and ineffective. Because we are fighting with a false image of the world, we are overcome

[1] 'Analytical Psychology and *Weltanschauung*,' in *Contributions to Analytical Psychology* (Kegan Paul & Co., 1928).

by the superior power of reality. In this way we discover how essential it is to have a carefully founded and worked-out *Weltanschauung*. A *Weltanschauung* is essentially an hypothesis, not a creed.

A satisfying *Weltanschauung* necessitates a highly differentiated consciousness. I have already emphasized the fact that, whether we like it or no, the general attitude and standpoint of the analyst has a powerful determining effect upon the whole analytical process. Since, therefore, the question of *Weltanschauung* cannot be excluded under any considerations, we are not permitted to ignore the problem of conscious differentiation. This is not a side issue; it is central, and by it analytical psychology will be judged.

In his work, *Psychological Types*, Jung undertook and carried out the first systematic research of the various characteristic types of consciousness. It is a masterly analysis and description of the differentiated, as opposed to the merely elementary, aspect of the psychic process. He showed in careful historical studies the relation between a man's philosophical outlook (his *Weltanschauung*) and his psychological type. This work has been almost completely ignored by Freud and his school. The importance of this fact must not be ignored. For it indicates that the problem of differentiation has not yet entered the Freudian horizon.

The situation is exactly analogous to that created by the discovery of Copernicus. The geocentric assumption is the natural and instinctive one, and Ptolemy was able to explain the movements of the planets very ingeniously on this hypothesis. Only very gradually, and against great resistance, did the heliocentric hypothesis gain a foothold in men's minds. It was hard to give up the static conception of the earth as the centre of the universe, because we are identified with the earth. It is our inevitable standpoint. Men found it hard to conceive of motions or relations that they could neither see nor feel. But in precisely the same way a man is identified with his own conscious function. It is his inevitable standpoint. Therefore a condition of constant invariability can easily be assumed concerning the conscious function, and only those motions and modifications of the psychic process be taken into account that present themselves to consciousness. I do not of course mean to imply that the Freudian psychologist does not perceive the fact that different individuals perceive reality in different ways. But I do assert that he is not sufficiently curious about these variations to modify his psychological conceptions so as to include this factor of individual and typical differentiation. Jung's work on the types has brought this whole problem of psychic differentiation into the sphere of scientific classification, and psychologists who venture to ignore this fundamental addition to our knowledge of the mind are choosing to remain on an inferior level of consciousness—a phenomenon that surely demands some explanation.

In practical analytical work the question of function-type and basic attitude are considerations that are absolutely essential to a correct psychological orientation. These are determining factors which operate over the whole psychic field, whether conscious or unconscious. How, then, are we to explain the fact that a whole school of practical psychologists finds it possible to forgo the use of perhaps the most delicate and illuminating instrument of their craft.

Modern psychology is in possession of a new instrument, the full potentialities of which are still to some extent unknown, but our scientific conceptions must be based upon those eternal realities of our psychic life to which every mature human being can testify. Our science must be great enough to contain the greatness as well as the littleness of man.

Jung saw the greatness of the spirit of man, and he could not be satisfied with concepts that dealt solely with his elementary origins. Who will throw a stone at the scientist who risked his repute and standing among the orthodox rather than deny that greatness? He claims the right to use the heuristic principle for what it is worth. He claims that since the mind is purposive, psychological science must embrace this fact. Jung, in fact, is great enough to create concepts that accord with man as a totality. He will not accept the alternative that man must fit into an inadequate formula or doctrine, because it has been called 'scientific'.

In conclusion I would like to quote the words of a modern seer, Herman Melville, whose works are shot through with a visionary fantasy, which often amazes one with its range and depth.

I quote a passage from that strange work *Mardi*, which if systematically explored might teach us much of the deeper life of the unconscious. He says:

> And that which long endures full-fledged, must have long lain in the germ. And duration is not of the future, but of the past; and eternity is eternal because it has been; and though a strong new monument be builded to-day, it only is lasting because its blocks are old as the sun. It is not the Pyramids that are ancient, but the eternal granite whereof they are

made; which had been equally ancient though yet in the quarry. For to make an eternity, we must build with eternities; whence the vanity of the cry for anything alike durable and new; and the folly of the reproach—Your granite hath come from the old-fashioned hills.

A fundamental psychology must free itself from quasi-scientific notions that, at bottom, are symptomatic of a transitional moment in man's development, and take hold of the eternal nature of man, namely, those things which always have and always will characterize the human mind. Always in explaining the past man has formed some notion of a cause, and always in his concern for the future he has formed some notion of a goal. Thus the causal and the final conceptions of psychic events are given in the fundamental or eternal nature of man. Both views are therefore essential and, notwithstanding the resistance of the intellect to admitting the existence of two equal and opposite principles, their indispensability cannot be denied. The factor of opposition is not merely an opinion; it underlies the very nature of reality, and therefore a fundamental psychological conception, as Jung has shown, must always embrace a fundamental pair of opposites.

The Importance of Dream-analysis for Psychological Development

I. INTRODUCTION

The value of the method I propose to submit to you is based upon the proposition that the activity of psychic processes can be regarded teleologically. By teleological I mean that aspect of a vital process which suggests the influence of an end or purpose upon its activity or mode of development. We can as well use the term final. The principle of teleology stands in the relation of polarity to the causal principle. Both viewpoints are indispensable for the understanding of physical phenomena and, hence, both have attained general recognition. And yet logically they are irreconcilable, since the causal viewpoint applies only to phenomena, whether material or psychical, while the final point of view can arise only through an idea, in the proper sense of the term, and which cannot be merely phenomenal.

As natural scientists, we are naturally attached more to the causal than to the final viewpoint; perhaps because of an inherent piety which reveres the ways and methods of the ancestors. And yet it cannot truthfully be contended that the principle of causality is more scientific, in the sense that we know more about its actual operation than about that of its less favoured opposite. From the standpoint of cognition, we are just as ignorant of how any cause *A* can bring about the effect *B*, or of what the dynamic operation represented by *A*, *B*, *C*, *D*, actually consists, as we are of knowing how a goal, in the sense of a future potentiality, can activate a series of events in a certain specific way. Since we are ignorant of the nature of vital energy, we are also in the dark in regard to the essential nature of vital processes; even though the various transformations of energy in living matter are familiar and predictable phenomena. If, therefore, we make the mistake of identifying either the causal or the final viewpoint with the actual, objective facts of experience, we are both unphilosophical and unscientific. These two principles of explanation are, in short, reciprocal subjective viewpoints depending less upon the objective behaviour of things than upon the psychological attitude of the investigator. The insupportable contradiction between them comes about through our illegitimate propensity to project a mere way of looking at things into the object itself. We can preserve ourselves from the contradiction only by realizing that these explanatory principles belong to the psychological sphere, and are only hypothetically projected into objective events for the purposes of explanation.

This preliminary philosophical warning is, of course, only for the benefit of those who feel prompted to defend either the one or the other principle as though its validity were guaranteed by the unshakable order of nature. Having affirmed my belief that both views are equally possible, I must confess to a temperamental partiality for the final viewpoint. The study of vital processes from this standpoint gains a particular interest from the fact that an unknown potential factor may be constellating the situation. Not that I find myself lacking in the detective's delight in tracking an obscure and reluctantly visible tendency to its last infantile stronghold. But the teleological vista seems to be richer in problems of interest, and the following of a definite direction into the future seems more humanly profitable than the tracing of a line backwards to a theoretical cause in the past. To my mind this preferential accent of emphasis on either principle should be ascribed to one's individual psychological type.[1] When, therefore, patients come to me who show a pronounced predilection for the causalistic explanation, I advise them to study some of Freud's admirable researches into neurotic causation. If they find these works completely satisfying I advise them to go to a Freudian analyst. To my mind this is the only honest course to take; inasmuch as my own psychological bias can easily present an obstacle to one who leans consistently towards the opposite standpoint.

As a rule, we find that the psychological attitude which favours the causal principle of explanation also embraces the mechanistic, the reductive, the retrospective, the objective: that attitude, in short, which tends to reduce the psychological field to a mere extension of the field of biology. This is the obvious way for a Western mind trained in the natural sciences to approach a new field of vital

[1] Although it is advisable to account for a preferential emphasis by reference to the type problem, it would none the less be fatal to any possibility of agreement to identify the principles themselves with individual factors. Every biologist and every psychologist must employ both standpoints in order to render an adequate account of vital processes.

phenomena. But though it is the obvious way, it does not follow that therefore it is the most fruitful.

If, for any reason, we have cause to suspect that the basic assumptions of our mind are insufficient to yield us a true understanding of the facts of experience, it behoves us to examine or re-examine their validity. Let us, therefore, make a short detour in order to inspect the philosophical credentials of the mechanistic hypothesis, upon which biological study has mainly relied for upwards of three centuries. But first let us consider the particular grounds on which psychology has reason to suspect the validity of the mechanistic hypothesis. When we contemplate the field of psychic phenomena we have absolutely no means of conceiving how psychic events, namely, affects, thoughts, feelings, images, can be related to physical events, as, for instance, biochemical changes in the cells of the brain and nervous system. The one category belongs to the unextended, the intangible, the imponderable: the other belongs to the extended, the tangible, the mensurable. We possess, in fact, no mediating function by which the one series of phenomena could be intelligibly articulated with, or superimposed upon, the other. How, then, is it possible to assume that the hypothesis and methods of natural science, which have been adapted exclusively for extended, tangible bodies, are equally valid for this other field of phenomena, which corresponds with the first in none of its attributes beyond the fact that both can be regarded as processes of vital energy?

The apparently inescapable dualism of mind and body goes back to the famous Cartesian postulate *cogito ergo sum*. The argument of Descartes can be briefly stated as follows: I know that I exist because I think. But, in knowing myself to exist, I do not know myself to be extended in space, because, while sure of my own existence as thinker, I can still be doubtful of the existence of all bodies. It was therefore concluded that the 'I' which is known to exist is a thinking thing, but not an extended thing—in other words, an immaterial mind. This conclusion was based upon the fallacy that doubt is knowledge; namely, that if we do not know with certainty that something is the case, we certainly know that it is not the case. For example, if I know that I exist, but do not know whether or not I am extended, I know that I am not extended. The only thing that has been proved is that thought and extension are logically independent attributes. Descartes was really wanting to find with his dualism a secure basis upon which natural science could rest, and the best way to circumscribe and simplify the field of study was to disallow all and every contamination from life itself, i.e. from the experiential.[1] The Cartesian dualism, though arbitrary, was absolutely essential for the purpose of creating scientific thinking. Without circumscription scientific concepts are unattainable. Descartes assumed, then, that the behaviour of all extended things could be explained mechanically: which assumption, given the state of the natural sciences in the seventeenth, eighteenth and nineteenth centuries, was perfectly intelligible. But now that the classical mechanics is no longer the accepted model of all the sciences—when biology is claiming a separate hearing and even physics is having its doubts about 'physical causation'—it is time to wonder whether psychology must still be harnessed to an argument that has lost its exclusive validity even for the physical sciences. I am indebted to Mr. A. M. Maciver and Professor J. M. Thorburn for the foregoing criticism of the mind-body dualism. In a symposium on 'Is there mind-body interaction?' at the Aristotelian Society, Maciver suggested that the teleological, as opposed to the mechanical, can be applied to extended things just as well as to the unextended. In other words, living bodies can act purposively quite independently of mind. There are certain developmental processes, as for instance, the development of the eyes in the embryo before there is any occasion to see, which are clearly teleological. In the experiments of Driesch, who sliced an embryo at the post-morula stage into two or more sections and found that each section developed into a complete embryo, we have clear evidence that the pattern of the total organism together with the purpose to achieve individual totality w as potentially present in every part of the embryonic tissue. The late Dr. Canti showed a film in which the complete femur of a chick with its trochanter, condylar processes, etc., was seen developing in a culture medium (i.e. quite detached from its normal articulations) from a thin slice of embryonic mesoderm. Similarly, in the case of the restitution of lost parts in certain amphibia. If a newt's tail is amputated, the cells restore the missing piece. But suppose we take the cell mass which is growing out to replace the amputated tail, and graft it on to the stump of a freshly amputated leg, it will restore a leg and not a tail.

[1] Kepler, for instance, did not sufficiently purge his material from this subjective contamination, and consequently made serious scientific mistakes. Descartes, realizing that complete confusion was likely to submerge science, rejected uncompromisingly anything that could make such mistakes possible. Hence the establishment of his dualism.

In the presence of such facts, which can be multiplied indefinitely, we must accept the validity of the teleological explanation within the domain of biology.[1] And these teleological performances can be related to the concept of mind only through the fact that the organism's inherited reproduction, or its inherited modes of ancestral reaction are not without the co-ordinate of experience. But if it is no longer possible to identify physical processes exclusively with mechanism, still less are we beholden to the mechanistic hypothesis as a sole means of approach to psychological events; although we reserve the right to employ the concept of mechanism wherever, and in so far as, it fits the observed facts.

Having broken the back of mechanism as a totalitarian hypothesis, purporting to explain the nature of all extended things, we therewith liberate other concepts which have suffered a mean bondage under this monster's tyranny during the biological dark age. If, for instance, we examine the traditional arguments against materialism, we find that most of them are not arguments against materialism at all, but against mechanism. To quote Maciver again:

> It is argued, for instance, that materialism cannot account for thought, because a thinking thing must be a unity, and materialism can only offer an aggregate, whether it be the brain, or the whole nervous system, or the whole body. If this argument is valid at all, it is valid against any theory which makes the thinker an aggregate, whether material or immaterial: it is valid (as is generally recognized) against any theory, such as that of the Associationists, which makes of the mind an aggregate of immaterial 'ideas' acting upon one another in a mechanistic way. But if we understand by 'materialism' simply the doctrine that every concrete existent must be extended, without taking it for granted that the activity of every extended thing must be determined mechanically, there is no reason why materialism should not provide a thinker who is a unity just as well as immaterialism. On mechanical principles, certainly, the only 'whole' is the aggregate, logically posterior to its parts; to explain mechanically the behaviour of a whole is just to explain severally the movements of all its parts and sum them together. But where process is teleological, all the parts of a whole may be united by a common purpose and the whole logically prior to them, in the sense that the behaviour of the parts cannot be explained except by reference to the purpose of the whole.

[1] The problem, as I see it, is that, although there can be no possibility of progress in embryology or biology unless we construe the embryonic process teleologically, it is extraordinarily difficult to determine the relation of the teleological explanation to the scientific concept.

If we take, once again, the development of the eye in the growing embryo, this development is unintelligible so long as we consider only the particular cells which go to form the eye, but it is immediately intelligible when we consider it in relation to the individual totality. And the teleological unity is the same, whether we are viewing the individual being as an extended body or an unextended mind.

I believe the whole problem of the action of mind upon body, or of body upon mind, will assume an entirely different complexion if we can rid our thought of the underlying assumption that body is identical with mechanism. Individuality, embracing the whole, provides a unified conception wherein the body represents its manifestation in the space-time continuum, while the mind represents the same totality in the unextended condition that is characteristic of the image or idea.

Resuming now our psychological theme, we have seen that there exist two quite characteristic attitudes which tend to regard mental phenomena from opposite standpoints. The one attitude which we might call the causal-reductive, tends to view the mental construct in terms of its elementary components, to lead backwards from the complex totality to its functional origins, and to see in the activity of these elementary root-processes a satisfying explanation of general human behaviour. This attitude is clearly indispensable when we are concerned with the aetiology of any given psychological condition. The other attitude is essentially complementary to the causal-reductive. We may call it the energic or teleological attitude, since with it one tends to keep in view the purposive nature of psychic activity, to regard the psychical product as a complex manifestation of various functional elements which are combining or interacting in accordance with some end that is intelligible, not by reference to past determinants alone, but also to future possibilities. This attitude is indispensable, therefore, for providing that aspect of the psychological picture which is the correlate of the aetiological.

Proceeding from such different premisses, it is hardly surprising that the accounts of mental functioning offered by these contrasting attitudes will have, on the whole, very little in common. Ostensibly both are handling psychic material for the sake of therapeutic requirements, yet the selective valuation that is inseparable from any specific attitude, tends to emphasize such different aspects of the material that the resulting pictures are quite remarkably dissimilar.

The notion that the causal picture has greater scientific validity because it emphasizes the objective environmental factors that have had a hand in producing the given state of affairs, is counterbalanced by the fact that our understanding of the laws of psychical causality is admittedly hypotheical. And furthermore, we cannot exclude the possibility in a particular case, where objective images and data are employed in the complex structure of a dream, that these may be utilized for the sake of a subjective purpose: a purpose that completely escapes our vision when the objective data are regarded as, in some way, causing the dream.

In the foregoing comparison I have permitted my temperamental bias a certain freedom because I am aware that the teleological position and the necessity for subjective understanding has rarely, if ever, been presented from this platform. May I remind you, in justification, that a scientific hypothesis requires no further advocacy once it has been accepted. Actually I regard, and make use of, the two methods of approach as mutually indispensable instruments. If we are reproached with offending the law of parsimony by introducing a new and troublesome hypothesis into the scientific field, I need only point out that our last offence against this law, namely, the introduction of the psychogenetic hypothesis into the aetiology of disease, has already borne abundant fruit. I must also remind you that no energic conception of mental functions is possible without admitting the concept of teleology. Freud himself has always accepted a teleological conception of libido. But whereas Freud restricts the teleological function to the specific striving of certain libidinous components, Jung expands this function to comprise the co-ordinated expression of the total psychical subject. Hence the only possible disagreement is found to centre in the relative values we ascribe to the two principles. It cannot be a matter of either-or. The law of parsimony is frequently introduced into a discussion as a hired bailiff, to keep marauding feet from trespassing on preserved ground. Kant's definition of comprehension is, I think, a more humane custodian of scientific truth; namely, 'the perception or realization of a thing to the extent which is sufficient for our purpose'.

If, then, our understanding of psychical activity requires the teleology of individuation, just as much as it needs the causality of the instinctive drive, is it not possible to modify our conception of scientific truth to include both these instruments?

Psychology, as you know, does not and cannot rest upon the same four-square foundations as the so-called natural sciences. We are confronted at the outset with the very reasonable doubt whether it is ever possible to achieve a purely objective evaluation of psychical processes and events. For psychology is the only science in which the function of cognition is at the same time the object of cognition. In every other science the immediate difference of the object defines it from the psyche apprehending it. But the psyche can be approached apparently from almost any angle, a fact to which the almost endless variety of 'psychologies' at the present time bears witness. Since however every possible approach is, as we have seen, necessarily conditioned by the particular psychological bias of the investigator, the problem of psychological types is absolutely fundamental to any mutual understanding of the ground covered by the several investigators.

So far as my knowledge goes, Freud has not concerned himself seriously with this problem, but has assumed his hypotheses to rest on purely empirical foundations. Approaching the psychological field from the established ground of clinical medicine and biology, he apparently concluded that the problem need not be faced. From this angle, the motivation of human activity is assumed to originate in the same instinctual sources as those postulated in biology as activating the behaviour of animals. But the science of biology specifically limits its scope to the empirical description and classification of living forms and their behaviour, excluding the philosophical problem of being. In dealing with the psyche, however, this limitation, proper to a purely descriptive science, is felt to be somewhat arbitrary and unreal, because the psyche, which we are attempting to observe, is also our experience, our being. We have to choose, therefore, either to limit our study of the mind to the terrain which is accessible to biological, neurological and physiological methods, or to employ borderline conceptions which, although empirical and descriptive in character, embrace none the less the irrational factor of experience.

To the psychological investigator who is concerned only with the study of the mental apparatus under laboratory conditions this dilemma does not arise; since he can always limit his experiment to the field of observed behaviour. But to the psychotherapist, who, from the practical necessities of his *métier*, must render to the patient some cogent explanation of the difficulties and experiences which have brought him to the doctor, this dilemma is painfully real.

Ideally, a scientific concept contains no more and no less of observed and verifiable data and inference than has been put into it. It is a parcel of fenced land reclaimed from hitherto undefined territory. But science also has to employ borderline concepts which subsume certain unknown, but inferred, factors under a known and recognized category. The very conception of the unconscious is such a borderline concept, since by definition it is held to contain factors, elements, processes, whose nature and extent are alien to consciousness, and whose activity is beyond conscious control. The danger of losing ourselves in this vague, uncharted dimension of experience is almost as great as our chance of getting lost in the continent of Africa. The only possible way to safeguard ourselves from luxuriant speculation in this indistinct and undefined realm, is to submit to the limitation of a definite standpoint and to state at the outset what this standpoint covers. Having made this limitation, we then know that we are observing certain psychological events or processes under a certain definite aspect, and we can then form a certain judgment about them. If we do not submit to this limitation, we are liable to become the victims of our own limitations in a negative sense. By assuming our standpoint to be all-sufficing, we unwittingly betray a one-sidedness of judgment which is plain to all beholders. When, for instance, psycho-analysis carries its scientific pretensions to the point of passing judgment on the subjective values which form the essence of religion and art, presuming to regard the whole realm of religious symbolism and experience as a demoded style of infantile thinking, this judgment merely recoils upon psycho-analysis with damaging results. For it betrays such an embryonic crudity of feeling behind the intellectual arrogance that no sensitive observer could possibly accept it as a mature human judgment.

With all seriousness, then, I contend that we do not further psychological science by claiming universal validity for any standpoint, but rather by affirming the relativity of our approach, and by stating our premisses as clearly as possible. Such a preliminary confession is like the map or chart given by an explorer in the frontispiece of his book, in order to show the reader the route he has travelled. By so doing, he invites the reader to accompany him along the path he describes, and with it he defines the limits of the territory he has observed for the benefit of subsequent travellers.

II. CONSIDERATION OF THE DREAM

Now that we have blown away the last possibility of misconception in respect to the claims of either principle to be identified with science, we are free to consider the dream without prejudice, as a complex, living formation proceeding from an unknown part of the mind. I use the word *unknown* instead of *unconscious*, because the dream-experience, being itself a partial state of consciousness, contradicts the notion that the dream-mind merits the description unconscious. Positive terms of description are, on the whole, more trustworthy than negative and, since we are now regarding the dream with a fresh, unprejudiced vision, it is advisable not to handicap our understanding with a word which contains contradictory implications. When we say that a dream is a product of autonomous psychic activity, we are on undebatable ground, and the only practical question left to discuss is whether or not this autonomous formation can legitimately be regarded as a teleological process conditioned by the potential goal of totality, in much the same way, albeit on the psychic level, as the cell processes in embryonic development.

We know that every organ and process of the body is constantly governed and regulated by the co-ordinated requirements and purposes of the whole. And if we attempt to resolve the life of an organism into a number of separate processes we reach no intelligible understanding of this inherent principle of co-ordinated wholeness. This wholeness is an essential phenomenon of life and not merely externally imposed, as in the case of a machine. So that, if we ignore the principle of totality we are also neglecting life itself. Hence, whether we are considering the complex organs and processes of this body, or the complex formations of the psyche, if we exclude the key-principle of totality from our reckoning, because it savours of teleology, we merely amass a meaningless jumble of unconnected observations.

But the entelechy of psychological development, though it embraces the same principle of co-ordinating totality, goes beyond the limits of physiological analogy through the fact that psychical potential is made actual through the transforming medium of imagination; wherewith I include the whole image-forming process of the mind. It is as though in the bodily processes we are viewing the operation of entelechy from without, while in the psyche we glimpse it from within. We even experience it as a compelling force.

With this conception of entelechy in our minds, the plastic objective character of the dream gains a new significance. Fundamentally the dream is an objective mental process, projecting into the visual and auditory fields subjective processes and conditions which must otherwise remain entirely subliminal. In so far as consciousness must itself be regarded as the most significant expression of individual totality (since no single part of the body possesses consciousness but only the living whole), we can regard this objective character of the dream-experience as directly subserving the integrating function of consciousness. We might even say that the dream is the manifestation of entelechy within the psychical process. This point of view runs directly counter to Freud's original conclusion; namely, that the dream-thoughts were masked in an irrational disguise in order to protect the dreamer from becoming aware of their contents and, thus, being aroused from sleep. In arriving at this conclusion, Freud seems to have overlooked the fact that dreams frequently present their contents in a fashion so dramatic and arresting, even though anxiety is totally absent, that the dreamer is instantly awakened. But apart from this imperative character of certain dreams, we know that human wisdom, both in civilized and uncivilized communities, has shown a strong inclination, particularly at critical moments and phases of life, to listen to the dream, to give it honour, and to try to fathom its meaning. These well-known facts are in keeping with the idea that certain dream-formations contain intuitions which, if apprehended, can add a new and significant content to consciousness. They do not accord with the conception of the dream as a mechanism which disguises the play of repressed tendencies for the purpose of maintaining a state of unconsciousness. Though it must, of course, be admitted that a very large number of dreams are symptomatic in character and, apart from the special interest of psychopathology, seem to make no particular claim upon consciousness.

This objective character of the dream is of the highest importance from the psychotherapeutical standpoint; for it is common ground with every school that the therapeutic result hinges very largely on the possibility of raising unconscious motivations into the conscious field where they can be assimilated by the ego. In borderline cases of schizophrenia the dissociating power of the pathogenic complex frequently has the effect of withdrawing the contents of the complex from objective manifestation in dreams. In these circumstances the objectifying function often manifests itself in quasi-autonomous drawings and paintings in which the dissociated contents are graphically presented. Experience has shown that the analytical handling of these drawings is of the greatest therapeutic value. This faculty of the autonomous psyche to objectify subliminal processes or events in plastic symbolism, whether in dreams, in active fantasy production, or in free-association, must be regarded, therefore, as an essential condition of analytical therapy. That these autonomous or semi-autonomous products should, as far as possible, be understood and interpreted in a secondary process of conscious elaboration is another condition of therapy about which diverse opinions are held.

Another character of the dream that tends to bear out the teleological hypothesis is the selection of the particular objective impressions that are introduced into the dream-structure. The appearance of these objective figures in dreams has led some people to believe that a dream is nothing more than a fortuitous and confused reproduction of certain sensory objective stimuli. But, since we know that nothing happens fortuitously in the mind, we must inquire why, out of the endless variety of possible impressions, just these particular images have been selected for reproduction. Their selection does not accord with conscious valuation, because a large number of these so-called reproductions produced only a minimal effect upon waking consciousness. Moreover, when a dream is faithfully reported, we find that the dream-figures are practically never a mere reproduction of the external impression. As a rule, they have undergone a 'sea-change', and the dream-mind is using them in an entirely new connection which has no obvious relation to that from which they have been abstracted.

There is also the problem of the energy-content of the dream. For it cannot be denied that the denizens of the dream seem to live and move and have their separate being, quite regardless of the dreamer's will or convenience. In fact, they appear to be independently activated with energy, in much the same way as the denizens of the external world appear to our waking senses. Again, we may assume with Freud, that all this manifold activity consists of frustrated or repressed instinctual tendencies achieving a complex drama of wish-fulfilment. But why reserve this explanation to the dream-life? Surely it is equally possible to explain the whole vast drama of human history, indeed, all human and animal activity whatsoever, along the same lines. A superior non-human intelligence might most reasonably conclude, if it had no access to our subjective feelings and purposes, that the whole of our human science and culture was merely a fantastic attempt at wish-fulfilment.[1] It is, indeed, perfectly possible to contend that all cultural achievement has been effected from the surplus of the primal *libido sexualis* that was not used up on the biological level. But if we assert this to be the whole truth of the matter, we cannot hope to convince our fellow-men that we have reached an 'understanding', to use Kant's phrase, 'that is sufficient for our purpose'.

It may be objected that this analogy is not valid because in regard to cultural achievement, a coherent purpose is demonstrable and self-evident. But can we not say the same for the cell formation that replaces the amputated leg in the newt? No, the only convincing reality which lends any real meaning to our cultural labours is the subjective value which we, individually and collectively, confer upon the whole human experiment. A non-human intelligence which had no means of comprehending this subjective value would be guilty of an 'unscientific' assumption if it ascribed to our cultural edifice any 'transcendental' motivation. That human society is a complex kind of mechanism is a self-evident truth. But if it were that *and nothing more*, psychology would not only be superfluous, it would be impossible. A purely objective biological account of any complex mental structure can deal only with the question of how it operates and how it came about. It must always exclude the problem of why it was created and what it intends. For the whole question of meaning is bound up with subjective feeling values; and just because these are in the highest degree individual, they are not representable in general biological categories.

Here, then, we come to the crux of the whole argument. For if we decline to admit the possibility of a subjective, teleological under-

[1] This concept offers us a good example of a scientific explanation that aims at excluding subjective valuation. When we reflect upon it in a human way we are chilled by its bottomless stupidity. A dream concerned with the plan and structure of a potential creative achievement is made to appear essentially indistinguishable from a dream on the lavatory level: since both are expressing an instinctive need. This conception has an almost uncanny silliness, reminding one of those substances of extremely low temperature which create a sensation that contradicts all normal opinion of cold. It is indeed so intensely banal that people even mistake it for a profound truth. As soon as one realizes, however, that it is a scientific concept of the mind that attempts to exclude all psychological values, we know why we are chilled. It is the *reductio ad absurdum* of science.

standing of psychic material on the grounds that this involves an unscientific method of explanation, we therewith exclude the psyche itself from our so-called psychology, since, by definition, the psyche means soul, life, breath, spirit; in other words, the inherent purpose of a living being.

The very word 'understanding' implies a certain attitude of apprehension that accords rather with the inner nature of a thing than with its outer behaviour: an attitude of standing under or within a thing, rather than viewing it from above. It implies an intuitive attempt to come within the limiting conditions and scope of the subject, with the object of achieving a comprehending parallelism, before attempting a critical objective judgment. Criticism, of course, cannot be suppressed, but until we have understood the individual nature of the experiment that is being attempted, we are not in a position to pass judgment.

Approaching a dream, then, with this attitude, we shall view it primarily as an experience of an individual psychology. First we may note that it is pervaded by a certain definite emotional tone. This may be either agreeable or unpleasant: it may be arresting, threatening, stimulating, sinister, haunted by anxiety, or frankly erotic. The affective content of the dream-experience helps us to understand the dreamer from a new angle. It tells us not only the character of the complex which conditions the dream, but also the peculiar attitude of the dreamer's personality to the complex. We may observe, too, the dreamer's attitude in the dramatic sequence or movement of the dream. Does he participate actively in these dream-events, or is he indifferent to what is happening in his own psychological kitchen? We note also that the various personalities of the dream are animated independently of the dreamer's control and their action is seldom aimless. They are 'up to something'. We may infer from these observations that the dream is a process of energy, and that each personality in the dream manifests a specific quantum of energy. It is, therefore, fitting to inquire whether the energy manifested in the dream is spending itself aimlessly, or whether a conversion of energy is taking place; as, for instance, where a transformation from a lower to a higher type of organism is being represented. From this we can decide whether a progressive or regressive evolution is in progress.

As an example of the way in which a dream represents the transformation of energy I shall briefly mention a dream of my own.

It occurred while I was engaged upon an attempt to give an analytical demonstration of a sequence of drawings from a schizoid patient. The dream was concerned with a sluice gate that had recently been constructed between a large pool (like a mill pool in a river) and a lock, into which the water of the pool flowed. In the pool there was a large number of snakes, eels and various kinds of fish. There was an idea that their presence in the pool was a seasonal occurrence in the course of migration. A kind of eel-basket had been constructed in this sluice gate to catch the snakes and eels, and a second contraption on top to catch the fishes. This whole construction was in the charge of an old Indian, who raised and lowered the eel-trap with a definite purpose in view. This purpose was to feed a number of water fowl, ducks, divers, grebes, cormorants, etc., who collected in the small lock, waiting for the snakes and eels to be released from the eel-trap. When the old man opened the basket there was a tremendous commotion and activity among the birds. But since it all happened under the water one could see nothing but the troubled surface. Then it occurred to me that it would be an excellent idea to dig a gallery underground up to the side wall of the lock and insert there a large sheet of plate-glass, so that one could actually see what was taking place.

I shall not burden you too much with my personal psychology, but I must explain that in my younger days I collected lepidoptera, and that the breeding of moths and butterflies from the egg through the larval and pupal stages held, at one time, an absorbing interest for me. You will understand, then, that in my own analysis the phenomenon of histolysis provided a kind of *leit-motif* for the analogous process of libido transformation. The association with the underground gallery with its glass wall is concerned with a device used by an inquiring fisherman who wanted to observe the behaviour of salmon in river pools, particularly in regard to their response to various lures. A glass-bottomed, watertight box was inserted under the water, thus fulfilling the purpose of a subaqueous observation-post. As for the other ideas in the dream, cormorants are used by the Chinese for fishing, and the old man was thought of as a native of India. With regard to the notion that the snakes and eels were migrating I have often observed that animals, as well as men, behave in a regardless, reckless fashion when migrating *en masse*. An irresistible collective momentum, however it may originate, sweeps every individual unit along in a blind compulsive urgency. A purely collective, undifferentiated aspect becomes apparent which cannot be reconciled with the vigilant, adapted behaviour of the same creatures when in their accustomed *milieu.* The sluice gate and lock suggest an artificial contrivance whereby energy potential can be liberated or dammed back at will, a constructional idea which gains a special significance from the nature of the foregoing association. There are, naturally, many subjective reverberations relating to this theme of energy-control. But since these belong more to the personal aspect of the dream, they are scarcely opportune to the present occasion.

I feel inclined to submit this dream to you because, as you see, its whole character is provocative of a teleological explanation. It is perfectly possible to ignore this aspect, and to stand in wonder before such a wealth of so-called sexual symbolism. Yet to do so, though it might corroborate a theory, would not deepen our understanding; whereas, regarding it teleologically, this dream contains much that I needed to know. To my subjective feeling there is a clear analogy between the snakes and eels of the pond and the caterpillar stage of the lepidopetra; between the eel-trap and the pupa; and between the process known as histolysis (viz. the disintegration of the organism of the caterpillar within the pupal case) and the assimilation of the snakes and eels by the birds: i.e. by a more differentiated, winged form of life. This part of the dream, then, appears to represent a conversion process whereby libido-components from an undifferentiated, general origin, represented as denizens of water in a state of migration, are assimilated by (hence, transformed into) ideational or conceptual elements, symbolized by the birds. Water, as you know, is the classic symbol of the unconscious, affective element, while air and light are symbolic attributes of consciousness.

The association with the Chinese cormorants adds the idea of control to the activity of the birds. The idea of a controlled energy-process is further elaborated in the making and operation of the sluice gate and trap. This symbol also contains the idea of a cultural machine by which the latent energy potential of the unconscious can be made use of. But the sluice gate and lock are used, not only for the control of the water level, but also for the catching of the eels and the feeding of the birds. Hence, we have here a condensation in which the conversion of energy, as a natural biological process, is identical with an artificial machine for energy-control.

I should have mentioned that the divers and grebes immediately suggested to my mind the lake of Zürich: so that these creatures are closely associated with the period of my own analysis with Professor Jung. This association implies that this whole hydraulic construction is directly connected with the analytical process. Yet there was no suggestion of Professor Jung himself about the little old man from India. This omission is significant: for my whole conception of the psyche as a process of energy is derived directly from Professor Jung. We might therefore anticipate that the dream-mind would have associated this introverted construction with him. Why, then, is an Indian introduced in his stead? At first I assumed that this was an allusion to the fact that India is the classical example of an introverted culture. But this seemed too vague and insubstantial a ground for substituting a shadowy general figure for the very positive figure of Professor Jung. It was not until I was actually elaborating the dream for this paper that I remembered I had stumbled upon several remarkable allusions to the symbolism of the *Kundalīnī Shakti* in my schizoid patient's drawings. The *Kundali* Yoga is, as you know, one of the classical Yoga systems of India. The patient had no knowledge of this system, or its symbolism, and yet the parallelism was so clear that I could not ignore it. In my written discussion I had drawn attention to these analogies and had suggested that it was not necessary to assume an unconscious penetration of Tantric ideas into my patient's psychology, but that we could more easily explain the existence of these parallel ideas on the hypothesis that the process of psychic evolution activated through the purposeful introversion of the libido in analysis is, at bottom, identical with that of the classical introverting systems of the East and, therefore, finds expression in parallel symbolism. Since, however, I was presenting my material to psychiatric colleagues who profess a profound scepticism in regard to just such correspondences, I was considering deleting this discussion from my study.

The basic conception of the *Kundalīnī* system is the awakening of *Shakti* (viz. the static or potential power in the body), symbolized as a serpent coiled three and a half times around the *linga*. *Shakti* is the undifferentiated, generalized energy potential of the unconscious that is aroused from a latent, slumbering condition at the base of the spinal cord by a deliberate introverting technique. Being aroused, a certain migration or upward movement of the *Shakti* energy takes place (*prāna*) through various centres (*chakras*) situated at definite levels of the body. This energizing of the *chakras* also effects a gradual transformation of the unconscious primordial energy (*Shakti*) into the conscious principle (*Shiva*) which is represented symbolically as a thousand-petalled lotus on the crown of the head. Both *Shakti* and *Shiva* are conceived as pre-existing primordial principles, and the psychical evolution instigated by the introverting attitude is regarded as the result of the activation of this pre-existing but latent polarity. There is a downward movement (*prāna*) emanating from the *Shiva* principle and a corresponding upward-moving *prāna* from the *Shakti* principle. Thus, in the symbol of the union of *Shakti* and *Shiva*, which is the central symbol of the traditional Tantric system, we recognize the same fundamental ideas Jung has described as the reciprocal action of the conscious and unconscious functions.

I have given but the briefest, hence quite inadequate, account of this Eastern system, but sufficient, I trust, to account for a certain aspect of the dream which would otherwise be inexplicable. Snakes are not normal inhabitants of water and one does not usually associate an Indian with mechanical or engineering ability. But if we regard the Indian as personifying the idea of psychological development as represented in this classical Indian culture system, we gain a most important sidelight on the dream-content. From this viewpoint the snakes and eels are manifestations of primordial instinctual energy (*Shakti* principle). Their migration is paralleled with the *prāna* which, in our terminology, would signify the kinetic manifestation of hitherto latent energy-reserves in the unconscious. Their entry into the eel-basket would correspond, though in a familiar Western guise, with the dynamic penetration of the *chakra* by the migrating *prāna* of the *Shakti* principle. And their assimilation by the birds would represent the union of *Shakti* and *Shiva*; namely, the natural intuitive process whereby the function of consciousness is fed by the deep activity of the unconscious. The fact that these particular birds, namely, grebes, divers and other water fowl, are associated with my introverted education by the lake of Zürich, gives to them a rather special character. It is entirely in keeping with the natural realism of the dream-mind to represent the specialized function of introverting intuition, which has become adapted to fishing for unconscious contents, by a species of bird which has developed the faculty of diving under the water for the purpose of vital supply.

By accepting the possibility that these correspondences which we have now developed are inherent in the spontaneous structure of the dream, we gain an insight into the operation of the autonomous psyche which has a general, as well as a personal, value. All the contents we have so far dealt with are more or less general representations of psychical activity. But the idea of making a gallery and a subaqueous observation-post is clearly a special improvisation answering my requirement of the moment; namely, to devise some means by which to demonstrate visually the way the unconscious develops under analysis. The material I am engaged upon is, in fact, visually demonstrable; because it consists of a sequence of drawings in which the evolution of the unconscious during analysis is artlessly depicted. The great difficulty with which I have been faced in the work springs from the peculiar condition of insulation which surrounds our analytical researches. It seems almost impossible to present the actual evolutionary process which we see developing under our eyes in an objectively demonstrable way. The dream is telling me that this is feasible, so long as the sensitive conditions inseparable from a subjective emotional experience are respected. The operation of refraction which hinders the eye from seeing what transpires under the surface of the water, is exactly similar to the action of what is termed the threshold resistance between the conscious and the unconscious. In order to circumvent this difficulty, the idea of extending conscious insight underground, as it were, is represented as a special kind of device. The underground chamber would be cut off from the brilliant illumination of daylight, as at the aquarium in Regent's Park, in order that the feebler subaqueous illumination can be effective. This would surely imply that the attitude of the observer in regard to the fluid activity of the unconscious must be adjusted to its special conditions. Thus the dream gives me a most valuable hint as to the manner in which the deep introverted activity of the unconscious life could be presented to the outside observer.

III. VALUE OF CONSTRUCTIVE OR ANALOGICAL METHOD

This dream is more valuable in demonstrating the possibilities of the constructive method of approach than a whole volume of closely reasoned argument. This is my excuse and, I trust, my justification, for introducing this material to you. I have naturally a certain diffidence in submitting to your critical judgment a living fragment of my subjective experience, but as we have already remarked, the dream-structure, as well as the character of the associations, suggests that a general or impersonal process is under review. I infer from this that the dream presents a problem of general interest. The transformation of the libido, the control of energy flow, the principle of equivalence (namely, the energy released or withdrawn from one psychic level, manifesting itself on another): these deductions are germane to the essential nature of the dream-structure. Whereas if we insisted at all costs upon a personal interpretation, in the support of some presupposition that every dream is solely concerned with personal and private affairs, we should have to force this explanation upon the dream, in spite of its manifest impersonal character. Naturally, every dream has a certain individual aspect, since an individual mind has dreamed it, but if we ask ourselves 'What does the dream say?' instead of 'What should the dream be saying according to this or that authority?' we find that dreams are concerned with impersonal and general problems just as much as, and perhaps even more than, with the personal. A dream, after all, is a natural product of the psyche, as a flower is a natural product of the earth, and the fact that a flower grows in a certain individual garden does not excommunicate it from the general family of living things.

Symbolic formations and mythological figures belonging to the general psychic inheritance are often clearly manifest in the dream-structure, and these formations demand a correspondingly impersonal treatment. In the Zürich school, therefore, we make use of the method known as *amplification*, whenever these myth-like formations make their appearance in dream or fantasy. The method consists in applying to the dream-myth the parallel cultural pattern from general mythology, in a somewhat similar way to the use of specific dye stains in histology. The developed myth-pattern brings into relief just those elements of the dream-structure which correspond to it. By this means the embryonic or immature components of the patient's psychic equipment are related to the more developed, cultural forms of mythology. The therapeutic value of this procedure rests upon the fact that a neurotic personality is attempting to live his life on too narrow a basis. Whether his insulated psychological condition is the result of his abnormal fears and anxieties, or whether his fearfulness and his other complaints are symptoms of his restrictive psychological habit, is a problem about which different views can be advanced. But about the actual condition which we have to treat, there is general agreement. The constructive method of handling the dream invites the patient to emerge from his twilit neurotic sanctum, where he is closeted with his personal inadequacy, into the wide field of human history where he is likely to find just that symbolic creation which, through its inherent correspondence with his own myth, will possess for him the redeeming value.

On the other hand, the reduction and disintegration of pathological archaism and infantilism is, of course, an indispensable part of the method; since no new attitude can be achieved so long as the psychic energy is invested in a complex that is insulated from any positive participation in life.

To recapitulate the general trend of the argument: there are a number of physical processes as, for instance, the development of the total organism from any section of a divided morula or the restitution of lost parts among the amphibia, which can only be explained on the hypothesis that the totality-pattern of the individual is potentially present in all its parts. How this can be, we do not know; but we have to assume that the morphological archetype is an inherent factor of the developmental process acting upon the developing organism as a teleological goal. The existence of the archetype of individual totality can be demonstrated in the autonomous products of the psyche in much the same way as Dr. Canti demonstrated the presence of the femur-archetype in his film of the embryonic mesoderm. For if we examine the developmental material, yielded by the unconscious during the analytical process, under the light of this hypothesis, we find the following evidence. Let us call this archetype of the integrated whole, the Self. We observe that certain influences, events, impressions, certain acquired ideas, tend to be projected upon the dream-stage under a critical, ludicrous, or sinister light. Other figures, personalities, influences appear consistently under a favourable aspect. The former represent psychic factors either inherited or acquired, which have had the effect of alienating the subject from his original natural wholeness: in other words, of separating the ego from the Self. The latter represent the harmonizing, integrating, concerting tendencies which assist the realization of psychic totality. Frequently the idea of a concert, an orchestra, or an organ, is employed by the dream-mind as symbolizing this harmonizing tendency. The very fact that schizophrenia, or the problem of the split mind, occupies so much of our psychiatric interest, provides further evidence that the goal of totality is our therapeutic criterion.

When observing this teleological process in the embryo or the newt, we do not confuse it with a mental tendency, but we regard it as an inherent property of the living organism. In the same way we are permitted to assume that the goal of individuation, by which we mean a process of differentiation having as its aim the development of the total personality, can be present in the psyche as an original life-tendency. From this point of view the retrogressive movement of the dream-sequence back to childhood and infancy, can be viewed as a teleological quest for those functional elements of the original nature which have become dissociated and repressed and, therefore, need to be restored. The theme of the search for the hidden or buried treasure would correspond to this motivation.

It has been objected that such amplifications of the given dream-structure as I have demonstrated in regard to my own dream, are unjustifiable from the standpoint of science and that we merely indulge a wayward imagination in following these intuitive allusions. My answer to this objection is that, scientifically, we are not permitted to assume that nature ever means anything in any of her spontaneous products. The fact that we actually do perceive meaning belongs to the nature of consciousness, and, since we cannot explain consciousness, we have to accept this fact as given. We cannot go behind it. But we also know from experience that the giving of meaning, or value, to a thing brings about a certain change in our view of the world and enhances individual distinctiveness. In other words, the more value we give to a thing, the more it lives for us and the more it imparts. When we pour an absorbing concentration of interest into an object or goal, that thing becomes pregnant and inevitably bears fruit. This psychological truth is implied in the etymological kinship of the German words *Betrachtung*—'concentration', and *trächtig*—'pregnant'.

It is an undeniable truth that the more value we give to the dream or to the function of imagination, the more is reciprocal activity between the conscious and the unconscious enhanced. The neurotic sense of inferiority which so cripples our patients can certainly not be mended unless we have some means of increasing the subjective feeling of value, or distinctiveness. The method of amplification helps to achieve this end by relating those elements of the patient's dream which contain mythological allusions *in embryo* to the fully developed analogue to be found in parallel cultures. If the allusions are not present in the dream, no parallel can be drawn. But if the seeds are present, is it not our psychotherapeutic task to incubate them?

Finally, Jung's constructive system is the practical method *par excellence*. For he maintains that dreams develop directly out of the patient's attitude to the critical problem of adaptation, by which his character is being tested at this actual moment. Even though the dream sequence runs backwards into early life, this movement must either be a retreat from the critical problem or it is *reculer pour mieux sauter*: in other words, an attempt to go back to an attitude that was still simple and whole, before the pathological inadequacy had developed. Thus the backward movement of the dreams into early life may carry the signification 'as then, so now'. Under this viewpoint the dream remains constantly in allegiance to reality and the work of salvage of deformed or neglected functions is undertaken with this end always in view.

Whatever method we adopt, this work of psychological salvage unites us fundamentally in a common goal, and, in spite of our psychological diversity, I believe that a syncretism can be achieved under a single embracing principle, if we can once accept the relativity of our respective standpoints. For, whether we are reducing our patients' pathological formations to their instinctual components, or whether we attempt to incubate functional embryos by means of analogous amplification, our aim is at bottom the same—namely, to assist the patient to construct or to reconstruct an effective psychological attitude that can withstand the divers and complex strains of modern life and at the same time provide him with an increased capacity for experience.

I have left the philosophical argument for the use of the analogical method until the end; since my paper was concerned more with its practical application in psychotherapy. The old scientific contempt of analogy—'a buttered slide to anywhere' as a witty colleague termed it—was aimed, and rightly, at the slipshod, illegitimate use of analogy as an escape from fact. At the present time, however, teleological concepts and analogical methods are being applied in history, philosophy and psychology by the very greatest minds.

They are receiving fullest justification by the most careful philosophical writers. One might even say that the whole problem of analogy—which is the instrument of teleological thinking—versus the scientific concept is engrossing the philosophical world of to-day. We have to realize the fact that, notwithstanding the difficulty of relating analogy to the scientific concept, the analogical method, when rightly understood and used in the proper place, is an instrument of the very highest precision. We can go further and say that where the application of the scientific concept in the wrong place hampers and muddles our intelligence, the application of analogy, with due recognition of what analogy is, clarifies and reduces to order.

Dilthey distinguishes the *Naturwissenschaften* from the *Geisteswissenschaften*, with which term he embraces those disciplines which, like history and psychology, cannot proceed on the same lines as the natural sciences. He asserts that their respective methods of approach must differ radically because the categories of reality of the *Geisteswissenschaften* are nowhere the same as the *Naturwissenschaften*. This division accords with the view I expressed at the beginning, namely, that the causal and final viewpoints exist in the relation of polarity, one to the other. If such a relation can be demonstrated to exist as an essential condition of our psychological thinking, the task before us is not to identify with either viewpoint, but rather to learn to handle these instruments with timely precision.

The Ghost as a Psychic Phenomenon[1]

It would be not only reckless but unprofitable to embark upon a discussion of the spirit-world without first circumscribing the terrain. As a physician approaching the field from the side of medical psychology I find, however, a piece of ground already cleared. But this claim does not correspond altogether with that of psychical research. Our psychological investigations have unwittingly quickened an interest in ghosts, because these play a symbolical role in the subliminal dramas with which the psychotherapist has to deal. Psychical research, on the other hand, tends to pursue its interest in the ghost as an independent phenomenon, existing in and for itself; its relativity in the scheme of general psychic causality being a secondary consideration, if not ignored altogether.

The psychotherapist encounters certain psychoneurotic states which, by their very nature, compel him to make use of the primitive concept of possession. These ghost-effects are very real. A psychoneurotic personality often behaves as though an alien will possessed him. He also has dreams in which a ghost appears in his room, or in which he is being pursued by a sinister daemonic figure whom he cannot evade. But, although the effect is alien in character, its causation is intelligible, and the conditions of its appearance are sometimes predictable.

We have the advantage, therefore, of being able to study the natural history of the ghost from an inside position, whereas the scientific investigator, who has to sift the accounts of a number of excited witnesses who may or may not have seen apparitions or heard strange noises, is in a different case. For he must needs determine how much or how little should be ascribed to general suggestibility, how much of the experience has been unconsciously trimmed to suit the supposed expectations of the investigator, and, even where a relatively convincing *consensus gentium* exists, he has to determine where a line can be drawn between the subjective constellation in the witnesses' psychology and the unknown factor which can be regarded as an external activating force. In these cases the psychical

[1] A paper read at a private meeting of the Society for Psychical Research on 25 November 1936.

context, by virtue of which the ghostly appearance would fit into a relatively intelligible sequence of events, is usually lacking and, therefore, the apparition is left suspended, as it were, in a super-normal or sub-normal unreality.

The question of setting, or frame, or context, is the primary consideration in the understanding of all psychic phenomena. In the field of natural science we are accustomed to draw certain logical conclusions from the objective aspect and behaviour of the things observed, since natural science proceeds on the assumption that nature is rational. But as soon as we cross over into the field of so-called psychic phenomena, a purely objective account of the phenomena is found to be inadequate. For example, an objective record of Saul's critical journey to Damascus, including the subject's account of the divine apparition in heaven and his subsequent change in character and attitude, savours of the miraculous only because the full subjective context is lacking. If this be added, we can get a glimpse of that split-off subliminal personality which was gradually assimilating the Christian spirit, while the conscious personality was fanatically over-compensating his own doubt by drastic persecution of the Christians. We might be able to detect certain signs, as the nascent Christian complex waxed in power in the unconscious subjective hinterland, until it finally broke through the threshold of consciousness, throwing Saul to the ground and declaring its superior energy-content by its apparitional manifestation in an aura of white light. From now onwards the previous conscious personality and standpoint is repressed as an unworthy antithesis to the victorious Christian thesis, finding only a spasmodic pathological expression in the guise of epileptiform fits.

The very fact that we are able to make this fairly intelligible reconstruction of what seemed to our forefathers a miraculous occurrence does not mean that we have, thereby, explained the overwhelming impression of a genuine religious experience. But it does mean that we are able to rescue a large tract of human experience from the realm of magic and mystery, and to bring it within the province of understanding. Instead of viewing an isolated disjuncted marvel in the skies, we are able to piece together an orderly sequence of events which reveals an inherent purposiveness. This has been made possible by carrying the agnostic spirit of scientific inquiry into the realm of psychic events.

In psychological practice we frequently encounter facts that seem scarcely credible; facts that appear at first so irrational that we almost despair of embracing them in a scientific corpus. But in so far as the living individual, who alone is able to provide the psychic context of these strange events, is sitting solidly before us, the lamp of reason refuses to be extinguished, and with it we are sometimes enabled to find the rational thread of continuity. The hypothesis which has supplied the golden thread in the labyrinth of the psyche is the conception that all psychic activity is purposive. This golden thread of purposive activity is, however, rarely supplied by the patient's conscious account of his experience. The clue is usually found in his dreams or fantasies. These spontaneous products of the mind reveal the unconscious causal nexus which makes the conscious history intelligible.

The unconscious is merely a term which comprises everything that exists, that has existed, or that could exist beyond the range of this individual consciousness. It is therefore a relative condition, since what is unconscious to-day may be conscious to-morrow, and vice versa. So long as consciousness, as in the early days of last century, was limited by the concept of miraculous or divine creation, the continuity of the evolutionary process was an unconscious content, but it was none the less a fact. And in so far as general consciousness to-day still regards the mental process as synonymous with consciousness, it must necessarily regard every projection of unconscious psychic activity as aspects of objective reality. For if the continuity between the emergent form and its antecedent germination in the unconscious is not perceived by consciousness, it is held not to exist. And when this continuity is demonstrated, it frequently happens that the individual concerned feels that in some way his faith has been undermined. Very few can tolerate the truth that what is attributed to fate represents the sum of unconscious psychic motivations, and that the all-embracing paternal image is a condensation of inherited experience. I believe everyone resents these psychological explanations, because in the West the concept of the psyche has been cheapened by a whole host of opinion-pedlars and wisdom-mongers who offer cheap explanations with the air of a scientific pundit. A cheap explanation explains things away, whereas our best scientific theory merely removes one veil from the muffled figure of truth. We use the term psyche as though the name gave us power over the thing named. But in fact we cannot even locate the psyche, while its contents and activities are, to a large extent, unknown to us and beyond our conscious control. When science invades the province that hitherto has been guarded by religious taboo, it has to tread warily; for it is sacred ground.

In certain Eastern countries, or amongst savage peoples, the voices of the insane are regarded as the utterances of a spirit, and arouse veneration and awe. Whereas with us, who know that the state of insanity means to be in the grip of irrational ideas, no heed is given to what issues from the mouths of the possessed, unless one happens to be a Dostoievsky or a Jung.

Psychological explanation is a scientific attempt to make the sequence of psychic events intelligible. But a purely rational account is never satisfactory because the nature of unconscious activity is primitive and therefore non-rational in character. Our best hope, then, is to make use of the non-rational symbol-language of the unconscious, even though a symbol can never be completely transposed into intellectual terms. Our experience of our underlying primitive psychology consists at times of ghosts, demons and other mythological denizens. During the experience these things are our reality. Hence our conscious reaction to these experiences must take into account the non-rational, dynamic character of the pure experience. And yet, because the ruler of consciousness is the reason, our account must also be essentially reasonable. Our worst danger is to use our scientific intellect as a defence against the experience of the primordial unconscious. Science is knowledge, and to experience ourselves must involve a certain responsibility concerning the knowledge we have gained. If I know, for instance, that certain so-called accidents which befall me, or certain bad effects I see in my children or my household, have their source in my unconscious psychology, I must choose between making my children my scapegoats or taking responsibility for my own psychology. I cannot any longer assume that I don't know.

Now this is the situation in which the problem of the ghost has placed us. There is not one of us who is free of responsibility concerning the ghosts of the past. We imagine we have bought off fate by our superior education, but actually we are haunted by bewildered and dissatisfied spirits. Ancestor-worship is to be found wherever culture has spread. Gifts and food and funerary rites, as are to be seen in China to-day, did not spring solely out of veneration for the honoured dead. Originally they were the means of satisfying the ghosts, in order that they should not afflict the living with their ghostly craving for life. When Dr. Jung and I were camping among the Elgonyi on Mount Elgon, we frequently came across little ghost-houses by the side of the path leading to a house or village. The little houses had two or more rooms, and milk and corn and other attractions were placed in them, so that the spirits might stay there and not go on to the village and make people sick. The ghosts of dead relatives and ancestors are particularly to be feared as the cause of illness. The most difficult and responsible office of the *shaman* among Siberian tribes, or of the *laibon* in East Africa, is literally the cure of souls. Healing the sick is considered to be a relatively elementary art. *Shamans* of the lower grades can undertake doctoring, but only the highest grade of *shaman* can shepherd the souls of the dead. In Lamaism, also, the ultimate store of traditional wisdom is reserved for instructing the dead. The spirits have to be enticed or led away from the habitations of the living to the place where they can dwell in safety. In Uganda we were allowed to see one of these houses to which the ghosts are led. They are really churches. Often a considerable amount of art and devotion has been given to these ghost-houses where the spirits of the ancestors are housed. The churches of our English shires, standing in consecrated ground among the graves of the dead, are really ghost-houses.

From this point of view God would be the great ancestor-spirit who must be very securely housed, lest He should wander into the village and make people mad or sick. The act of consecration is a magical ritual designed to set apart this special plot of ground in which the ghosts of the dead are magically contained. We have lost sight of the original psychological necessity which set apart the *Gottesacker* with its graves and spirit-house as a piece of consecrated ground; but comparison with the primitive homologue shows us that in spite of our ideal superstructure, the ground-plan of our civilized religious structure is identical with the primitive conception.

Mr. John Layard tells me that in Malekula, an island of the New Hebrides, the most pressing need in every person's life is to have a pig or pigs which, in the event of death, can be sacrificed to placate the bad female ghost Lehevhev, so that the soul may travel safely to the volcano where the ancestor-spirits dwell. At the end of the great Sumerian epic, *Gilgamish*, we find the closing stanzas concerned with the description of the ghosts found in the underworld by Enkidu's spirit, and how their fate is determined by the way they died and the way in which they are remembered by their surviving relatives.

Just as good manners consist in bearing in mind the shadow of the living, as, for instance, face-saving in China, or in Africa the careful avoidance of a man's shadow, and here at home the instinctive consideration for the complexes of one's friends; so piety consists in taking care of the ghosts. Many primitive people will never chastise their children because the child is inhabited by an ancestor-spirit. Similarly a snake that comes into a house is protected and fed, because it contains an ancestor-spirit. Then there is the care of sacred animals,—for instance, the sacred cows and apes of India, the totem animal, or the creature who becomes your *tinihowi*, if you are an Achumawi Indian—all these pious exercises are inspired by veneration for the spirits.

Nearly all peoples in whom ghost-psychology plays a vital role discriminate between bad ghosts who seduce or in some way alienate the living from their proper way (often they are vampires and werewolves), and the good spirits who want to be reborn or to participate positively in life. I remember a paranoid case of dementia praecox who three times attempted her own life. After leaping from the top of a house, she told me that her mother and her lover were calling her to join them in the spirit-land, and that her leap was done in pure ecstasy. On one occasion during the Easter Passion-week she attempted her life because Our Lord was calling her to join Him. At other times He spoke to her out of heaven, revealing to her the inner nature of the universe, a kind of secret doctrine which she had to teach to all who could listen with their hearts. Thus, in this woman's experience, Christ was at one time a bad ghost seducing her to suicide, at another He was a celestial source of illumination and guidance; in other words, a guardian spirit.

Luther had this same ambiguous conception of God. He said that when God was in the heavens He was all majesty and power; the God of our ideals. But sometimes He absconded and in a concealed form drove men mad or compelled them to every kind of irrationality. He called this nether aspect of God the *deus absconditus*.

The Chinese also make a distinction between the *shen* soul and the *kwei* soul. The character for *shen* means to expand, to rise up. It is the divine substance which rises up and leads to deliverance.

The *kwei* is daemonic, compulsive, and clings to the concrete and earthy. The meaning of *kwei* is ghost-being. In Egypt the ka-soul was the double or shadow, and tended to cling to the material body.

This ambivalency also appears in the primitive attitude to spirits. It is illustrated very beautifully in an account of a Siberian *shaman*, given by Leo Sternberg, the Russian anthropologist, in a paper on Divine Election in Primitive Religion. He was impressed by the fact that behind all the favourable or unfavourable events in a primitive man's life the activities of good or bad spirits are always presupposed. As an example, he cites the case of a young *shaman* of the Gold tribe whose sincerity attracted him. He records this man's life-history as follows:

My ancestors lived in the village of Urmil [15 versts from Chabarovsk]. Their gens is said to have migrated there from the lower reaches of the Amur. Long, long ago, we were Ainu. The old folks say that some generations back there were three great shamans of my gens. No shamans were known amongst my nearest forefathers. My father and mother enjoyed perfect health. I am now forty years old. I am married, but have no children. Up to the age of twenty I was quite well. Then I fell ill, my whole body ailed me, I had bad headaches. Shamans tried to cure me, but it was all of no avail. When I began shamaning myself, I got better and better. It is now ten years that I have been a shaman, but at first I used to practise for myself only, and it is three years ago only that I took to curing other people. A shaman's practice is very, very fatiguing, it is much harder than felling trees, but there is nothing to be done about that.

Once I was asleep on my sick-bed, when a spirit approached me. It was a very beautiful woman. Her figure was very slight, she was no more than half an arshin [71 cm.] tall. Her face and attire were quite as those of one of our Gold women. Her hair fell down to her shoulders in short black tresses. Other shamans say they have had the vision of a woman with one-half of her face black, and the other half red. She said: 'I am the ayami of your ancestors, the Shamans. I taught them shamaning. Now I am going to teach you. The old shamans have died off, and there is no one to heal people. You are to become a shaman.'

Next she said: 'I love you, I have no husband now, you will be my husband and I shall be a wife unto you. I shall give you assistant spirits. You are to heal with their aid, and I shall teach and help you myself. Food will come to us from the people.'

I felt dismayed and tried to resist. Then she said: 'If you will not obey me, so much the worse for you. I shall kill you.'

She has been coming to me ever since, and I sleep with her as with my own wife, but we have no children. She lives quite by herself without any relatives in a hut on a mountain, but she often changes her abode. Sometimes she comes under the aspect of an old woman, and sometimes as a winged tiger. I mount her and she takes me to show me different countries. I have seen mountains, where only old men and women live, and villages, where you see nothing but young people, men and women: they look like Golds and speak Goldish, sometimes those people are turned into tigers. Now my ayami does not come to me as frequently as before. Formerly, when teaching me, she used to come every night. She has given me three assistants—the 'jarga' [panther], the 'doonto' [bear], and the 'amba' [tiger]. They come to me in my dreams, and appear whenever I summon them while shamaning. If one of them refuses to come, the ayami makes them obey, but, they say, there are some who do not obey even the ayami. When I am shamaning, the ayami and the assistant spirits are possessing me: whether big or small, they penetrate me, as smoke or vapour would. When the ayami is within me, it is she who speaks through my mouth, and she does everything herself.

This, as you see, is an interesting case because it is an uncontaminated psychological record of the conversion of a daemonic, obsessing ghost into a helpful, guiding spirit. Furthermore, it supports our idea that the possessing-ghost is a manifestation of the familial or racial unconscious. In general, there are two distinct causes of sickness among so-called primitive peoples. The one is the loss or absence of a soul, the other is possession by an alien spirit. In the former case a man feels he has lost something which is normally his: virtue has gone out of him. In the latter he is invaded by some influence or power which has estranged him from his normal being. Something, in fact, has got into him.

From this point of view *the soul* in the former case represents a certain quantum of vital energy which receded out of consciousness into the personal unconscious, where it was no longer immediately available.

The concept of spirit or ghost, on the contrary, always represents either a welcome or an unwelcome intrusion. The Holy Ghost and the hierarchy of angels and archangels on the one side, and Satan the Evil Spirit with all his host on the other, are highly elaborated conceptions of universal psychic factors which appear under analogous forms in every human society.

In everyday psychotherapeutic practice we encounter precisely similar conditions to those described above; namely, losing a soul or being invaded by a spirit. A patient, for instance, complains that her interest in her work and in her friends has disappeared. Her voice has no resonance, her narration of the events of her life is a dull monotone, her face is expressionless and her outlook is that of an imprisoned victim. She is afflicted by a profound sense of inferiority which constantly insinuates that she has no right to burden me or anyone else with her misery. When we look at her dream-life we find a copious activity in the unconscious which flows along entirely independent of consciousness. Consciously she finds no interest or meaning in her dreams, but she records them dutifully. From her dreams it is quite clear what has happened to her. She is the daughter of a policeman and was brought up on the supposition that what was required of her was to behave in a certain way. Value was not given to her as a unique individuality, but only in so far as her behaviour conformed to collective requirements. In fact, she was not loved, but merely drilled. She had a good intelligence, and with it she was able to gain a certain independent position, but only as an intellectual machine in scientific institutions.

This way of life offered no possibility at all for her emotional and instinctual needs. Therefore her soul flew away. In other words, the flow of instinctive energy receded into the unconscious and left her bereft like a marooned mariner on a desert island. This patient dreamed that her blood was being sucked by a vampire ghost. The soul that flies away is apt to become a renegade.

This case is an example of a great class of disabled individuals. The sense of insufficiency or inferiority (what is termed the inferiority-complex) is, according to our experience, always due to the fact that an essential function has dropped away, or has been left dormant in the personal unconscious. It is a part of the personality which needs to be lived and, therefore, its absence from consciousness is felt as a crippling loss.

With such cases the therapeutic aim is to recover the lost function, first by a thoroughgoing recognition of the actual condition, and then by a work of assimilation or reintegration of the absent function into the conscious personality. An attitude of acceptance of the unconscious is the primary necessity in these cases.

With the other type of case we find that the normal, healthy personality has become infected by an archaic, daemonic and highly irrational complex which is liable suddenly to invade consciousness in the form of an obsessional idea or craving, sometimes in outbreaks of explosive violence which have apparently no rational cause. The effect of these irruptions is to alienate the personality to such an extent that the whole expression undergoes a change. One can tell in an instant whether the real personality is present or the invading one. With these cases the mental disturbance affects other people in the *milieu* and, in the worst cases, may even tyrannize like the evil spirit which from time to time inhabited King Saul, or like the demon Asmodeus who possessed Sara.

Jung demonstrated, in his researches in the field of dementia praecox, that this phenomenon of possession was due to the spasmodic activation of an autonomous complex. He also showed that the hallucinatory projections and the unbridled force of the complex were due to its pathological independence from the normal self-regulating co-ordination of the psychic contents. As soon as the complex can be pierced by the full rays of conscious insight, it gradually assumes a relative character and loses its daemonic power.

Occasionally a split-off function assumes a relative autonomy, thus borrowing the character of a familiar spirit, without pathological consequences. The *daimon* of Socrates would be such a case, in which the intuitive function takes on a kind of separate activity in the marginal region of the mind.

In certain hysterical patients, where there is a one-sided and abnormal activity of the sympathetic system, and a correspondingly defective conscious function, the surplus of energy is liable to explode or spill over in a quite irrational way. In such cases it is by no means uncommon for objects in the immediate environment to be broken, or for an animal in the patient's neighbourhood to behave in an erratic symptomatic fashion.

It seems to me probable that this externalizing of vital energy in hysterical patients is of the same order as the various manifestations of aberrant energy in mediumistic séances. They are equally devoid of purpose or psychical content, and their sole interest rests upon the fact that energy, which is normally organized in a psychological system, suddenly assumes an erratic behaviour in the objective field. From the psychological standpoint this spilling over of psychic energy on an infra-psychic level must be regarded as pathological and also, in a sense, as rather tiresome. One soon wearies of stunts which, at bottom, have no aim or purpose other than challenging one's credulity. In saying this I do not, of course, include the genuine psychic experiments that have been seriously conducted for a number of years, and the results of which have served to expand our conception of psychic possibilities in a very remarkable way. But everyone will, I think, agree that in the realm of so-called psychic phenomena, there is a considerable portion which belongs properly to the province of physics. In all probability these manifestations of erratic energy in mediumistic séances will eventually be measured by physical instruments and the whole atmosphere of the super-normal will depart from them. If we leave this aspect of spiritistic experiments to be taken care of by the physicists, we come to those borderline phenomena which really demand a thoroughgoing psychological investigation. This research should embrace all the dynamic psychological factors present in the séance-group, particularly the origin of the main trend of interest by which the control of the evening has been constellated. It has often been observed how the presence of a particular personality in the group activates a sympathetic complex in the group-unconscious.

Every avenue of psychological exploration should be exhausted before the alternative hypothesis of an extra-psychic presence can be established.

In making these explorations we have to take into account two kinds of subjective ghost-complexes which are liable to become activated in individual participants by the highly suggestible atmosphere of the séance. The one is the complex of a specific bereavement in which the psychic energy that was invested in the dead person is held in the unconscious and therefore excluded from active participation in life. This is the ghost-effect coming from the past. The other is more difficult to explore, because it arises from a future potentiality that is not yet active in consciousness. As a rule, we can only understand these manifestations by subsequent observations of the life-interest of the persons forming the group.

It might be well to discuss the psychology of these ghost-complexes in more detail. What may be termed the psychological ghost-effect appears in one form or another throughout civilized psychology. It is, in fact, an aspect of primary human experience from which the particular attributes of the legendary ghost are derived. The ghost-effect is liable to appear under the following conditions:

(*a*) When an essential instinctive relationship is severed by death. The vital energy that was identified with the loved parent or child, etc., no longer possesses the living object. By virtue of its energic momentum this specific energy-content produces an image of the person which may either be projected into space as an hallucination, or appear as a revenant in dreams or séances.

(*b*) In cases where the investment of vital energy is centred in an unborn child and a miscarriage occurs, the ghost-effect often takes the form of profound and sometimes suicidal depression, occasionally with auditory hallucinations, and often there are characteristic ghost-dreams.

(*c*) When an essential function or phase of the individual life is ignored or repressed, resulting in a characteristic attitude of resentment or self-pity. In the dreams of such persons the excluded function frequently takes on the aspect of a pursuing or haunting ghost.

From this point of view every psychic element or function which, by virtue of the vital energy it contains, demands to become incorporated in the complete personality, is liable to develop certain sinister properties of the ghost when excluded from life. The bitter, resentful moods of unfulfilled personalities are due to the tauntings of these psychological ghosts. The chronic bad conscience, the man with a chip on the shoulder, the person who reviles his fate, etc., are typical examples of this condition.

In cases where a man has been prised away from his ancestral background and attempts to live in total disregard of the qualities of his inherited psychology, it is usually ancestral figures that haunt and accuse him in his dreams.

What is termed a complex is, at bottom, a specific functional potentiality, involving a certain quantity of energy under the tension of the opposites, yea or nay. In so far as this function has been repressed, it is a ghost seeking redress. In so far as it represents a future potentiality of increasing life and consciousness, it is a spirit seeking life. The one effect causes resentment, the other the birth-pangs of creation. In so far as they are unconscious, both can appear in the form of projections in the apparitional sphere, the character of the projections differing according to the nature of the complex from which it springs.

From these fragmentary examples it will be immediately clear why in every country and period the most malign ghost is that of the man who took his life, or of the man whose life was violently cut short of its natural fulfilment. In that famous account by two English ladies[1] of the ghostly appearance of Marie Antoinette's court

[1] Morley and Jourdain, *An Adventure* (Faber & Faber Ltd., 1937).

in the Trianon, we are instantly reminded of the fact that the people who figured in those scenes met their death under the guillotine.

But although we can appreciate how the ghost-effects I have described in the psychological sphere inevitably and logically result from an arbitrary intervention in the natural development of a vital process, in other words a kind of partial suicide, we are no nearer to an understanding of what constitutes the ghost as an objective or extra-psychic entity. In the one case our subjective understanding of the individual psychic history gives us the necessary clue, whereas the problem of the ghost as an independent entity brings us face to face with an enigmatic psychic occurrence without a subject to interrogate. As a psychologist I cannot conceive a more extravagant situation. Give me a ghost who will stand and answer like a man. What then? you ask. Well, in that case we shall have a human document we can understand, instead of a supernormal phenomenon.

At the word 'supernormal' we can almost see the door of our inmost mind being opened by an unseen hand, and the dark individual problem, which underlies all our discussion of ghosts and spirits, steals silently among us. Like the haunted sun-hero Gilgamish, our mind at one time or another is liable to be invaded by the doubt: 'My brother is dead; does he survive? And if so, can I reach him?' In the presence of this all-too-human preoccupation, science can say very little. With regard to the effective survival of the spirits of our dead *within the psychic sphere* there can be no doubt at all. There is abundant evidence on every side from living men and women that their lives are influenced, guided, and in a certain sense controlled, by persuasive or malign forces which they identify with the spirits of their loved dead. There are abundant and, I believe, quite genuine communications which contain descriptions and impart certain knowledge that has the self-evident character of transubjective information

The difficulty we have in drawing decisive conclusions from this evidence arises from the fact that, so far, we are quite unable to define the frontiers of what we rather naïvely term the unconscious. We think of the psyche as a totality embracing the whole subject. But within this totality that complex we know as our personality is only a small fragmentary item. Beyond our personal psychological domain there extends a vast, indefinite psychic hinterland whose contents are no more a part of our personal psychology than is the Tower of London or Stonehenge. Normally, we are like caddis-worms, completely protected and covered in by the contemporary factors of our personal life. At certain moments, however, we stumble unwittingly into this impersonal, transubjective dimension and we then experience the events of that realm in an immediate objective sense. When a man has experienced this realm of the collective unconscious he knows he has been beyond the normal framework of our three-dimensional reality. He can never express or communicate his experience in ordinary language. Like Blake, or Melville, he feels isolated and somewhat alienated from his contemporaries. His attempts to express his experience are usually highly symbolical, and the irrationality of his creations often raises the suspicion of insanity. In the Middle Ages the experience of the collective unconscious took on the peculiar symbolism of alchemy or of some mystical quest, as in the Quest of the Holy Grail. In the East this whole dimension of spiritual experience has long been explored and highly elaborated in the Tantric and other forms of Yoga.

The limits of this primordial ocean cannot be set. All we can know of this realm is by the empirical way of experience, and naturally the accounts of subjective experience are subject, to some extent, to individual psychological constellations.

There is no doubt that our lives are conditioned far more deeply by the events of the impersonal psyche than from purely personal sources. It is, in fact, the primordial oceanic basis upon which our little personal craft ply their ceaseless activity. What we cannot determine is whether the spirit-world, which appears to be inhabited by the spirits of those who have died, is an aspect of this vast hinterland of the psyche, or whether it can be regarded as existing independently. All we know is that the spirits of the dead can become part of our experience only by means of our conscious psychic envelope, and just because of this inevitable condition it is practically impossible to determine whether they exist independently of the psyche, or whether they live because the living give them life.

Jung's Conception of the Structure of Personality in Relation to Psychical Research[1]

I wonder at my own temerity in daring to handle this theme in the discussions of this Society. Firstly, because I am not adequately informed with regard to what has already been published by our Society in this special field of research. Secondly, because I am not altogether clear what bearing Jung's conception of personality has to do with your investigations. With these rather formidable obstacles in my path, I find myself uncomfortably aware of my incompetence.

In regard to the main structural principle of quaternity, which forms the basis of Jung's conception of personality, I can assume that this is generally known. The four main psychic functions appear empirically in dream and fantasy material as the four pillars of the house, or as the four cardinal points of the psychical universe. The problem of individuation invariably begins with this foundation as the groundwork of the idea of totality. The fact that these four main functions, thinking, feeling, intuition and sensation, never appear in any human subject in a state of equally balanced functioning, is bound up with the unavoidable one-sidedness of conscious development. To analytical investigation the psyche appears as a complex molecular formation, containing the generally human qualities, functions, and instinctual strivings in a more or less integrated combination. Theoretically, we cannot escape the conclusion that every individual contains all the generally human elements, and that what constitutes the uniqueness of individuality is the particular grouping or combination of elements within the individual molecule. It must also be self-evident that in one individual these elements will be more stable and harmoniously integrated than in another. Because there exists no human striving which is not countered and opposed by its opposite, it follows that the central striving for unity or integration encounters an almost equal tendency towards dis-

[1] From the *Proceedings of the Society for Psychical Research*, vol. xlvi, Part 165, September 1941.

solution or disintegration. In general it is possible to allocate the positive quality of integration to the function of consciousness, and its opposite tendency, that of dissolution or dissociation, to the autonomous or unconscious psyche.

We have to remind ourselves at this juncture that the duality of the mind, i.e. consciousness versus the unconscious, must not be conceived statically or structurally, but rather as a condition that is constantly undergoing change. What is conscious at this moment may be unconscious to-morrow, or in an hour's time; and what is unconscious now may, at some future moment, become conscious. But although mental contents are constantly changing from one sphere to the other, the condition we call conscious can, none the less, be represented as a more or less integrated field. The condition of mental contents in the unconscious, on the other hand, is rather that of fishes or marine organisms existing in a more or less dissociated and fluid state in a dark and essentially primitive underworld.

This inherent duality is not as a rule admitted or understood by the scientific investigator and this is the primary cause of that obstinate mental opacity which still makes it necessary for us to attempt to prove a number of facts which are, psychologically speaking, self-evident. In everyday experience with patients, for instance, the incidence of telepathy is in no sense a supernormal occasion. The synchronous apprehension of the same fact, word, experience or idea, by two people either intimately involved or potentially related, is hardly a matter of special comment. The activation of the unconscious during analysis seems to favour this primitive or instinctual operation of the mind.

When I spoke of the condition of the unconscious or autonomous psyche as essentially primitive, I was alluding to the fact that the basic premisses and modality of expression of the unconscious are characteristically those of the primitive mind. Civilized consciousness, for instance, has accepted reason as its ruling principle. It seeks to see and plan ahead. It aims at adaptation, relatedness, regularity and integration. It believes in caring for the whole and in safeguarding relations to the objective world. In pursuing this reasonable policy consciousness tends to exclude the irrational and ignore the unpredictable. In its totalitarian attitude of control towards every factor within its peculiar framework of time, space and causality, rational consciousness is even inclined to deny the existence of things and events which, by their nature, are antipathetic to its rational structure, and to hold as unreal everything which appears irrational. Since the numinous experience (i.e. an overwhelming psychical tendency or experience of an irrational kind) cannot be fitted into any plan, the rationalist will tend to deny its reality. Similarly, because a dream, vision or hallucination happens outside the sense of time, at no particular place, while its causality is obscure, it is also regarded as merely imaginary and of no particular significance. The events that are liable to take place in a mediumistic séance are also subject to the same prejudice, since they cannot easily be roped into the time, space and causal compound.

Thus we see that the structure of our rationally controlled personality is such that the fundamentally irrational or primitive nature of autonomous psychic activity is sensed as alien and suspect and, therefore, must be as far as possible excluded. When it is seen that this dualism of the mind rests upon the existence of antipathetic premisses, it will be understood that the scientific mind can become attuned to the alien character of autonomous events only through submitting, either willingly or unwillingly, to the experience of the other side of the mind. But since even the most complete rationalist has at some time in his life been a child, has presumably dreamed, and is, moreover, subject to the unpredictable and irregular factors of experience as much as everyone else, it is clear that something more is needed than the mere fact of experience. Consciousness has not only to participate in, it has also to value the experience as significant. The physicist Helmholtz, for example, is reported to have said: 'Neither the testimony of all the Fellows of the Royal Society, nor even the evidence of my own senses, could lead me to believe in the transmission of thoughts from one person to another independently of the recognized channels of sensation.' Similarly, an eminent colleague of mine, belonging to the mechanistic school of psycho-analysis, when asked by a friend, who was observing the analyst's delight in whirling a stick between his fingers, whether he was free to waggle the stick he held in his hand in any direction he chose, replied: 'Naturally I have the feeling of freedom, but I know it to be an illusion.'

Everyone must have observed numberless parallel examples of the way in which the confirmed rationalist continually prejudges his actual experience in accordance with the demands of certain theoretical preconceptions. It is as though he felt a perpetual need to sterilize his mind from any possibility of a sympathetic understanding of the opposite principle. The totalitarian type of consciousness is, as we know from bitter experience, deeply averse from admitting the independent activity of any elements beyond the scope of its control.

I must confess that it seems to me as unprofitable to attack this curious blindness by argument and demonstration as it is to try and convince the savage mind of Africa of the irrationality of witchcraft, or the mind of Nazi Germany of the stupidity of its totalitarian prejudices. A scientific colleague of mine told me of an attempt he made to persuade an intelligent African chief of the wrongheadedness of his belief in witchcraft by the direct means of a post-mortem demonstration of the lungs of a man who had died of tuberculosis. He pointed out the nature of the disease by contrasting it with normal lung tissue and the demonstration was clear and incontestable. But the intelligent African, with the polite smile of superior knowledge, replied: 'You see now how this man was bewitched.'

We come, then, to two fundamentally contradictory modes of explaining the nature of human events. The civilized mind operates from the postulate of natural cause; the savage from that of witchcraft or, in other words, the power of the wish. Assuming the self-evident superiority of the rational standpoint, we are all, to some extent, infected with the belief that the primitive mode of explanation is the product of ignorant superstition. The affirmation: 'I am right' includes the presumption: 'You are wrong'.

At bottom it is the absolutist claim of either principle which confounds understanding. So long as any attitude claims to be absolute, intelligence is imprisoned within its prescribed limits and no further understanding is possible.

Our objective, scientific way of approach is the result of a prolonged and exhaustive investigation into the nature of the objective universe. In the Middle Ages, it was still possible for men of the finest intelligence to project the contents and processes of the unconscious into matter, because at that time the nature of matter was fundamentally mysterious. When we try to follow the alchemical quest of the mediaeval philosophers, we get lost and bewildered in the almost inextricable confusion of chemical procedures and of psychical or spiritual admixtures which seem to us to vitiate the whole method of approach. For them chemistry provided the field into which the psychical processes of individuation were projected.

The science of chemistry finally succeeded in reducing the material matrix to its elements, and in so doing it revoked the psychical projections into the unconscious. Yet the essential psychological goal which created alchemy was not thereby satisfied. It survives still in the unconscious, appearing to-day in that central striving for totality Jung has called individuation.[1] In the same way the science and technical means of astronomy penetrated the starry vault of heaven, which had previously invited the projections of the gods and the whole astrological cosmogony. But the quest of the supra-personal determinants of human fate, which had in fact created astrology and the celestial home of the gods, is not fulfilled by the objective discoveries of astronomy. The quest still survives, although it has been shifted back from the objective into the psychical sphere.

It is as though the civilized mind, having to a large extent conquered the realm of matter by reducing it to known and predictable laws, is now faced with the vast and terrifying forces of primitive unreason which it succeeded in expelling from its rationally ordered universe. It is indeed undeniable that the unconscious of civilized man has become dangerously overcharged, and we have at present no adequate means of handling those irrational contents which the scientific *Weltanschauung* detached from their objective matrix and repressed into the unconscious. Thus, on the one side stands the force of reason, intellect, and law-abiding conformity: on the other, we see the forces of the pagan and quasi-primitive unconscious engaged in world-destroying rebellion.

This terrifying activation of the unconscious is not resolved by abusory epithets levelled at those who have become possessed by it. We are more liable to survive the flood if we attempt to understand the manifestations of the unconscious, whether on the larger scale of world-events or in the sphere of individual psychology, as something essentially antithetical to our rationally conceived and ordered world. It is the unpredictable and irregular which now challenges our understanding.

Freud has attempted to read the riddle of the autonomous psyche with his comprehensive concept, wish-fulfilment. This conception can be regarded as a valuable pointer or directive principle, since we see that the power of the wish is, in fact, the ruling idea in primitive mentality. Indeed, the whole belief in witchcraft has developed

[1] The reader is referred to Jung's discussion of alchemy in his work, *The Integration of Personality* (Kegan Paul & Co., London, 1940).

from empirical observation of the incalculable power of the wish. Given the extreme suggestibility of the savage mind to certain classes of ideas, the power of suggestion has, in fact, an unlimited effect. That this is by no means limited to Africa and other uncivilized lands is shown by the fact that Hitler, using precisely the same means as the primitive medicine man, converted German inferiority and self-distrust into a wellnigh invincible force, by suggesting to the German people that they were the children of the pagan gods, that they had never been beaten in battle, that they were the Chosen People and that he stands in direct relation with the heavenly powers. What better example can history supply of the dynamic power of the wish? Without presuming to claim any precise etymological kinship between the words, it is literally true to say that Hitler has bewitched the German people by the magic of *wish*craft.

To the rationalist mentality suggestion represents a kind of bogy. For better or for worse, it is in point of fact one of the most powerful instruments of consciousness and is in constant use in education, advertisement, public policy, preaching and propaganda. In spite of the fact that it is often abused by unscrupulous manipulators, its dynamic potentiality, when properly appreciated and safeguarded, makes it an invaluable means of guidance and control. The goal of self-discipline is also implemented in considerable measure by deliberate auto-suggestion. When some intellectual purist interrogates me anxiously as to the possibility of suggestion creeping into the analytical treatment, I reply that suggestion does not creep in; it is welcomed as a royal principle. Behind this fear of evil suggestion there lurks the whole sectarian fear that innocent people, in a plastic vulnerable state, are being got at for sinister power purposes. Even though it is admitted that devotion to the work of healing is not invariably accompanied by an adequate measure of self-criticism, yet the very need to achieve positive results will tend to ensure that those ideas will be brought out from the patient's material which carry the suggestion of healing and value. Why should one forgo this most effective means of reaching the required goal? This positive use of suggestion is altogether different from hypnotic suggestion which always seeks to enter by the back door. I try to show my patients how to honour it as the means provided by nature for bringing about the rule of harmony and order in place of chaos.

At bottom, the fear of suggestion comes from the very reasonable fear of using primitive unconscious means. But people who have lost contact with their instinctive roots have to learn to go with and trust their nature and not assume that it is invariably evil. I cherish the hope, therefore, that science will some day accept the hypothesis that wisdom and understanding are more precious in the psychological field than a sterile attitude of exclusion. We have to know the truth of the psyche and this will always escape our grasp if we attempt to deal with it from the basis of distrust. In order to understand the pristine character and operation of the sympathetic nervous system we must not insist that its mode of functioning shall be identical with that of the brain and central nervous system with which consciousness is directly related. Like the autonomous psyche, its operation is fundamentally independent and we must therefore approach it with a sympathetic attitude.

The conscious function is under the directive control of the will, whereas the unconscious is the home of the wish or, to put it more correctly, instinctual striving. The antipathy which rationally minded people have to anything coming immediately from the unconscious has to do with these unpredictable, independent, and amoral activities of the underside. A philosopher once said to me with passionate intensity: 'If I find I want to believe a thing I know it must be false.' We even suspect ourselves of wishful thinking when we allow our minds to dwell, for instance, upon the obvious instability of the enemy's morale. In both these examples we detect the firm resolution of consciousness not to be influenced by the primitive or childish character of the natural mind. But supposing what we wish to believe happens also to be true? And conversely, what if a certain aspect of scientific truth can be apprehended only by a correct appraisal of the power of the unconscious wish?

These questions bring me to the specific problem we are here to discuss, namely, the relation of the structural personality to the work of psychical research. Everyone who has ever had to do with mediumistic séances will have become aware of the peculiar tendency of the medium's so-called 'controls' to become psychically sensitive to the most eminent, distinguished, or dynamic personality in the group. The medium tends to respond to the unconscious wish of this dominant personality and to give it voice in a transposed or symbolical fashion. It is almost as though the medium gave utterance to a dream-content of the psyche to which he had tuned in.

The wish or tendency may also be that of the whole group, or it may be merely a general expectation or curiosity. It may be that the *mana*[1] which clings to the significant personality produces a wish in the medium to become related to the *mana*-object in this oblique fashion. In Jung's paper on the Psychology and Pathology of so-called Occult Phenomena[2] this phenomenon of oblique relatedness is clearly discernible. For example, on one occasion after the medium (a girl of fifteen and a half) had evinced acute emotional symptoms in a somnambulistic trance, she awoke in a distraught and rather confused state of mind. She said she had seen all sorts of things but would tell nothing. Only after urgent questioning she related how with extraordinary clarity she had seen her grandfather arm-in-arm with Jung's grandfather. Later, in a detailed system of relationships, elaborated in a visionary retrospect of various incarnations, she discovered that in the eighth century she was the mother of her present father, of her grandfather and of Jung's grandfather. Hence the striking friendship of these two old gentlemen, who were otherwise strangers. Moreover, in the thirteenth century she was a certain Mme de Valours who was burnt as a witch. In this incarnation she had been Jung's mother.

In her waking state her adolescent personality was restricted by social, educational and personal factors from making the desired intimacy. The erotic transference could, therefore, exist only in a dissociated, repressed condition in the unconscious. Clearly this girl inherited a mediumistic capacity and the greater part of her psychology expressed itself in mediumistic ways. She had, in point of fact, very considerable potentiality existing in a more or less undeveloped state in the unconscious. At the period of the séances, this potential caused the unconscious to be preponderant in energy-value over the conscious. Because of their dissociation from consciousness, these personality-elements could appear only in a relatively timeless, mythological state. Once in the waking state after a trance she said: 'I do not know if what the spirits say and teach me is true, neither do I know if they are those by whose names they call themselves, but that my spirits exist there is no question. I see them before me, I can touch them, I speak to them about everything I wish, as naturally as I am now talking to you. They must be real.'[3]

[1] A primitive energy-concept which connotes impressive or supernatural effect and is usually associated with some outstanding personality.

[2] C. G. Jung, *Collected Papers on Analytical Psychology*. [3] Loc. cit., p. 22.

By pointing out the presence of this specific wishing potential in the unconscious of this medium I do not thereby mean to imply that the whole of the mediumistic phenomena described by Jung can be explained in terms of an unconscious erotic transference. This would be to fall into the fatal trap of the 'nothing but' type of rationalization. I merely seek to demonstrate that the dissociated potentialities in a relatively undeveloped personality exist under the condition of the wish. These contents have no integrated relation to consciousness and, therefore, can only come to expression in their own twilight world of the dream or trance. The transference creates a bridge of fantasy whereby the dissociated potential seeks to find a point of interest or attention in the objective world. Jung's personality, with all his dawning realization of the importance of the unconscious, would clearly provide that point of commanding interest about which the whole mythological development could revolve.

From the standpoint of the girl medium's personal development, we could regard this as the phase of the transference, by means of which the developing ego is able gradually to assimilate the inherited potential in the unconscious. From the standpoint of individuation, however, we must conclude that the medium's attempt to relate to the unconscious contents of different personalities in the group in a more or less systematized unconscious way, could be a definite hindrance to the development of the medium's personality. Inasmuch as the expectation of the group tends to give a kind of cultural value to the dissociated condition it will hold the personality at a lower and less organized level of consciousness. From another point of view, it must be admitted that, by refining his faculty of adaptation to the subliminal and potential, rather than to the actual factors of the contemporary scene, the medium performs a valuable function.

The case of Hitler provides, however, a very significant example of the two-edged value of mediumship. Hitler has undoubtedly a mediumistic psychology. He was born at Braunau in Austria, the home of the well-known Schneider brothers. This coincidence lends colour to the possibility of a certain local suggestive influence which might favour mediumistic development. Whether this was so or not, there is abundant evidence to show that Hitler attained his formidable power over the German nation by acting as medium, as well as primitive medicine man, in relation to the German unconscious. On the other hand, we have watched his destructive attempt to obliterate the critical, structural aspect of German psychology and culture, in order to give unrestrained licence to the hitherto dissociated pagan elements of the racial unconscious. There could be no more eloquent example of the danger of permitting the amoral dissociated elements to become paramount in human affairs. This sudden unchecked eruption of the pagan myth, leading to the complete submergence or overwhelming of the previous conscious ideals, is essentially similar to an outbreak of acute mania. So long as consciousness adapts to the uprising urgency of the unconscious with insight, and more or less sympathetic control, a new structural integration is always possible. But when the repressed forces sweep everything before them and brook neither opposition nor control, catastrophe is due.

Another interesting fact about the nature of dissociated contents can be learned from the behaviour of the various voices or personalities which take the stage in the mediumistic séance. As a rule the voice speaks with absolute authority. The note of the categorical imperative is unmistakable. In spite of the fact that these dissociated entities appear to want nothing better than to become related to the living, it is only with difficulty that they are taught to converse. Their style is that of downright affirmation, like Jahveh thundering from Sinai. On the first appearance of one of these so-called controls one often gets the impression of an attitude of intolerance towards any other spirit, as though two spirits of opposite character could not coexist in the same universe. Moreover, people like Joan of Arc, who are in the habit of listening to the voice of the unconscious, are inclined to accept its claim to absolute authority, and are often prepared to suffer rather than admit even the possibility of their voice being mistaken.

Here again, then, we find a significant contrast between the condition of the dissociated complex and that of the conscious personality. The training of a disciplined personality very largely consists in learning to adapt to a number of disparate claims, tasks and expectations in the spirit of relativity. We try to create plans and systems in which these mutually antipathetic factors can be interrelated. In strong contrast to this mitigating principle of relativity, the dissociated complex is characterized by an absolutist all-or-none claim, a character which is also native to the child. Thus we see that the unconscious content enjoys the primordial simplicity of an unrelated existence, while consciousness is marked by its ability to create a complex co-ordination of related elements.

The labour of creating an increasingly complex system of adaptation represents a very serious strain on psychical resources. It is, therefore, intelligible that a number of individuals should recoil from the strain, even though escape means a relatively complete surrender to a psychotic or psychoneurotic condition. On the other hand, there are, as we know, certain vital occasions when the terse simplicity of a categorical injunction is exactly what one needs. Many people inhabit a needlessly complicated world of cares, scruples and superfluous expectations. A strong pristine wind of affirmation, like the voice which said: 'I am that I am', is needed to sweep away the clutter of neurotic reservations. People who try to create a too complicated or ideal conscious house are liable to become imprisoned in a defended fortress where they die of boredom. Similarly a marriage that aims at being ideal and perfect in all respects becomes an impossible burden for human nature to sustain.

The primitive unconscious insists on being admitted whether we like it or not, hence the wiser choice is to strive not for perfection, or for an ideal plan, but for totality. And in order to accept the totality of one's nature it is essential to give value to the specific needs, urgencies and potentialities which at first make their appearance in a more or less crude and dissociated form.

If I were to presume to apply these general considerations to the actual investigations of our Society, I would say that the primary factors to be considered are the psychological ones, both in respect to the actual human material of the medium (the degree, for instance, of conscious discipline and integration) and to the possibility of specific unconscious potentialities existing in other members of the investigatory group. The fact that these potentialities are liable to become apparent under the guise of wishing, or in some projected form, is simply the inevitable condition native to dissociated complexes.

To my mind the real object of psychology at the present time is the unconscious or autonomous psyche, and if we are able to discover under what psychical conditions such phenomena as telepathy, exteriorization of energy (e.g. poltergeists, mediumistic phenomena on the physical plane, etc.), phantasms of the living, precognition, etc., are liable to make their appearance, a most valuable contribution to science will be in our grasp. The practical difficulties, so far as I see them, reside in the fact that before we can reach even an approximate estimate of the psychological factors actually operative in any investigation of group phenomena, we should need to conduct a preliminary analytical survey of the medium as well as of each member of the investigating group. If, for example, in a preliminary survey of the dream-material of the individual participants we were to discover personalities which corresponded in general characteristics to those which appeared in the mediumistic séance, we should be in a position to equate the autonomous activity observed in the séance with certain specific urges or tendencies in the psychological sphere. Whether this method of approach would prove feasible in practice depends upon a degree of willingness which is not easily available; not because of any lack of devotion to truth, but rather because the idea of admitting the possibility of dissociation of personality-elements in oneself is liable to meet with determined resistance on the part of every rationally organized consciousness. What is beyond the limits of conscious introspection is still held to be non-existent by those who have not yet had the experience of being separated or prised away from the safeguarding limitations of their rational envelope.

It would be alien to the positive spirit of analytical psychology to discourage the enthusiasm for research which animates our Society. I simply wish to emphasize the psychological postulate that whenever and wherever the phenomena of dissociation are encountered we have to deal, not with the free denizens of the spirit-world, but with specific psychical factors belonging to analysable human subjects. That these factors can be constellated and brought to manifestation only under certain peculiar conditions pertains to the character of the dissociated state. In order, therefore, to be able to explore the whole field of so-called supernormal phenomena we need to extend our knowledge of the psychology of dissociation. With this end in view it is a pity that the deep investigation of human psychology has been till now almost exclusively in the hands of the doctors, since this has fostered the prejudice that dissociation is invariably a pathological condition which ought not to exist. Inasmuch as every potential or emergent factor in the unconscious exists in a dissociated condition before it is realized and accepted by consciousness, it is clear that this consulting-room prejudice is frequently liable to obscure our vision of the real facts. It is to be hoped that we may eventually cleanse the medical mind of this prejudice in order that a clear collaboration between medical psychology and psychical research can become a realizable objective.

On the Psychological Origins of Divine Kingship[1]

The fact that a psychologist is invited by an anthropological society to contribute a paper for discussion is in itself a significant occurrence. It amounts almost to a confession that the necessity for scientific syncretism, by which both disciplines are impelled, is felt to be of greater moment than the difference of their respective postulates.

In anthropology we can point to the contributions of distinguished writers brought together in the two volumes *Myth and Ritual* and *The Labyrinth*; to the invaluable works of Professor Hocart, e.g. *Kingship* and *The Lifegiving Myth*; to the works of Perry, Elliot Smith and others testifying to the vigorous syncretistic spirit in this discipline. The method consists in analysing a traditional pattern in such a way that inner correspondences are revealed between the elements of the given pattern and other forms in an analogous field of reference. Hocart's work, *Kingship*, is an excellent example of this method. Through a careful analysis of the rites of coronation, marriage, ordination, etc., in many cultures, he discovered a convincing series of correspondences with the primitive pattern of initiation; concluding therefrom that these were all cultural variants of a fundamental ritual pattern of initiation.

The existence of a basal or archetypal pattern from which a number of traditional rites have developed, presents us with a highly interesting and hence highly disputable problem; namely, do these cultural variants point to a world-wide migration of ideas from a single cultural source, or have they developed autochthonously out of the relatively uniform basal structure of the psyche? Our preference for one or other side of this ancient debate depends, I believe, more on one's fundamental psychic disposition, or type, than upon the value of the evidence. The proof of autochthonous creation, it is true, must rest largely on the absence of the possibility of diffusion —a negative condition that is exceedingly hard to substantiate. But the autochthonists are not really interested in this type of evidence,

[1] *Folk-lore*, vol. xlvii, March 1936.

a fact which by itself reveals the existence of a temperamental rather than a rational preference. The introverted thinker (a good autochthonist must surely have strong introverted sympathies) viewing things from the standpoint of the subject, realizes that vital forms of expression are created out of vital needs. He knows that the vital needs of human beings are relatively few and remarkably constant. If a visitor comes to his house who possesses a better technical equipment for expressing a vital human need than the one he has hitherto employed, he may or may not adopt the better technique. But never for a moment will he allow that the borrowed, or adapted, technique was anything more than a modification of his own original. Whereas the thoroughgoing extraverted diffusionist tends to assume that the presence of the more cultivated visitor in the house provides an adequate explanation for the need as well as for the equipment, as though invention were the mother of necessity.

The controversy continues to rage, because a rather specious loyalty to one's temperamental viewpoint urges one unconsciously to emphasize the arguments that favour one's own psychological predilection, and to depreciate those of the opposite type. Neither side can conclusively prove its case; since the autochthonists are faced with a bulk of irrefutable evidence for the historical fact of diffusion; while the diffusionists are bound to admit that the very fact that certain specific cultural patterns have achieved a world-wide distribution points to the existence of a correspondingly universal vital need. Whether such a need creates a spontaneous cultural expression, or selects its form from a visiting culture, is not a matter of very great concern for the psychologist. It is different for the anthropologist. In his attempt to trace the successive migrations of early cultures, the distribution of identical forms is highly significant. But, for the psychologist who is concerned more with establishing the basal uniformity of the human psyche, the influence of cultural diffusion assumes a secondary role.

Jung's theory of the basic uniformity of the psychical structure is grounded on the fact that a comparison of the mythic patterns gathered from every part of the globe reveals a very high degree of uniformity of structure. When we reflect upon the great differences of climatic and vegetational conditions, from the arctic to the equator, to which mankind is adapted, the relative uniformity of man's physical structure is a surprising fact. The uniformity of cerebral structure is such that it requires a skilled eye to detect the differences between the brain of an Australian aboriginal and that of a Harley Street specialist. In respect to the physical structure of man we can, therefore, speak of an archetype, in so far as a high degree of consistency is maintained under a great variety of conditions.[1] Inasmuch as the psyche is nothing else than the response of conscious human existence to the conditions of life on this planet, it would be surprising indeed if its basal structure did not bear witness to such a uniformity as we find in the human body. But when we speak of the basal psychic structure it must not be supposed that we assume identity between psyche and brain. We cannot even say that the psyche is the function of the brain: we do not know. All we can know of the nature of the basal psyche is from its products, particularly from spontaneous natural products such as dreams, myths, visions, etc., not to mention that vast store of legendary material which Sir James Frazer has brought together within the pages of *The Golden Bough*. By sifting and collating this material we find, just as Hocart discovered in his research into the ritual connections of kingship, that certain *leit-motifs*, certain basic images and patterns, reveal themselves as the elementary components of which the almost infinite variety of mythological forms is composed. These basic structural elements Jung has called archetypes or primordial images. He regards them as emotionally toned psychic entities which have been developed in the general psychic structure through the endlessly repeated occurrence of certain typical needs, relationships and adaptations in the totality of human experience. Thus, just as the structure of the heart bears witness to the immense variety of strains which human enterprise has imposed upon it through untold ages; so, in precisely similar fashion, the basic psyche carries the record of man's instinctive adaptation in the form of these collective images.

For this evening's discussion I have selected the archetype of the king; and I propose to inquire into the psychic origins of the king-idea from the standpoint of racial experience. According to Elliot Smith's account in his valuable work, *Human History*, there are certain indigenous tribes, as, for instance, the Eskimos; certain tribes of North American Indians; the Punan of Borneo; the Bushmen of Africa; food-gathering peoples living on the outskirts of civilization,

[1] In comparative anatomy the term archetype signifies 'an assumed ideal pattern of the fundamental structure of each great division of organized beings' (*Oxford Dictionary*).

who have no idea of the king as a hierarchical figure. These people live in small communities in a state of natural communism. Produce of the hunt is shared; women have as a rule equal rights with men, and the leader, or head-man, is merely the man of ripest experience. He possesses no magical qualities. There is no hierarchy of power, because social organization has never become a problem. These people still preserve a natural human piety, and appear to reject the proffered boons of civilization as something dangerous, if not actually impious. To maintain the integrity of their natural condition is their one guiding principle. Nature is their wisdom and their safeguard, and they refuse to improve upon what she provides, or to build up civilized ramparts from which to defy her wrath.

If we compare this picture, which is vouched for by a variety of competent observers, with the collectivized races who, by the practice of agriculture and other cultural inventions, gradually erected a counter-position of civilized security over against the original mother-deity, we can readily grasp how the need of a protected, hence rapidly growing, population for an infallible safeguard from the devouring and ruthless aspect of nature came to be invested in a magical or divine personality. There would necessarily devolve upon this being the function of fertility and security that had been previously guaranteed by the state of unity with nature. When we study the myths of early civilizing races we cannot but be impressed by an inescapable feeling of dread of this vengeful, destroying aspect of nature. We might almost suppose from this evidence that civilized man is burdened by a bad conscience in relation to his original animal state.

In the Gilgamish epic, dating from early Sumerian civilization, we are the fortunate possessors of invaluable psychological evidence of the hybris-guilt which accompanied every encroachment of early civilizing man upon the hitherto unchallenged primacy of nature. Gilgamish is the cultural hero-king, two-thirds divine and one-third mortal, who tyrannically forces the people of Erech to incessant and arduous toil in the building of his city. In his attempt to erect an impregnable counter-position over against the seductions of the primordial natural existence, Gilgamish violates every natural relationship.

> Gilgamish leaveth no son to his father. . . .
> Gilgamish leaveth no maid to her mother, nor daughter to hero,
> Nay, nor a spouse to her husband.

In opposition to the original instinctive pattern of the natural community Gilgamish has set up an artificial cultural pattern in which all loyalty and allegiance is centred in the king. In other words, the civilizing genius of man has revolted against the original submission to nature and her laws, laws that are written in the unconscious inheritance of instinct. In place of his original allegiance man is seized by an idea forcing him to some unknown destination; an idea of such immeasurable power that it could only have been fathered by the sun. This belief is asserted in the divine nature of Gilgamish and in the fact that Shamash, the sun-god, is mentioned as his father.

Like Zarathustra, Gilgamish manifests the one divine attribute of man, namely, the power to transcend himself and thus to create the beyond-man. But prophetic ideas are tyrannical. Accordingly Gilgamish, who personifies the civilizing idea, becomes a dictator, attempting to displace every former allegiance, in order to make his rule absolute. The civilizing genius of mankind has thrown up innumerable dictators who have, likewise, attempted this wholesale displacement of pre-existing natural loyalties, only to find their rule eventually undermined by the same underground secession of collective libido to the older gods as is portrayed in this myth. This recession of the libido is represented by the prayers of the people of Erech ascending to Anu, imploring him to raise up a champion in their defence. He calls to Aruru:[1]

'Twas thou, O Aruru, madest primeval seed of mankind,
Do now make its fellow, so that he happen on Gilgamish,
Yea, in the day of his pleasure, so that they strive with each other,
And he unto Erech give surcease.

Out of the clay Aruru created Enkidu, a being who accords with the primordial image of the natural man.

Sprouted luxuriant growth of his hair like the awns of the barley,
Nor knew he people nor land; he was clad in a garb like Sumuqan.
E'en with the gazelles did he pasture on herbage, along with the cattle
Drank he his fill, with the beasts did his heart delight at the water.

Gilgamish has a dream foretelling the advent of this champion of nature, and thereupon sends to the drinking-place, where Enkidu comes with the wild animals to drink, a hunter accompanied by a

[1] Citations are from R. Campbell Thompson's translation, *The Epic of Gilgamish* (Luzac and Co., 1948).

courtesan of Ishtar's temple. The woman seduces him from his original virginal state, and when, finally, he realizes that the animals no longer accept him as one of themselves he follows the girl to Erech. The renegade recession of libido back to the primitive state would imply a complete rejection of the whole civilizing experiment. But even in the harshest moments of the Taurian age this was no longer possible. Mankind is irredeemably committed to the civilizing experiment, even though it destroy him. Therefore Enkidu cannot stay in the absolute primitive state. The true indigenous, food-gathering primitive is hardly seducible and cannot be enslaved, for he is still simple and whole. But Enkidu is a product of resistance. He is composed of opposite elements: Ninurta the warrior, Sumuqan the agriculturist. Cain and Abel, the first protagonists of the problem of the opposites in civilizing man, have entered into his composition. Therefore is he seducible. The role of the courtesan is as old as civilization; but assuredly not older. She is the snare to catch the renegade impulse in man. It is notorious that the courtesan's clientele consists mainly of married men. That is to say, men who have subscribed to the civilized pattern which entails allegiance to the civilizing goal. The renegade impulse as such stands in contradiction to this pattern. But since both cannot be lived at the same time the renegade is trapped in a mean and unconvincing compromise. Therefore is the courtesan dishonoured. She offers no solution to the conflict, but merely provides expression for a pathetic gesture of regret for a state that can never be recaptured.

The courtesan of Erech reminds Enkidu of the power and luxuriance, the heroic splendours of the city of Erech, and he has to follow her. Gilgamish and Enkidu fight for possession of the woman, and after a terrific encounter, in which Gilgamish appears to get the better of his adversary, a mutual pact of brotherhood is sealed. From the moment this pact is made energy is released, and a new attempt at extending civilized lordship over nature immediately begins to revolve in the mind of Gilgamish. He proposes an enterprise against Humbaba, the fearful monster who guards the Forest of Cedars. There are certain points concerning this enterprise about which the myth is quite definite. First, when Enkidu tries to dissuade his friend from pitting his power against that of an elemental daemon —'Humbaba, his roar was a whirlwind. Flame in his jaws, and his very breath Death'—Gilgamish replies with matter-of-fact precision: ''Tis that I need the rich yield of its mountains I go to the Forest.

We are actually living in a historical moment when the modern representative of Gilgamish gives the self-same reply. The second clear statement of the myth is that the Forest of Cedars enfolds the sacred precincts of Ishtar the nature-goddess.

Eke they beheld the Mount of the Cedar, the home of the Immortals,
Shrine of Irnini[1] the Cedar uplifting its pride 'gainst the mountain.

Thus we can infer that the monster Humbaba is again a projection of the abysmal dread that accompanied every new advance of the civilizing rebellious son against the domain of the original mother-goddess.

If we regard this myth as a collective human document—and how else are we to understand a myth?—we see that the characteristic opposition of the civilized mind between instinct and culture was already a formidable problem in the third millennium before Christ. Gilgamish personifies the power of the cultural idea. Enkidu that of the primordial unconscious. As the one urges forward, the other pulls back. Enkidu, representing the standpoint of the primitive soul, is won over to the civilizing idea only when the validity of his standpoint is given due tribute. But the pact of brotherhood has something of coercion in it, since Gilgamish always holds the whip-hand and Enkidu is never completely convinced. He seems to have much the same reserve and foreboding in respect to Gilgamish's grandiose schemes as the indigenous food-gatherers (according to Elliot Smith's account) manifest towards the proffered boons of civilization.

When we identify ourselves wholly with the magnificence and power of our civilizing mission, we always tend to do violence to our basal primitive nature. The bombing of Abyssinian villages by Italian aeroplanes fills us with intense anger and shame because we too are involved. There is a million-year-old human being who lives in us, who shares like Enkidu in the fundamental virtue of the animal state and in whose eyes the civilizing hero, who knows neither ruth nor fear, and who disowns the original law of reciprocity, is a rebel and a criminal. But just because the civilizing hero at every bound oversteps nature's law of reciprocity, he is tormented by a bad conscience with regard to nature. Hence the crime of hybris has always been followed by compulsive expiation. So in the end Gilgamish the hero becomes Gilgamish the victim. The death of Enkidu is a direct result of heroic hybris, in other words, the

[1] A form of Ishtar.

arrogant defiance of the gods. The loss of Enkidu means the loss of the guarantee and support of the basic instinctual energy. Gilgamish becomes a restless, driven creature, like Orestes pursued by the furies, eternally tormented by the longing for immortality which had been previously guaranteed by the instinctive covenant with nature.

Throughout mythology we find the hero who attempts the impossible inseparably joined to his compensatory figure; namely, the helpless victim of fate. We need only mention the tragic fate of Prometheus; the humiliation of Heracles, bound to serve Omphale, the luxuriant Queen, in a menial capacity as penance for his crime; the fall of Icarus; the betrayal of Siegfried; the killing and dismemberment of Osiris. The traditional killing of the king, which later developed into the sacrifice of criminals and other human victims in place of the king; the ceremonies of public humiliation of the king, an example of which was given in *Myth and Ritual*; all these examples, which can be multiplied indefinitely from the pages of *The Golden Bough*, point to the same fundamental pyschic conflict that has obsessed man since his first faltering steps along the path that estranged him from his original unconscious unity with nature.

Moreover, this intimate connection, amounting almost to identity, between the hero and the victim is not merely an archaeological curiosity. It is an inescapable condition of our actual psychic economy. Examples will be familiar to everyone of the individual in whom one function attains heroic status, or is exalted by an heroic aim, while its opposite function lies prone and passive as a helpless victim of circumstance. What woman does not know the man who fills the hero role in the disciplined realm of the intellect, but feels himself doomed to be a scapegoat in the opposite realm of feeling? In certain affective conditions in both men and women we can observe the manic, exalted mood of the hero followed directly by the depressive, impotent mood of the victim. This ambitendency of mood is symbolized in the mythic figure of the hero, who always has a vulnerable spot where the lurking traitor can plunge his spear, or the venom of the snake can find an entry. Thus every hero is eventually betrayed by his opposite principle; a fatality which brings us back once more to the fundamental conflict of the civilized mind; namely, the heroic, tyrannical idea, which aims at perfection, warring against the primitive unconscious, which still clings to the primordial, instinctual simplicity of life. Thus the history of civilization should be written from opposite standpoints, from the angle of the slave as well as of the ruler, from the psychology of the renegade and scapegoat, of the two million witches burnt in a single century in Europe, of the tortured suspect, of the victims impaled for the sake of an absolute truth, of the lunatics, criminals and neurotics, as well as from that of the law-giver and law-abider. Viewing history from this angle, it would seem that the cruelty and ruthlessness of the tyrant spring from the sense of guilt and insecurity by which the civilizing experiment has been burdened since its first beginnings.

For the tyrant is never a mere solitary individual lusting for power. He is also the voice of a vast animal which is afraid of its own double nature. Is not Gilgamish described 'as the shepherd of Erech, the highwall'd. He is their shepherd . . . masterful, dominant, subtle'? Mankind is also a herd, an irresistible collective momentum, a streaming of vital units demanding a leader, in whom the prestige and power of man, the successful gregarious animal, can become manifest. Thus, at bottom, the great shepherds of mankind, from Gilgamish to Hitler, are mediums of a vast collective force or tendency which they can neither control nor understand, even though they become its voice. They are possessed by it, and are usually destroyed by it. Collectively mankind has a quite different psychology from that of any of its individual units. Mothers and fathers never want to cast their children into the flaming belly of a demon-god. The individual African negro would never dream of inflicting the cruelties and mutilations which the youths and maidens have to undergo in their tribal initiations. The holocaust of victims offered up to tribal deities, or slain to accompany the spirit of the dead king, are terrifying and unintelligible facts to every individual heart and head. And no man has ever been able to say why these things are done; just as no man in Italy to-day can provide any convincing reason for the slaughter of the people of Abyssinia.

When I was with Jung on his expedition to East Africa in 1926, we frequently asked *laibons* and head-men to tell us why they had to subject their youths to such frightful ordeals in their puberty initiations. The only reply they could offer was, 'If we did not do these things, they would be no better than the animals'.

This reply is a good example of what Lévy-Brühl has termed '*représentation collective*'; namely, something which everyone believes, but no one thinks. It is not thought; it is merely said. And just because it is a collective representation it brings us, in my view, quite near to the solution of the problem. If we had the power to evoke this evening the spirits of the most abominable tyrants in human history, and could compel them to answer for their worst deeds before the tribunal of our individual feeling, would they not all say as with a single voice, 'If we had not done these things, then this or that worse consequence would have followed'? They would all instinctively claim the necessity of prophylactic bloodshed—against what? Are not the magical offices of the king-sacrificer also at bottom a prophylactic measure against this same menace?

My professor of zoology at Cambridge oncc said to me, with the hope perhaps of discouraging my uneducated importunity: 'Young man, if you want to be popular among your fellow-men, ask no questions which cannot be answered.' You see now where my intemperate mind has led me—into the dark underworld of the human unconscious. Perhaps I should have done better to listen to his counsel! But occasionally it happens that questions which seem altogether beyond the rational scope of isolated, individual consciousness are solved in an irrational way by a vision or dream from the collective unconscious. I should like to describe to you a dream which came to me after a long discussion I had had with Professor MacDougall in Switzerland. We had spent a Sunday on the Rigi, and the problem of the collective psyche had been uppermost in our discussion, since it was a matter about which we found the utmost difficulty in arriving at any agreed conception.

Two nights later I dreamed that I was on the slopes of a mountain and was pointing out to my companion how a great spur of the mountain resembled the shape of a vast animal. As I watched I saw that it actually was an incredibly huge beast, for, looking carefully, I observed the slow heaving of its flanks. It seemed to be embedded in, and almost of the same nature as, the mountain itself. The jaws of the creature were like a triangular pit at the other end, a mile or so away from where we were standing. Three robed figures stood in a triangular disposition about the yawning mouth. A high barricade, or screen, was erected to the left of this sacred enclosure, and I saw on the horizon a great hurrying stream of human figures, like a stream of ants, moving towards the barricade. Again like ants they clambered over the barricade, and as they dropped to the ground on the other side, they were picked up by the priests and thrown into the monster's mouth.

I could not conceivably explain such a dream as representing an aspect of my personal psychology. Twice, it is true, I have witnessed hordes of men and women streaming in a demoralized rabble without aim or consciousness, and doubtless such experiences make an unforgettable psychic impression. Moreover, I have observed that the collectives migration of animals, and insects, as well as those of man, are usually attended by a reckless spirit that is frequently suicidal. In particular I might mention the migration westwards of the lemmings in Norway, which often ends in their being drowned in the sea.

We have absolutely no means of knowing how these incalculable collective motivations originate. We only see effects which we, rather blindly, ascribe to instinct. But the term instinct is also used to explain the orderly and discreet behaviour of these same creatures when they are adapted to their specific environment and manifest therein a totally different individual character from their migratory recklessness.

The contrast in behaviour between creatures adapted individually to their natural *milieu* and the same creatures under a collective motivation, whether of panic or any other mass-urge, is so striking that we are justified in concluding that the one state is safeguarded by an instinctive state of awareness, while the other is conditioned purely by the state of collective participation which is without safeguards.

So far as I am able to understand my dream at all, I regard it as a graphic representation of mankind in this state of collective unconsciousness in which individual awareness and responsibility are submerged by a mass-urgency that is symbolized by a vast, archaic, devouring beast without heart or head. Our own experience shows us with what slow and arduous pains even a relative detachment of individual consciousness from the original matrix of unconscious participation is at last achieved. In primitive societies individual consciousness rarely goes beyond a certain degree of personal awareness. The collectivized savage cannot be said to have any individual standpoint of thought or feeling, though naturally he has the instinctual awareness of a separate creature.

Is it possible now to relate these somewhat random reflections about the collective psychology of mankind as a gregarious animal to the function and nature of the king? First let us ask the question: Why is the king almost universally conceived as divine? Everyone knows the king to be a man with precisely the same body, the same human needs and limitations as all other mortals. He is born, he eats and sleeps and weds, grows old, and dies like other men; and yet, in so far as he is identified with the idea or image of kingship, he is without question divine. Before he was king, he had no special divinity. But from the moment the image clothes him he is immortal. No rational explanation which depends upon the fact that he has to perform ritual and executive functions vital to tribal welfare will really suffice. The Governor of the Bank of England or the Prime Minister has equally vital functions to perform, but these persons have never been regarded as in any way divine.

No, we have to seek the answer to the riddle in the significant fact, so well elaborated by Hocart in his work, *Kingship*, that the ritual of coronation is at bottom identical with that of initiation.

The psychology of initiation is a vast subject. It would, therefore, be vain to launch our craft on that relatively uncharted sea. But this much we can say without fear of contradiction, initiation is always a *rite de passage*. It is a birth-defile through which the raw human product is passed in order to emerge a neophyte. The neophyte is, as you know, instructed that his old self, or previous state, is dead and that he is now an entirely new creature. In many cases he is smeared with white clay, and has to be taught how to speak and eat and wash himself, as though he had actually not existed before.

You will remember what the head-man told us in Africa. 'If they do not go through these things they are no better than animals.' To a white man this answer would immediately be interpreted as an assertion of human superiority over the animal kingdom. This is precisely not what the African feels. He would not dream of putting man at the top of the animal hierarchy. Those animals he kills, he puts below him, but those that are able to kill him he sets above him. It is not, then, the arrogance of human power that prompts the above reply, but rather the deep collective fear of the animal state; namely, that state of frenzied possession by unconscious daemonic forces when all safeguards are abandoned. Again this has to be qualified, since the animals have their own instinctive awareness as safeguard, and this the African knows perfectly well. It is rather the state in which a man goes off by himself, listens to the bad spirits, becomes a renegade, goes back on the tribal solidarity, gets fascinated or bewitched. That which threatens collectivized mankind is the force which breaks the human ranks and drives men back to the wild, undisciplined state of a rogue elephant. This atavistic mood is dangerous to more than the individual inasmuch as these daemonic states are highly contagious. Like a fire panic may start at a definite spot, but it easily becomes a conflagration. It is this fact which proves that these irrational affective states, although apparently localized in the individual psyche, are actually collective in character and origin. The collectivized man who breaks away and goes back to the solitary reptilian level where no loyalties or allegiances or obligations have power to hold him, is, of course, incomparably more dangerous than, and vastly inferior to, a wild animal. Moreover, the animals will no more accept kinship with the human renegade than the proud savage will accept the white man 'gone native' as his equal. We often say of the degenerate white that he is no better than a savage. But what we mean is that he is incomparably more degraded. He cannot be a true savage; he is essentially a counterfeit, a renegade without safeguards.

These distinctions are psychologically of vital importance for the understanding of our problem, since it is clear that the danger which the initiation rite is directed against is the sinister lure of the retrograde path. There are only two paths for the libido to follow; either it goes onwards through its various phases and transformations, or backwards through a retrogressive evolution. The one we call evolution, the other atavism. Thus the rite of initiation into manhood is a forced introversion, a psychological histolysis, that is precisely analogous to the histolysis of the pupal state in which the organism of the caterpillar is transformed into that of the butterfly. It involves a kind of mitigated frenzy and insanity, whereby the lad is inoculated with the dread of the spirit world, with panic, with the fear of death, in fact with the terrible destructive aspect of the collective unconscious, but under safeguards. He is, as it were, passed by the priests, who represent traditional wisdom and tribal authority, into the very jaws of the great spirit monster. But even in the worst moments of fear, he is safeguarded. He can face the Minotaur just because he has in his hand a silken cord. This cord is the authority and continuity of tribal tradition. He is covered by the human pact. Thus, at the same moment that the lad is detached from the safeguard of the parents, he is inoculated against the worst dangers which beset human consciousness, namely, the danger of being sucked back along the retrograde pathway by the fascination of the archaic images of the collective unconscious. Initiation, then, from the psychological angle is an indispensable prophylactic measure against the lure of atavism; and we can surely ascribe the sinister increase in mental disorders throughout all classes in our civilized Western communities to the decay of the traditional form of religious initiation and to the absence of any other cultural form which could take its place.

We are now in a position to appreciate how the idea of kingship necessarily became identified with that of divinity, which also includes the attribute of immortality. The king-idea is the silken thread. The safeguarding power of the continuity of tribal authority and tradition from earliest times is concentrated by means of mass-projection upon the person of the king. The distant heroic ancestors, the mighty figures of the mythic past, are alive and present in the person of the king. He is the master symbol just because he is living history. The stability and continuity of the warm-blooded human pact, upon which the whole morale of the race depends, is present in the king as a living fact. Therefore allegiance to the king always means submission to the pact: and what is this pact but the means by which man, as a relatively weak and defenceless creature in the order of nature, is able to maintain a biological status which otherwise he could never achieve?

Thus we see that fundamentally the function of the king is religious in character. He is the integrating focus of authority and power, the spiritual talisman against the daemonic fascination of the collective unconscious, or world of the spirits. He is the defender of the faith *par excellence*, and since he is the symbol of the continuity of tribal life, he is also, necessarily, immortal. Let me read the opening lines of the Gilgamish epic, which describes the essence of the king-idea as man conceived it in the dawn of civilization:

He who the heart of all matters hath proven let him lead the nation,
He who all knowledge possesseth, therein shall he school the people,
He shall his wisdom impart, and so shall they share it together.
Gilgamish—he was the Master of wisdom, with knowledge of all things,
He 'twas discovered the secret concealed . . .
Aye handed down the tradition relating to things prediluvian.
He is our shepherd—masterful, dominant, subtle.

Hocart corroborates this same conception of the king-value where he points out that the king-sacrificer re-created the earth by the same methods[1] as were used by the original creator. The ritual he employs is the traditional way, and the king-sacrificer is the one person empowered to enact it. The ritual, then, is the silken cord of continuity connecting the living tribe with its original source. It symbolizes a tribal memory of the victorious human pact, upon which their whole existence depends.

Here I should like to quote from Hocart a Brahmanic myth-ritual which affords highly suggestive testimony to this psychological value of the king, which we are attempting to reconstruct. The myth runs as follows: 'The gods and titans strove together for these worlds. They strove for the eastern quarter. The titans beat them thence.' And so they went fighting round the compass until 'they strove for the north-eastern quarter; they were not beaten thence. This quarter is the unconquerable. . . .' The gods said, 'through our lack of a king they beat us; let us make a king'. They made Soma king. With Soma as king they conquered all the quarters. He who sacrifices has Soma as king. They place Soma on the cart as it stands facing east; he conquers the east. They carry him round by the south; thereby he conquers the southern quarter, and so on round the compass. The conclusion is, 'By Soma, the king, he conquers all the quarters who knows this'.

This myth tells us a great deal if we can attune our minds to the universal language of the myth. The titans are relatively familiar figures. We know from analogy with Greek mythology that they represent *daimones*, namely, vague personifications of elemental powers. In his excellent work, *From Religion to Philosophy*, Professor Cornford demonstrates the evolution of the elementary *daimones* of primitive Greek thought to the fully anthropomorphized figures of gods and heroes. There was a *daimon* of fire, of the gens, of mystical fraternities, of the sea, and of the wind. They are, in fact, the elementary psychic response to certain overwhelming or dynamic impressions. The titans are vast, because they are overwhelming. Therefore to the loosely organized, relatively primitive mentality anything which could produce an overwhelming effect, either for man's good, or for his destruction, was conceived as divine or daemonic in character. Let me give you an example from my own observation. When camping on the slopes of Mt. Elgon in Kenya, we were living among the Elgonyi, a people closely related to the Masai. We observed them

[1] "The Life-giving Myth" in *The Labyrinth*, edited by S. H. Hooke, M.A., B.D. (S.P.C.K., London).

at sunrise prostrating themselves to the sun. Before doing so they breathed or spat on their hands and then, extending the palms towards the sun, exclaimed *Adhista*, which means Lord. The new moon was greeted in the same fashion and the word *Adhista* was also uttered. When at last these people came to trust us, they explained that only when the sun first leaps over the horizon is it *Adhista*. When it is high in the heavens, it is no longer *mungu*. It was the first appearance of the sun and the new moon that meant god. Similarly in their description of *Ayik*, the evil power. He was not the origin of pestilence and catastrophes or evil events. They disliked to speak of him. They described him as the bat's wing that strikes your face in a dark cave. Or, making a low whistling sound, they said he was the cold wind that comes out of the graves and runs up your spine, when no one is near. When they dramatized *Ayik*, their teeth chattered with terror. It became perfectly clear that, for these people, god and devil were psychological moments. God was not the sun, but rather the moment of re-created morale, when the light and warmth of the sun banishes the fearful denizens of the night. And *Ayik* was the moment of panic, when the spirit is congealed and a man is spellbound, overwhelmed, dismembered by blind terror.

Obviously these conceptions of the Elgonyi are identical with Horus and Set of the Egyptians. It seemed to us more than probable that there, in the depths of Africa, we had stumbled upon the original religious experience. To the primitive mentality autonomous psychical events form the primary condition of life. The primitive has no trained, reliable, detached, intellectual function which can be relied upon to operate satisfactorily irrespective of the underlying subjective emotional state. He is literally at the mercy of psychic forces and, therefore, those things which can re-establish and evoke morale belong to the category divine; while those forces or conditions which overwhelm or undermine his morale are simply the devil.

The battle, then, between gods and titans symbolizes the struggle between opposing libido tendencies; the gods representing the inherited psychic elements that are experienced as helpful powers, while the titans represent aspects of nature which have the power of forcing a man into renegade panic or frenzy. In the battle the overwhelming power of the titans drives the gods backwards until the last barricade is reached. The eastern quarter was the first to be vanquished; therefore, the north-eastern sector would represent the last stand. This is when the real mettle of a man or a creature comes into action, and it is at this point that the divine symbol is evoked. A superior power is needed to vanquish and transform the daemonic in man. Thus the myth shows us with clear precision that the king-idea was born, like the divine sword, *Nothung*, out of utter need.

In this connection I should mention an interesting parallel mentioned by Richard Wilhelm, the eminent German sinologue. He said that the north-eastern point of the compass is regarded by the classical Chinese diviners as the favourable spot where new beginnings originate. It represents the dawn-point, or the point of the new moon; hence it is identical in meaning with *Adhista* of the Elgonyi, or Horus of the Egyptians.

The myth not only tells us of the primitive psychic necessity from which the king-idea sprang; it also tells us the name and character of the first king. Soma, as you know, was a plant, from which an exceedingly powerful spirit was distilled. It was the juice which inspired mortals and was also the nectar of the gods. It is identified with the sap of trees and the seminal fluid. It is said that when Indra in the form of a falcon stole the soma drink, the herdsman, Kricanu, wounded him in his foot with an arrow. Thus soma is equated with the fire stolen from the gods by Prometheus. Soma was the *Φάρμακον ἀθανασίας*, the stimulating wine, the holy drink of inspiration, the mead of immortality. Soma is also identified with Agni—fire in Hindu literature. When men drink it

> They feel the god within their veins
> And cry in loud exulting strains;
> We've quaffed the Soma bright
> And are immortal grown;
> We've entered into light,
> And all the gods have known.
> What mortal now can harm,
> Or foeman vex us more?
> Through thee beyond alarm,
> Immortal god, we soar.[1]

Certain gnostic communities drank soma in their feast of communion, holding the same belief that when the exaltation of the soma drink possessed them they participated in divinity.

When we combine all these attributes, fire, fertility, the sap of life, immortality, divinity, inspiration, we see at once that soma is a

[1] Muir's Original Sanskrit Texts.

libido-symbol of incalculable efficacy. These attributes can only mean that under the influence of the soma drink, men experienced the fullest possible enhancement of vigour and spiritual power.

But how cool these words sound and, therefore, how far away from that original divine frenzy which seized hold of the worshippers! We have no introspective means by which we can recapture this central religious experience, though the dynamic idea which informed it we know without the shadow of a doubt. It was identification with, or partaking of, divinity. The fullness of godhood was known to man, not because theology was taught him by the priests, but because he actually experienced it. Let us not wince at this intoxicated experience of divinity. We think of alcohol as a chemical substance which, when administered in sufficient quantity, produces certain specific effects. This is a good example of how hard it is for the unaided reason to know the kingdom of heaven. If we have never once permitted our individual particularity, our detached personality, to dissolve in the golden tremors of a wine-lit feast, we cannot know what mysteries are concealed behind the word intoxication. No man can reach that state by himself. Wine is the god of communion. It is essentially the maker and renewer of the human pact. Dionysos never revealed himself to the secret drinker or to the dipsomaniac. The antique world had a truly moral attitude to the most intense sensory experiences. They valued self-discipline as we do; but they gave the highest possible honour to those symbols which had the power of releasing instinctual energy as though under divine aegis. The significance of the communion ritual as a *unio mystica* with god is at bottom sexual and very corporeal. Jung writes in his *Psychology of the Unconscious*: 'The primitive significance of the communion is that of a *Hierosgamos*. Therefore, in the fragment of the Attis mysteries handed down by Firmicus, it is said that the mystic eats from the tympanon, drinks from the kymbalon, and he confesses, ὕπο τον παστον ὑπέδυον, which means, "I have entered the bridal chamber". . . . Irenaeus mentions some more of the initiatory customs of certain gnostic sects, which were undoubtedly nothing but spiritual weddings.'

This concrete honouring of the libido is found also in the *Shakti* ritual of communion, where the worshipper partakes of the five elements, grain, meat, fish, wine and woman. The essential idea of this communion feast is that the goddess *Shakti*, being the latent primordial energy of nature, manifests herself in these ritual elements and, therefore, in the moment of participation, the worshipper not only partakes of, or has union with, divinity, but also in so doing he offers the goddess a moment of completion or self-realization. But Shakti, as you know, is by no means a merely benign deity. She is also the devourer, the destroyer, the terrible one. She is as much daemonic as she is divine.

From these somewhat discursive reflections we can rejoin our discussion of Soma as king. We came to the conclusion, you will remember, that the titans represent the daemonic powers of the primitive unconscious, which very nearly overwhelmed and disrupted early civilizing communities. But where does the daemonic, archaic power of the unconscious chiefly lurk but in just those overwhelming psychic tendencies we call animal instincts? When we discuss sexuality we enter the realm of daemonology, and our rational weights and measures become quite ineffectual. Everyone who has had experience of those tragic lives in which sexuality or alcoholism has assumed an archaic or, as doctors express it, pathological character, knows only too well the meaning of the term daemoniacal possession. Continuity of personality is broken, and in place of the known, and perhaps loved, individuality, a strange and devilish being inhabits the house of consciousness. This is the renegade, the betrayer of the human pact. When this daemonic complex is uppermost, one can believe nothing. There is no dependable self present, and, therefore, no undertaking will be carried out. An archaic spirit of uncontrollable power and urgency has taken possession, and if it gets too deep a hold in the psychic economy, the retrograde path to lunacy or suicide becomes more or less sure.

It is this fascination or possession by the archaism of the unconscious which has constantly threatened the integrity of the human society, whether savage or civilized. The danger is not that someone gets excited, or inspired, or begins to talk in strange tongues; rather it lies in the deep renegade tendency to withdraw stealthily from the human pact, and to go off with the devil. The man who broods and glowers in a mood of hostile isolation, and will not say what is in his mind, is committing emotional blackmail: inasmuch as by arousing the primeval dread in those around him, he compels them either to placate him, or to have him certified. Whereas the man who is gripped by a terrible mood, but none the less communicates the fact to his wife, or to his friend, is still observing the human pact. He has not gone over to the devil, and therefore there is no fear of treachery or conspiracy.

Soma, Dionysos, Attis, Aphrodite, the whole pantheon of so-called orgiastic divinities, represent, therefore, the absolute need of early man to create a divine symbol whose divine power consisted in the fact that it could hold the dark, archaic tendency from its renegade path, and bring it within the sovereignty of the human communion. Thus the real stroke of genius which came to the gods in that north-eastern quarter, when the titans had pressed them against the wall, was to make Soma king. By this act of giving royal honours to the very thing which possessed daemonic powers, the daemon was transformed into a god. Psychologically, it was the discovery that, by raising the idea of communion, relatedness, the human pact, to the highest possible value, those forces of the unconscious which held for man the greatest danger were transformed into the safeguarding power of divinity. Thus also in historical times predatory and undisciplined savage chieftains and clans were transformed under the aegis of the same divine symbol into disciplined subjects of the king.

We are now in a position to understand why *Shakti* without safeguards symbolizes the uncontrolled destructive energy of primordial nature, while *Shakti* under the safeguard of communion is the creative energy of life.

I have tried within the limits of a short paper to reconstruct for you the original psychological condition out of which the king-idea arose. I trust you will not charge me with attempting to formulate a psychological hypothesis that runs counter to the accepted anthropological conception of kingship, as presented in *Myth and Ritual*, and *The Labyrinth*. Anthropological research has been concerned with a more or less exhaustive account of the manner in which the divine function and nature of the king has been manifested in all its manifold character and world-wide distribution. The question I have attempted to answer is why the king-idea was identified with divinity. Psychology and anthropology ask different questions and, therefore, they must necessarily have different ways of approach. But they need not clash.

Hocart opens his second chapter on the 'Divinity of Kings' with these words: 'The earliest known religion is a belief in the divinity of kings. I do not say that it is necessarily the most primitive, but in the earliest records known, man appears to us worshipping gods and their earthly representatives, namely kings. We have no right, in the present state of our knowledge, to assert that the worship of gods preceded that of kings; we do not know. Perhaps there never were any gods without kings, or kings without gods. When we have discovered the origin of divine kingship we shall know, but at present we only know that when history begins there are kings, the representatives of gods.' When I read that paragraph I thought to myself, How can archaeological research ever discover the origin of divine kingship? Divinity is not a concrete object to be discovered. Originally it is always a psychological experience, the meaning of which could be recaptured only by the intuitive faculty which enables one to partake, in some measure, of past experiences that express a recurrent human necessity. Every reconstruction of historical moments which carries conviction to our feeling, as well as to our reason, is actually achieved in this way.

As you have doubtless guessed, the reconstruction I have attempted to-night is also a condensation of a very great number of empirical observations gathered from patients' material, as well as from my own. As a medical psychologist I am, of course, vulnerable to the criticism that constant experience of pathological mental processes has warped my vision and, therefore, I see things in a queer light. But I must point out that battling with titans, or the act of mystical union with the god, or the flame of divine intoxication, are not the ingredients of normal experience, and that only those minds which at certain crises have been carried over the line that separates reason from unreason can give us a first-hand account of what these irrational experiences signify. Anyone who has known in his own life the wellnigh irresistible force of a daemonic complex, and has learnt that by bringing this daemonic influence under the sovereignty of human relatedness it has become transformed into a spiritual power of undeniable efficacy, will appreciate what divine kingship means as a psychological reality. But even in the realm of so-called normal psychology, the releasing effect of confession (and confession is precisely the sharing of something that wants to be withheld) is apparent not only in the Oxford Groups, or under the aegis of the Catholic Church, the historical *magna mater*, but also in the intimate sphere of personal relationship. I have observed a profound and enduring transformation of a man's basic attitude to life result directly from confessing to myself and to his wife an experience which had cut him off from human acceptance with an unbearable sense of guilt. Anyone, indeed, who has developed a fair measure of psychological objectivity can make the experiment in himself of contrasting those facts of his experience which he has communicated to, or shared with, another mind with those facts he has never been able to impart. He will observe that all those contents that come within the sphere of relatedness have a warmer and livelier complexion than those that have been withheld; and moreover there will be noticeable a certain apprehension of danger or anxiety clinging to this secret shadow-world of the psyche.

If these facts are true of individual morale, are we not also entitled to suppose that the morale of a tribe or a people is subject to the same conditions? We also know from our own experience that anything which can undermine our morale can also prejudice the effective performance of the tasks upon which our existence depends. Hence the need to create a king; namely, a symbolical representative of the ruling principle—that value which cannot be overthrown by daemonic influences from the shadow-world of the unconscious. This is a need that must be recognized as vital for all mankind.

From the psychological point of view, then, the symbol of the divine king is an archetype which has been created in the basic psychic structure as an enduring answer to a vital human need. It is a psychic heirloom handed down in the continuity of the psychic process, and has its origin in man's greatest peril. How, then, are we to explain the fact that, according to the various observers mentioned by Elliot Smith, there are a large number of indigenous food-gathering tribes who have never conceived the necessity of creating or acquiring the king-symbol? The only answer I can suggest is that these peoples have remained contained within the psychic safeguard of the primal condition. So far as my inquiries have gone, it appears that these indigenous people have no collective rites of tribal initiation. I can speak from personal knowledge of certain primitive tribes of Californian Indians. Among the Achumawi, for instance, there is a form of solitary initiation in which the boy is advised to go up to a distant crater-lake and seek there his individual *tinihowi*. He is told by his father or guardian to dive into the lake at sundown, and it is impressed upon him that he is going to die. But if the *tinihowi* likes him, it will fetch him out and bring him back to life again. The *tinihowi* is usually an insect, a fly, a grasshopper, or a butterfly. But it can be a lynx, or even a stone. He has to learn its nature, its needs and its language. He must never bring it back to the village, nor must he ever speak of it to anyone. When he goes out to talk with it, he must fast and purify himself. It cannot stand the odour of meat, or refuse, or fornication, and his whole success as a brave, a runner, a *shaman*, indeed his whole future morale as a man, rests upon this magical relationship. Moreover, it is optional. Many men never achieve a *tinihowi*; and then they are just ordinary Indians, no one in particular.

If we find that this interesting primitive form is at all characteristic of the indigenous peoples, we might be able to draw certain conclusions concerning the premisses of the genuine primitive psychology. Judging from this instance, we can say that, for the Achumawi at least, the magical relation which holds the safeguard of superior morale, is not with the king or any tribal figures, but with a magically endowed natural object. Through his *tinihowi* he re-creates the primal pact with nature, and feels the guarantee of a magical potency in so far as he maintains the pact; but if he breaks the pact, and loses his *tinihowi*, the magical potency departs. I can only offer this suggestion tentatively, because I have not sufficient evidence from other indigenous peoples to substantiate this conception. But the main thesis is not thereby affected. It is briefly this: human morale is the expression of an enduring safeguard. In the primitive, indigenous community man is still contained in the state of participation, or primal unity with nature: this is his safeguard. Whenever a relative degree of dissociation from, or opposition to, this primal condition is reached, the need for a magical collective safeguard against the avenging power of nature becomes apparent. This need created the symbol of divine kingship. Through the fact that the king represented the whole continuity of tribal life and tradition, this symbol also safeguarded the continuity with the original source, which is the very essence of the pact with nature. In certain enduring cultures, as, for example, that of Egypt, the divine king or cultural hero is wedded to the mother or nature-goddess. The union of Isis and Osiris represents this dual allegiance; namely, to nature, as well as to culture. In certain other cultures, as we have seen in the Gilgamish epic, the cultural hero is a tyrannical, arrogant figure, who consistently spurns the feminine deity, and who attempts to break every natural instinctive bond in order to intensify the power of his principle. This headstrong, civilizing impetus can produce a profound disunion in man between his cultural present and his natural past. Then a new pact with nature has to be achieved, or she assumes the aspect of a vengeful, devouring monster.

If these reflections seem to be rather specially opportune in the present phase of the civilizing experiment, it may be not unconnected with the fact that a very great number of my neurotic patients, who have somehow become prised away from their cultural background, manifest an overwhelming need to recover their natural birthright. They live in a civilization where thick layers of asphalt and concrete separate mankind from the fertile soil of the unconscious, and they simply have got to make their individual peace with nature, the original mother. This need to find again one's original being seems to be the basic theme of every dream and fantasy, and it often leads one far back on the path of man's ascent in order to recover the jewel that was neglected and left behind. I have come, therefore, to view the historical sequence of culture from this angle, and although the idea of the divine king has decayed in modern society to a more or less stereotyped convention, I find that the original *mana* of the king is all the more vigorous and alive in the individual unconscious. The king now becomes the symbol of the integrating individual principle, the concept of the impersonal ruler of the total subject, whose roots are strong in the inherited structure of the basic mind.

I trust this brief attempt at a psychological valuation of the king-idea will also contribute to the much-needed syncretism between psychology and anthropology.

What it is all About

(The first three chapters of an unfinished book)

Chapter I

In a moment of exasperation a well-known psychologist once blurted out 'I do not understand, nor do I want to understand, what Jung means'. It was not for me to question the intelligence of my colleague, but his obvious exasperation set me pondering. Why has the English mind been so resistant to any fundamental explanation of the unconscious? What, after all, has Jung done but blaze a trail through what had hitherto been an unknown region of the mind? Taking the experiences of himself and his patients seriously, he created empirical concepts which were fitted to deal with the facts he encountered. But he would have nothing to do with explanations that were not worthy of the experience.

Naturally, if a man is already wedded to a scheme of rational explanation which ignores the reality of a very large part of mental activity, he will not tolerate a standpoint which includes the part he omits. I doubt if my colleague would admit the possibility that his mind was prejudiced. But the only thing which prevented him from understanding Jung was the fact that the case was already prejudged. His exasperation, however, betrayed the presence of a prejudice which is to some extent typical of the English mind in general. He will serve well enough, then, as my starting-point.

Let us assume that the confusion people are liable to feel when they first encounter Jung's ideas is due to the fact they cherish certain unconscious assumptions about themselves which make it hard for them to see themselves differently. The possibility of enlightenment consists quite simply in the ability to see oneself differently. This is the basis of the whole business of psychotherapy. If one can achieve this one can be cured.

What then does it mean to see oneself differently? The kind of view a man has of himself and the world has been acquired in various ways. To a very large extent he takes himself for granted. He is born and reared in a certain family, and belongs to a certain tradition, class and nation. He inherits certain characteristics from his forebears. He is sent to a school where certain idealistic trends and class prejudices pervade the very air he breathes. All these factors of differentiation are more or less taken for granted. They represent the conditioning framework of one's fate as a civilized being. It is sound to regard them as the basic conditions which have to a large extent governed the architectural structure of the house one actually lives in. But individuality is not merely the product of certain conditions. It is something in and for itself. It is an inner nucleus or potential of decisive power. The total personality is the resultant of this creative centre acting upon and reacting against the basic conditions of one's fate.

Now the first thing to be quite clear about is that man is not just a mechanism. If that were true, your personality would be merely the product of certain conditions. Furthermore you would never have a neurotic problem. For how could the soul become a battleground of conflicting forces if it were a mere reflex of inner and outer determinants? In reality the human soul is like a snake. It has an immense continuity backwards, even into the pre-human past. And because of this agelong inheritance it has also an indefinite forward extension into the future. The instinctual behaviour of human beings is quite incomprehensible without some understanding of the snake-soul which still lives and operates in the background of the mind. Besides, therefore, all those conditioning factors mentioned above, we have also to take into consideration certain basic instinctual urgencies and patterns of behaviour which come from the whole evolutionary past of the species. These are also taken for granted in so far as no one is aware of their existence in himself until he finds himself behaving in a rationally unaccountable way.

When, therefore, the analyst talks about becoming conscious, he really means that you need to become aware and to take responsibility for these basic potentialities of the soul which are seeking expression in a more or less consistent path of life.

A very interesting pastime, favoured by certain islanders of the New Hebrides, is described by Layard in his work *Stone Men of Malekula*. The pastime consists in making tracings in the sand. He writes:[1]

> All the designs follow the same fundamental plan. First a framework is traced, consisting either of straight lines set at right angles and crossing

[1] p. 649.

one another, or else of small circles set in a regular pattern. The pastime consists in tracing round and round and in and out of these straight lines or small circles, a geometrical design formed of a single continuous line. In all cases the skill arises from the fact that once the continuous line is started the finger must not be withdrawn till the entire figure is completed.

In Seniang these designs are called *ni-tus* and

their importance can be gauged by the fact that *ni-tus* is one of the four things a man may swear when making promissory oaths. Deacon says 'each design is regarded . . . as a kind of maze' and he found that in the Seniang district of Malekula they were all connected with a special design called 'The Path', the drawing of which was an essential item in the journey followed by the ghost of every man to the land of the dead.[1]

The myth which explains the importance of these sand-tracings is given by Deacon as follows:

> Ghosts of the dead . . . pass along a 'road' to Wies the land of the dead. At a certain point on their way they come to a rock . . . lying in the sea . . . but formerly it stood upright. The land of the dead is situated vaguely in the wooded open ground behind this rock and is surrounded by a high fence. Always sitting by the rock is a female ghost, called *Temes Savsap*, and on the ground in front of her is drawn the completed geometrical figure known as *Nahal*, 'The Path'. The path which the ghost must travel lies between the two halves of the figure. As each ghost comes along the road the guardian ghost (of the rock) hurriedly rubs out one-half of the figure. The ghost now comes up, but loses his track and cannot find it. He wanders about searching for a way to get past the guardian ghost, but in vain. Only a knowledge of the completed figure can release him from the impasse. If he knows the figure, he at once completes the half which *Temes Savsap* rubbed out; and passes down the track through the middle of the figure. If, however, he does not know the figure, the *Temes*, seeing he will never find the road, eats him, and he never reaches the abode of the dead.[2]

Layard goes on to say 'The Path' is in fact a degraded form of labyrinth such as, in ancient Egypt and elsewhere, stood before the tomb representing the entrace to the future life.

Let this perfect myth from Malekula be our touchstone, for within the primitive labyrinth we may find the answer to our quest. Let me explain first of all that continuity of spiritual life is at the

[1] To the primitive mind 'ghost' really means soul, and the 'land of the dead' means the abode of the ancestral spirits. [2] Op. cit., p. 651.

root of all human piety. This may be represented in various ways as the immortality of the soul, as reincarnation, as the cult of the ancestors, or, as in the mystery initiations, as the idea of renewal or rebirth. With the Malekulans and the ancient Egyptians we may find it represented as the labyrinth guarding the future life with the ancestral dead. In every case we are dealing with one and the same basic conviction which I have termed *the continuity of spiritual life*. Taking this as our golden thread, we can see that the continuous line threading its way in and out within a given geometrical framework must represent a certain experimental individual something finding its way within the conditioning pattern given by fate. The symbol of the rock, which formerly stood upright but is now lying in the sea, can be taken as the major problem of this individual life; that troublesome and recurrent problem which so persistently betrays one's best efforts. The idea of the phallic rock immediately occurs to the mind, because this represents the most ancient and most universal problem of mankind. Moreover, since the myth is man-made, it is significant that the devouring ghost is female. We shall have more to say about this female ghost later. It has to do with the theme of the devouring mother which Jung has dealt with so exhaustively in his *Psychology of the Unconscious*. The ambiguous rock, which first stands and then is supine, suggests the effect of the incestuous mother-tie upon a man's virility. Just because the mother calls to his weakness and infantilism, she has the effect of undermining a man's spirit and seducing him back to a state of helpless dependence just at the moment when he most needs to know his own mind and follow his own path—as though the purposive desire of the soul, which would lead a man towards his realizable goal, fades away into childish passivity and inertia.

Thus the rock is the dangerous place guarded by a devouring ghost. The penetrating point of the myth is, however, found in the figure which the guardian ghost uses to snare her prey. The idea of rubbing out half the figure in order to gain her end reveals the nature of the ghost. The primitive psyche, being only loosely integrated, is particularly threatened by the danger of disintegration or discontinuity. African natives often describe this graphically as 'loss of soul', as though a soul had absconded, leaving them forlorn, without strength or purpose. Because of this fatal liability the primitive personality is readily vulnerable to panic and other powerful affects. Thus he is liable to states of possession which he ascribes to spirits or demons. With us this alteration of personality due to powerful affects is also indicated in such popular figures of speech as being 'transported' or 'carried away' or 'beside oneself'. Speaking generally there are two ways of getting sick among primitive communities. One is 'loss of soul' when something which should belong to you absconds, or goes with the unconscious. The other is when you are invaded or possessed by a spirit, where in fact something foreign has entered into you. The state of disintegration represented by 'loss of soul' is, of course, precisely the condition which makes one vulnerable to alienation by a foreign spirit. We shall discuss these two types of sickness more fully when we come to speak of the unconscious, because both types occur just as freely amongst civilized people, only we call them by different names.

With these facts in mind we can see that losing one's way and being eaten by the guardian ghost represents this very real danger of disintegration, with its loss of the safeguarding sense of continuity. The characteristic one-sidedness or loss of balance which overcomes one in a state of panic, is shown in the unconscious compulsion to move in a circle, instead of following a consistent direction. Whenever a man allows himself to be driven by storms of affect, giving way to moods or lusts or panic fears, this cyclonic tendency always becomes manifest. Hence the wisdom of the East is primarily concerned with teaching the way of detachment from the affects so that one may find one's individual way between the opposites.

We shall usually find that in the heart of a myth or dream a jewel is set. This one is no exception to the rule. For assuredly it is a basic truth that the way out of the dangerous impasse is to know the completed figure which is, as it were, engraved in every man's heart from the beginning.[1] It is this knowledge of the way one has to go which is called 'guidance' or the 'voice of the heart'. For the heart is situated, as it were, midway between the thinking head and the seat of the affects in the belly. Hence the 'voice of the heart' contains also the wisdom of the ancestors who have travelled the path before and know the dangers. Therefore the myth says, because his soul knows the completed figure, a man can find the middle way between the opposites. And the way through is also the road to the

[1] The writer of the twenty-second Psalm had this knowledge when he wrote: 'But thou art he that took me out of the womb: thou didst make me hope when I was upon my mother's breasts. I was cast upon thee from the womb: thou art my God from my mother's belly.'

ancestors; meaning that the continuity of spiritual life has been preserved.

I have put this nutshell myth at the beginning, because I want you to become accustomed to thinking by analogy. For you cannot go far without first becoming acquainted with the language of dreams and myths: it is the royal road to the understanding of yourself. The unconscious still retains the original picture-language of the primitive mind, and this is the idiom in which the most salient truths about yourself are couched by the dreaming-mind. For the unconscious is still primitive in its oblique method of approach. The dream-mind, using impressions, incidents and persons in the form of analogy, asks us to put 'It is as though' in front of the dream, before we try to understand what it is saying.

How, then, can this particular myth refer to you and your problems in this sophisticated modern world? There are of course a great variety of ostensible reasons why people come for analysis. But the only reason which makes them stick to it is because they have lost their way. Especially in times of transition, like the present, people easily get prised away from their containing background. They reject or relinquish the way and religion of their ancestors almost without knowing what they are doing. But why does one get lost psychologically? It is because the way of the ancestors had, for them, a real sense of purpose. They felt themselves to be performing and achieving God's will. When, therefore, one is still contained by, and integrated in, the ancestral pattern of life, one is sustained by this feeling of purposeful continuity, so that the ultimate problems of life are, as it were, taken care of. The question of finding the individual purpose of one's life does not seriously arise. But when the pattern fails to provide a sense of purpose, mere collective security is never enough to fulfil the need of the soul. It is then that the problem of individuation really begins. Because, logically, the very fact of having rejected the way of the ancestors, however unconscious this rejection may have been, imposes upon one the obligation of finding a better way: a way, that is, which is informed with a purpose which the ancestral way no longer possesses.

At bottom, therefore, the state we call neurosis results from the attempt to live one's life without a sufficient purpose. It is like the state of our world at the present time when the forms and, to a large extent, the spiritual values of the past have been carried away, and no one cay say with any certainty what is happening to us and what the future may hold. This is the rock where the danger of losing the continuity of spiritual life threatens our civilized world. By the people of Malekula this danger is expressed in their myth, through their own religious symbolism. The Malekulans are still living in the Stone Age, and the great megaliths, which are a feature of their central religious rite, are identified with the ancestors. When the men are initiated into the rite they take on a new name and this rebirth signifies being united or identified with an ancestral spirit. Hence, when the stone is upright it would symbolize a visible landmark which reaffirms the continuity of their spiritual life. It is the symbol of confirmation. But when it is lying in the sea it is as though this symbol had vanished from sight and was simply awash in the unconscious: only a latent, not an active force.

This, then, is the state of a person who has been prised away from his containing background. The symbol of virile, active or creative purpose is no longer visible, and all the values of the past recede away and lie more or less dormant in the unconscious. But a symbol of power which has ruled and directed the lives of our ancestors, filling the very centre of their world, does not, in fact, just die or go to sleep. It still exercises an equal power from the unconscious side; only its potency, which before was recognized and positive, is now unrecognized and negative. The true measure of this negative potency is actually experienced in the incalculable power of a neurosis which seems to lay a chill hand on the very sources of life. The doctor who tries to convince his neurotic patient that the neurosis is simply the result of certain mistakes, or baneful influences of his childhood, just that and nothing more, will inevitably arouse the most strenuous resistance in his patient. The neurosis has perhaps become his sole vocation. It devours all his powers and energies. It has demanded of him untold sacrifices of pleasure, life, fruitfulness and human fellowship. How can that be merely a mistake which can be reasoned away by a well-meaning outsider? No, the only way to cure a neurosis is to give it its value as a major power. It is as though the whole ancestral line were gathered together in the stone circle of the neurosis and were saying: 'If you cannot live in our way then, at least, you shall not be free to live in yours'.

Thus we have to realize at the outset that the problem of purpose and continuity is a fundamental issue in any system which attempts to heal the sick soul. The deterministic school has attempted to obliterate the thorny problem, seeking to re-establish life on a rational basis, from which the human soul with its agelong ancestral inheritance is simply excluded. The results of this method are well known, and the widespread resentment against the whole system is, in my view, wholly justifiable. Having thrown out the baby, it proceeds to analyse the bath water; as though the mysterious vitality of the soul could be found in those inevitable conditions of early life to which all babies are in varying measure subjected. This is not to say that increased knowledge of the ways in which the soul can be helped or hindered are not useful. These will become even more valuable to life than the improvements in physical hygiene have already proved to be. But conditions are accessory factors: they are not the essential thing. This is surely proved by the fact that a Freudian analysis goes on and on for years. So that the patient has to make his analysis the main preoccupation of his life. One can only imagine that the hope is somewhere entertained that the dragon of neurosis will be finally slain by sheer boredom.

How then is one to find again the completed figure which will guide one past the guardian ghost of neurosis? It must first be realized that life is not an isolated individual chapter, beginning with the cradle and ending with the grave.

Clearly the conception of God as the centre of the universe would be quite meaningless to us if there were no kindred centre of universality in our own psychology which could correspond with the universality of God. From this point of view, the egocentric personal conception of the purpose of life would be personified by the myth of the soul who gets lost because half the figure has been rubbed out. What I have termed the continuity of spiritual life is represented in the idiom of the unconscious by a figure of commanding authority or wisdom, and when it becomes active, its direction or utterances are as though a million-year-old human being were taking a hand in our life. Frequently the figure is represented in dreams by the king or some other royal personage. This is in virtue of the fact that the authority of the king is invested in him as a person only because he is the present link in a long dynastic chain. Moreover he is a good king only in so far as he is able to place his impersonal function above his own egotistical interests. In the East we find this impersonal dynastic centre represented as the Brahmanic or true self, as opposed to the ego, or false self.

It is most unfortunate that this larger conception of the Self, embracing the totality of one's being, past and future, collides against a violent prejudice of the Christian-trained mind. For just as 'mind' has become identified with the known confines of consciousness, the term 'self' has become reproachfully identified with the ego. In consequence, when we come to deal with the true Self—which is no more personal or temporary than the oakness of the oak—we have to overcome an ingrained prejudice which brands everything which comes from within as having no true validity. The conscious ego has even the audacity to identify its wishes with the events and experiences of the dream-world. Hence Freud's famous conception of unconscious activity as mere wish-fulfilment.

This grotesque undervaluation of the Self has resulted inevitably in the most damaging intrusion and interference of the ego in the sphere of the instincts whose natural spontaneity is blocked as soon as the ego intervenes. Harley Street is haunted by people who want to be told how and what to eat and drink, how to make love, if at all, how to combat constipation or frequency, or painful or irregular periods. Over the whole range of instinctual functions an atmosphere of fear and fuss prevails. The more disorderly these elementary things become, the more strenuously does the ego fuss and interfere. Thus the civilized man and his primitive elder brother in the unconscious have reached a state of mutual distrust. This has happened in a civilization where for centuries it has consistently been taught that to consider oneself or to reflect upon one's vital problems was a selfish morbidity. Is it to be wondered at that we should need to salvage some of the wisdom of our primitive forebears?

It becomes evident, therefore, that one of the first problems we shall have to deal with in order to re-establish a vigorous and natural continuity with the past, is how to deal with the nervous ego and its insistent desire to fill the centre of the stage. Again and again in the early stages of analysis the ego rushes in, claiming this, repudiating that, or going off on long, discursive attempts at self-justification, for ever side-tracking the real work of analysis.

The things to be underlined in this chapter are:

First, that the neurosis has arisen from a rupture in the continuity of spiritual life, and that life has come to a standstill because the feeling of purpose and significance has shifted from the objective field of life into the subjective field of the neurosis. In other words the neurosis has become, or tends to become, an end in itself.

Second, that the continuity of spiritual life does not pertain to the ego-centre, but to the impersonal Self in the unconscious, which is, in fact, continuous with the ancestral past.

Third, that in order to re-establish this continuity, we have first to deal with a gesticulating ego which always tries to monopolize the centre of the stage. In the next chapter we shall have to see what can be done about that.

Chapter II

THE PERSONA

Before we can discuss the detachment of the ego from the persona, we must first understand what the ego is. It has been defined as the focal point of consciousness, and just because it is this focus the ego is not unlike the eye of the body. All the ideas, feelings, impressions, strivings, memories, etc., which are integrated around the focus of 'self' go to form the ego-complex. Hence it is the most highly organized complex in the psychical hierarchy, and because it wields the executive power of deliberation and will, it is not fantastic also to compare it with the prime minister. For just as the power of the minister grows *pari passu* with the power of the state, so the ego has developed through the increasing organization of consciousness. Moreover, since consciousness is the cause of the ego-disease, only consciousness can cure it. The first step in the cure is to teach the ego its proper function as prime minister instead of fussing all the time about the opinions of society. Hence the problem of the troublesome ego is unavoidably linked up with its detachment from the persona.

Just as every organism and every kind of fruit has an outer covering in the form of a skin or rind, so also has the human personality. The persona, then, is the role one learns to play in adapting to the outside world, i.e. the social *milieu*. It is obviously as necessary to have a civilized persona as it is to wear civilized clothes. To attempt to do without it would be merely a bold bid for nudity in the psychological sphere. But just as a tough, indurated rind is a bad substitute for a sensitive skin, so an over-elaborated persona is like a mask which conceals or disguises the native individuality behind it. This probably explains why Jung gave the name *persona* to this complex; a term used by the classical actors of antiquity for the masks they put on when playing comic or tragic roles.

Lest the term 'complex' should cause confusion, let me explain that the structure of the mind has become integrated as a complex whole throughout an agelong discipline of adaptation in which certain partial systems, each following its own special bent or goal, have gradually acquired a certain relativity one with the other: as though a cabinet of ministers, each with the interests of his own department at heart, had to relate their several views and interests to a common policy. These partial systems of the mind are called *complexes* and, as one might expect in a living organism, which is ruled and centralized by purpose, each complex is energized by a specific dynamic nucleus that is instinctively orientated towards a certain goal. When any particular complex carries its inherent partnership too far, so that the balance of the whole is threatened, we may speak of a fanatical mind or one-sided psychology. The analogy of the cabinet of ministers is only true of a well-balanced and disciplined mind. More often we come across a dictatorship of one function-complex, the effect of which is to create acute opposition from the repressed minority almost amounting to a state of civil war.

Because of an inherent tendency of the mind to personify its contents, we actually find in dreams specific complexes being personified by figures suggestive of their actual purpose and character. Hitler, for instance, has been a favourite dream-representation of an overweening power-complex, while some beautiful, voluptuous woman will personify the sex-complex.

The persona is such a complex or partial system, and is usually represented by someone, known to the dreamer, who typifies in his manifest character the specialized role of respectability or worldly ambition, sophistication or whatnot, which characterizes the dreamer's outer role.

In much the same way as a statesmanlike prime minister handles the peculiar sensibilities of his colleagues, with the aim of holding them together as a team, the ego, as the effective voice of consciousness, needs to become conscious of its integrating role, in order to bring the various disparate strivings of this complex psychical organism into an orderly relativity. But the ego cannot achieve this degree of authority over the complexes unless it has received it from a higher command.

To anyone reared in a democratic constitution the relation of the ego to the Self should be easy to comprehend, inasmuch as it is almost identical with the relationship between prime minister and sovereign. The sovereign's power to choose his prime minister is vested in him by the constitution of the land. The prime minister then is chosen by the king and holds his office only so long as he is the effective voice of the whole nation. As soon as he ceases to represent the national will and purpose he ceases to be prime minister. Thus, just in so far as he respects and submits himself to the continuity of national policy, his authority is secure, and his subordinate ministers will bow to it. The analogy holds true in practice; because only in so far as the ego-complex submits to the impersonal direction of the Self (i.e. has a really impersonal attitude) can it effectively voice and control the heterogeneous components of the mind.

When I referred above to the necessity of the ego becoming detached from the persona, I knew that sooner or later I should have to elucidate that statement, or fresh difficulties would arise. The ego and the persona should, in fact, be separate and distinct systems. But unfortunately—especially among the English, where the persona-ideal of the gentleman has achieved a considerable vogue—it often happens that the ego identifies itself with the persona so completely that a man really believes himself to be the gentleman which he conscientiously shows to the world. From the point of view of social decorum and national prestige, this lifelong performance has doubtless a certain merit. From the standpoint of individuality, however, it is a disaster. For it rests upon the assumption that man is exclusively a social being and, therefore, that his social personality is the only function that matters. Let us suppose, for instance, that a certain prime minister gets into power with the express purpose of involving his country in every kind of expansionist scheme, so that all the resources of the country and all the best brains are employed in foreign commitments, to the complete neglect of home affairs. Just such a phase, for example, as Japan has been immersed in during the past decade or two. The nation may endure the sacrifices demanded for a time. But if his schemes result merely in war and general disturbance, with nothing to show for it but the distrust of one's neighbour, and misery at home, the day of revolution and retribution will surely come. In exactly the same way it is possible for a man to become identified with an expansive social persona, to assimilate himself successfully to a desirable social *milieu* and spend all his energies in ceaseless effort to keep up with the ever-increasing demands of his worldly function. He will probably go into parliament, buy a baronetcy, marry into a county family and be received by most of the people who count. Having achieved his ambition he may one day overhear his long-neglected soul murmuring: 'So what?' He may reason with his soul, explaining irritably that he has gained everything a man could reasonably hope to attain. Why in heaven's name is she not satisfied?[1] Or again, a man may cultivate a persona especially built for charm, so that no woman can resist him. After endless exhausting 'conquests' the soul drearily says: 'So what?' Another man has taken popularity with men as his goal in life. He belongs to a dozen clubs, has followed all the manly sports, prides himself on going everywhere and knowing everybody, and then, one day, people are amazed to hear that he has accidentally shot himself. What has gone wrong? Apparently nothing. Everything has gone according to plan: only it was the wrong plan, with all the essentials left out.

One is reminded of Jung's aphorism: 'Psychology only becomes relevant when a man has reached the end of his rope'. So long as a man can get along successfully on charm, popularity, success, being a good fellow, or any other of the gentlemanly hypotheses, who has the right to say him nay? Naturally there are always certain indications, red-light symptoms of warning, long before a man reaches the end of his rope. He will get 'nervy' and 'highly strung', will probably drink and smoke and eat too much. He may even go to his doctor, who will tell him to go easy for a bit, especially with alcohol. But these cannot stop him. He can still pull out a bit more rope. In my experience it is not until such a man is brought to a complete standstill by a knock-out blow from fate that he will stop and listen to what is going on within his own soul.

This, then, is what I mean when I say that to identify oneself with one's outer social role is easy to do, but is none the less disastrous. The fact that everyone else around one seems to be doing it, and getting away with it, only makes the danger greater and more insidious. Why, for instance, was the League of Nations impotent

[1] A man's inner character, or soul, is feminine in character. This will be explained in another chapter.

in the face of Japanese aggression, or when Hitler began devouring Europe? Simply because these crazy usurpations were the logical outcome of the whole social pattern of life in which we, and every other civilized nation, have evolved. These aggressive nations are simply carrying further and more ruthlessly the same policy of worldly aggrandizement which we followed in a more leisurely and gentlemanly fashion during the last century. We were helpless to stop the avalanche because in a sense we started it. It is hypocrisy for us to assume that we are fundamentally different. We too can be ruthless when our vital interests are imperilled.

In order to grasp the nettle firmly we need a standpoint of detachment from which to realize our own responsibility for the debacle. But this is impossible so long as we assume that others have the wrong motives while we have the right ones. In a work of thoughtful and constructive analysis[1] D. W. Harding has assisted the gaining of this detachment by pointing out that collectivized peoples are, in fact, governed in all social and international dealings by a pattern of domination or submission. This pattern has sway wherever human life is integrated according to a hierarchy of position and power. In so far as all one's social dealings are with people who are either above or below one there is an instinctual tendency to make use of the power motive which is inherent in the whole pattern. The result of this is that the healthy candour and spontaneity of free individual expression is constantly being held in check by the assumed requirements of social success and prestige.

In his analysis Harding comes to the same conclusion as Dr. Erich Fromm,[2] who traces the root of the trouble to a prevailing sense of insecurity and helplessness in the individual soul, over against vast forces which seem to lie far beyond the power of human control. It is certainly true that the smaller nations seem to find a balanced life and policy easier to maintain than the great states. It is always the conflict of ambition among the great world-powers which sets the conflagration alight.

This digression upon world affairs is not, as it might seem, irrelevant, because at bottom the same principle is at stake; namely, the problem of establishing the human limit. Any goal which is pursued fanatically, without consideration for existing rights and claims, leads inevitably to a human catastrophe. It is the absoluteness of the aim

[1] *The Impulse to Dominate* (George Allen & Unwin, London).
[2] *The Fear of Freedom* (Kegan Paul, Trench, Trubner & Co., London).

which is impious. The same goal followed in the spirit of relativity could have the opposite result. A desire that is followed with the idea of relating in a human fashion to the desired object, furthers or enriches life. But power or desirousness, taken as an end in itself, submits to no limits and therefore it tends to grow into a demonic appetite. Hence it is always dangerous when a small man of humble origin is able to climb to a position of great power. How can he avoid becoming inflated with limitless fantasies? Such men are not disciplined to wield power: hence they can never be relied upon to set a limit to their ambitions. So when fate offers them the possibility of harnessing their impossible fantasies to the terrifying potentialities of a modern state, the fate of Nebuchadnezzar surely awaits them.

The life-course of the successful man who identifies his ego with the persona (i.e. the worldly function *par excellence*) may also run in an ever-expanding spiral to which no limits are set. It is against this tendency of man to allow the world to alienate him from his original human shape that the Founder of Christianity so urgently warned mankind. To lose one's original unity and shape in a vortex of demonic expansion is surely the greatest danger to the spiritual life of man. For instead of being guided by a wise and helpful spirit he becomes possessed by a devouring demon. It is in the World and the Flesh that man encounters his devil. But the devil is his own desirousness.

The pursuit of unrealizable goals, then, is a kind of madness, and the moment of detachment we spoke of, whereby a man is able to cry 'enough' to his world-devouring ambitions, is like waking up out of a bad dream into a world of friendly and known reality.

So far we have been considering only the more extreme and morbid type of identification. There is, of course, the more legitimate type, in which the persona is a well-disciplined and socially impeccable outer form. But in these cases, too, the spontaneous individual expression is continually hampered or repressed by fear of social criticism. The persona ideal which prompts this very considerable sacrifice of individual spontaneity is a product of history and long tradition. This is the source of its power and prestige.

The training of the human ego from early childhood keeps the persona-ideal more or less constantly in view. The tradition of conformity to the recognized social pattern of behaviour naturally helps the ego to overcome the self-consciousness and crudities of adolescence. It supplies a ready-made role which the unsure adolescent ego can adopt by the easy method of imitation. The process of hatching out from the primordial freedom and spontaneity of the child-state can be a very painful one, since the lad is still in the dark as to what the world demands of him. The prestige of the social persona undoubtedly acts as a powerful incentive at this point, helping him to throw off childish ways and to take on some of the load of adult responsibility. When one sees a youth of twenty, fresh from his public school, taking complete charge of several hundred coolies and bringing them into line with assured mastery, one may well marvel at the success of the metamorphosis. It is hardly surprising that a thing of such power should be much coveted, and men naturally tend to identify themselves with implements of power. It is hardly an exaggeration to say that the British public school persona, based on the Arthurian myth, has been one of the most potent forces in establishing British rule and British fair-play throughout the Empire. Each of the great Services has produced its own specific variant of the gentleman-persona, and the successful career of the soldier, sailor or airman is very largely determined by his ability to run true to type. The persona-ideal operates just as powerfully and insidiously in feminine psychology as in the masculine. Only the types differ in character.

In order to do justice to the psychological pre-eminence of the persona-ideal during the earlier phases of life, a treatise on its historical and sociological derivatives would be necessary. But this would land us in problems far beyond the scope of this work. I must, therefore, confine myself to the historical indications already given. But before leaving the problem we must differentiate quite clearly the two types of persona I have outlined above. On the one hand we have the grotesque, inflated type, beloved of the cartoonists, whose worldly pretensions are completely and even ludicrously belied by his actual human quality. The bombastic display of uniforms, the dramatic ceremonials, and all the imposing fuss with which these little men festoon their illegitimate power, are quite obviously faked. It is a bluffing attempt to legitimize a power which is essentially illegitimate.

On the other hand, the impeccable persona of the second type has the character of a recognized and accepted style. Although this too must be regarded as a bluff, in so far as it effectually masks the individuality which uses it, there is in fact a vital difference, because this second type is the expression of a legitimate social form, belonging to an integrated order of society. It must be evident, therefore, that if civilized society devised effective means to prevent unscrupulous men from seizing power in illegitimate ways the former type would eventually become extinct.[1]

It is dangerous to assume that a function observed in the individual is identical with a similar function observed in the state. But in this matter of the persona, the temptation, I admit, is stronger than my powers of resistance. Is it not permissible, for instance, to link up the bombastic persona of a Mussolini or a Hitler with the characteristically false and exaggerated nature of Italian and German propaganda? The motive of illegitimate power which produces the cartoonist's delight is surely the same as that which inspires the whole policy of Goebbels. A discriminating scrutiny of the exaggerated persona will often light upon those very motives it was especially designed to conceal. On the other hand, the persona that is too meticulously correct is also suspect. It is liable to conceal a deep moral insecurity.

Civilized society has built up redoubtable fortifications against its underlying primitive psychology. The persona is merely the social expression of this achievement. But a fortress can only too easily become a prison, and the persona a strait-waistcoat. At bottom, therefore, the persona is really a civilized bluff. But if it is recognized as a social necessity, peculiarly adapted for a large variety of social and professional requirements, one can wear one's persona as one wears one's overcoat, putting it on and off at will. In this way it is possible to preserve the integrity of the ego from the allurements of the social masquerade and thereby also to maintain one's freedom. Generally speaking, the ideal of good behaviour is set at a higher value in the training of the young than spontaneity and originality. It is therefore possible to win high marks in the collective sphere without ever facing the problem of what one really feels or thinks *au fond*. But in the analytical session where the only thing that counts is the real, where truth is unveiled without witnesses, this excellent social function can be shed at the door.

Naturally a person does not come to a doctor just to chat. There

[1] If I were pressed to define what I mean by a legitimate persona I would say that a persona which pretends to no more than is given by one's integrated function and position in an existing social order would be legitimate. Whereas one that asserts a claim to power and consideration which does not rightly belong to its owner is illegitimate.

must be a real desire to get down to the causes of the problem or difficulty, otherwise why consult a doctor? Nevertheless, by dint of long habit one can become so completely identified with the persona that it is at first almost impossible to lay it aside. Moreover, the very idea of talking to a psychologist can have the effect of putting the ego on the defensive. This attitude of defence is not always secretive. Frequently it goads one to talk too much or too recklessly. But this kind of talk is always away from the point. It is like the mother bird trying to decoy the intruder away from her young. Sometimes it is enough for the doctor to say to a feminine patient who is struggling against this tendency to chatter, 'May I suggest that Mrs. So-and-so sits over there on the settee with a book so that you and I can have our talk without interruption'. Any means is worth trying which will assist the ego to lay aside the persona defences.

Naturally this method is only possible with the type in which the persona is a legitimate social façade. It would be quite useless with those people whose persona is based upon illegitimate power. But then such persons would only come to a doctor through sheer terror, when they have already seen Nemesis waiting round the corner. The last thing they want is the truth about themselves. They sometimes come, nevertheless, seeking a way of escape from their fate.

At the beginning of the chapter we said that the first step in the cure of the ego was to become conscious of its proper role in the mental hierarchy. We have now seen that its identification with the persona leads either to inflation or to some kind of worldly falsification of the personality. We also likened the function of the ego in the mind with that of the eye in the body. We know that the eye represents the reaction of the living organism to the properties of light. An organism that wants to make use of light for the purposes of vision must develop an eye. Consciousness is analogous to light, and in order to make full use of the properties of consciousness an integrated ego-function has been developed by man. But supposing the eye, in virtue of its specialized and vital function, should begin to put on airs, as though it were the whole body, we should have to subject it to a rigorous discipline in order to teach it its place. But when the ego, as the essential function of consciousness, assumes that nothing exists in the mind which it does not know about, it is behaving in exactly the same way. What does the ego know about the mysteries of the unconscious, or even of its own reverse aspect, the shadow?

I can use the analogy of the eye with all the more confidence because the unconscious continually reverts to the metaphor during that process of self-realization which we call analysis. Very few people, in my experience, go through an analysis without dreaming of having their vision corrected. Indeed, so intimate is this association, that ophthalmist colleagues have told me that the mere training of the eye, by means of spectroscopic exercises, etc., often has the effect of curing neurotic symptoms. It is almost as though a distorted or falsified view of oneself, or of life, made it impossible to see correctly. But however that may be, there can be no question at all that the first step in analysis is concerned with correcting the patient's view of himself and the world. Naturally there are a great number of people who come to the doctor to be cured, who have no desire at all to see things as they really are. An eminent eye-specialist informed me that often myopic patients are by no means moved by gratitude when given glasses to correct their vision. Sometimes they are furious when the warts and wrinkles on people's faces or the threadbare patches in their carpets are revealed to them. Having grown accustomed to a roseate fantasy they prefer this to the real world.

The ego also generates a roseate fantasy of itself and of its importance in the scheme of things; a fantasy which it is hard to forgo, particularly if no especial value can as yet be discovered in facing the naked truth. To satisfy this doubt, let us go back once again to the analogy of the eye. The eye is the chief means by which the peculiar nature and reality of the outer object becomes manifest to consciousness. It is the organ which first introduces the 'I' to the 'not I' and by which the dawning ego makes its first relation to the world it has to live in. But the eye can see without really seeing. In other words, if we see without interest or attention we are not allowing the reality of the object to enter the mind. The object as such is still irrelevant.[1] If, on the other hand, we allow our interest to be aroused by an object, then desire, apprehension, or the need to understand and relate to it are evoked by the act of seeing. Thus a psychical factor is introduced which we can think of as a streaming or flow of energy.

[1] I am reminded of an American woman who, after a few weeks' analysis, looked at me strangely and said, 'Dr. Baynes, I believe you are the first man I have ever really seen.' 'What then have you been seeing up to now?' I inquired. 'Oh, just coats and hats walking around.'

This flow of interest or desire is what we term *libido*. The neurotic individual who lives in a world of objects and people with whom he can make no vital connection is perhaps the most wretched of men. He lives in a challenging world of interesting objects without the wherewithal to meet the challenge. The essential charm and beauty of childhood resides in the fact that the stream of interest and desire flows out spontaneously in all directions and to all kinds of objects. The libido runs out to gain the world because the fantasy activity of the child-mind is completely unhampered by the load of responsibility. When the time comes for the child to take some responsibility for something so that he has to look after it, he will show the same capacity for not seeing things which the neurotic person has had to cultivate towards life in general.

We must conclude from this that everything we see with interest makes a certain claim, demanding from us some degree of responsibility. In other words, the flow of the libido which invests the outer object has also a retroactive effect upon our own character. In effect we are changed, moulded and shaped by the things or persons in which our libido involves us, either by attraction or repulsion. This is inevitable. But so great is the force of primeval inertia or, if you will have it so, of the lure of the irresponsible childish state, that a very great number of people refuse, in effect, to be changed or shaped by life. They want to maintain the eternal *status quo*. Here again is the problem of the ego, since it is primarily the ego that refuses to conceive of itself differently.

Being born into the world means to suffer change, and since one has presumably not willed to be born, there seems to be no sufficient reason why one should undergo the pains and tribulations of being changed in the service of some unknowable end. Thus we are faced with the fundamental question of being able to have faith in life; since apparently it is impossible to live one's life wholly or with any intensity of purpose unless one can believe that the whole human experiment makes sense.

One of the most striking differences between early mankind, up to the time of the Reformation, and modern man, is the fact that originally men possessed an inborn and self-evident conviction that they belonged to the cosmic order. They were integrated in life in a way which we are not, even to believing, as we see in the early dawn of astrology, that there existed not only a correspondence, but a synchronicity, between the inner world and the outer: that the deep determinants of human fate could even be read in the movements and relations of the heavenly bodies. This feeling of being deeply integrated in the cosmic order is clearly an expression of that same principle discussed in the first chapter, which I called the continuity of spiritual life.

The growth of science and the development of the sceptical scientific attitude of mind has had the effect of separating us from this inherent sense of continuity. But perhaps science, after all, did not produce the feeling of detachment. Was it not rather the sense of being cut off or severed from the natural, primordial state which necessitated the scientific view of life? If man had never been ejected from paradise he would not have had to become conscious. The geocentric fantasy of the universe—which even the Elizabethans still clung to—is simply another evidence of the myopia of faith. The short-sighted individual who prefers his rosy-tinted fantasy to reality merely exemplifies the truth that, in order to evolve, consciousness demands the sacrifice of every fantasy which can be used as a substitute for reality. Clearly this sacrifice cannot be made immediately or at will. If the immature mind of the child is suddenly confronted with something that is beyond its capacity to understand, it instantly defends itself by an artless rendering of the situation which brings it into relation with its picture-book world of childish fantasy. Fantasy is therefore nature's means of protecting the immature mind against the shocks of the real. But so deep is our veneration of childhood's innocence and charm that parents made it their aim to preserve their daughters from any real experience or from the true facts of life. Childishness has been deliberately cultivated and reality either bought off or kept at bay. Only men were fitted to know the world as it is. The necessities of war economy have changed all this, and immaturity is no longer prized as the mirror of heaven. Reliability, steadiness and endurance are needed instead.

These considerations have to be mentioned because the feminine persona has to a large extent been built up on this fantastic conception of woman's role. Fortunately women themselves are realizing that the world was not made, or intended, for grown-up children, and they are becoming more and more insistent upon meeting reality on equal terms with men. The liquidation of so many of our civilized defences is also effecting a change in the persona values. People begin to realize that it does not pay to cultivate a fantasy world in place of the real one. In the terms of our analogy, correct vision is increasing in value. To go on believing in a childish make-believe world in order to preserve a childish make-believe personality is, let us hope, the last stupidity of the age of faith. But let us be quite clear in distinguishing true belief from make-belief. It is a providential provision of the mind that one can only truly believe something which one knows to be true. True belief is essentially knowledge. How indeed could I believe something to be true which is outside human cognition? Make-belief, on the other hand, is a fantasy I make use of in order that I shall not know the facts. I do not really believe it. It is simply an umbrella which I put up in order to defend myself from the responsibilities of true vision.

Thus in our discussion of the persona we are led irresistibly to the basic tussle between fantasy and reality. Fantasy as we now see it, is a creation of the subject, and serves the needs and wishes of the subject. Reality, as we now see it, is generated by the object, or rather by an adapted relation to the object. All the discipline of education should be primarily concerned with leading the libido which is involved in fantasy, into objective channels where it can be gradually integrated in the living texture of reality. Fantasy is the expression of unconscious potential. It is the crude ore which has to be refined and minted and brought into general currency in the spheres of work and love.

In this second chapter the important things to remember are:

First, that the ego is merely the executive function of consciousness: it is by no means the whole of the psyche.

Second, that in order to be able to conceive itself differently the ego needs to be detached from the persona, viz. the worldly function.

Third, this means creating a psychological standpoint from which one can criticize the persona in order to judge whether its pretensions are valid or not. It is clearly impossible to shred away the substitute of fantasy-elements of the persona unless one can believe that reality serves as a better basis.

Fourth, if we follow the stream of libido we naturally become involved in real objects and real goals and thereby we become changed, *i.e.*, more real. If we deny or dishonour the libido we must necessarily take a substitute or fantasy-image in place of the real. This is the royal road to neurosis.

In the next chapter we shall see what is actually involved in this following of the libido.

Chapter III

FOLLOWING THE LIBIDO

All our talk in the last chapter about gaining detachment from the persona would remain in the air unless we followed it up with a discussion of how it can be done. Here we have to submit to the principle that one cannot empty an existing vessel of its libido-content without first creating a better or more attractive one to contain it. We have to go with nature; no good is achieved by arbitrary attempts.

Fundamentally the mind is a system of energy, in which a flow of energy, declaring itself in the form of attention, interest, desire, command, will, etc., proceeds from the experiencing subject to an object. Whenever we are conscious at all, there is always an object. The literal meaning of object is something thrown before the mind. What is actually presented to the mind is an image. These images may be derived from sense-perception, *i.e.*, visual, auditory or tactile images. Usually when dealing with so-called outer objects the mental image of the object is a blend of various sensory stimuli. These may be termed complex images, and the sense of immediacy they possess compels us to ascribe a higher degree of reality[1] to these objects than to any others. But in spite of this immediate sense of reality we have to recognize that we actually live in a world of images, and that the objects of consciousness can originate just as well in the world within as in the world without. We think we know these real objects outside us because we have created various means for adapting them to our purposes; human objects just as much as non-human. But on reflection we shall have to realize that all we can really know about them is how they appear to us. What they are, in and for themselves, is a mystery.

On the other hand, we have also to deal with a world of inner objects which become manifest in images that arise independently out of the unconscious in the form of ideas, reflections, intuitions,

[1] It is not without interest that, for the practical Anglo-Saxon mind, the word *reality* is derived from *res, thing*; whereas with the more introverted German mind the word *Wirklichkeit* derives from *wirken, to effect*. What has effect upon the mind, whether coming from within or without, is therefore the basis of reality for German psychology: not just the thing as such.

waking fantasies or dream images. Here again is another world of phenomena or appearances. We know just as little about the actual contents of our inner world as we do about the objects outside us, since our knowledge in both cases is confined to the manner of their appearance. It is therefore literally true to say that the psyche is the creator of our world: inasmuch as it builds up or creates, out of the welter of impressions and images which crowd into the mind, a coherent, associated and meaningful world. This is the miracle we take for granted and blindly depreciate when we assume that the mind is like a photographic plate, merely a reactive or reproductive mechanism. If the contents and experiences of our own mind are unreal to us, where then shall we seek reality? That is real, said Zeno the Stoic, which has the power so to seize upon the mind that one cannot disown it.

This definition agrees with our dynamic view of mental activity. Transposing it into our terminology, we would have to say that that is real for us which commands the greatest intensity of libido. As soon as interest, attention or desire is aroused by an object, that thing becomes part of our reality. Therefore when no libido flows out to anything outside us it is like being psychologically marooned in a subjective world of fears and fantasies. The neurotic fear of responsibility freezes the flow of libido at its source; with the result that all the functions of relatedness by which the human being naturally adapts to his environment are starved of vital energy and tend to atrophy. Just as love entails consequences which a man who is in love does not see, so fear can equally blind a man from seeing the fate that is in store for him. In his fear of taking responsibility, the neurotic person does not see that he is denying all purpose to life. The state of being cut off and marooned is the terrible nemesis resulting from this denial. It is the state where the beleaguered fortress becomes a prison.

There is the case of the young woman patient who has been unduly sheltered and cared for, and has received all this untold service without a single thought of what is due from her under nature's law of reciprocity, which is binding on every living thing. The more the debt mounts up, the more her fears intensify and multiply. She is like a frightened child marooned on a rock, watching the tide slowly rising. The world she lives in seems unreal, and nothing, not even her unearned food, satisfies her. It is a desperate situation which only a reborn attitude of faith in the purpose of life can remedy. All that is needed is the faith, which is also knowledge, that the sea can bear her up; but her whole refusal of life has already rejected this knowledge. She knows instinctively that to fight the sea means to drown in it. The ego is powerless to find the solution, but at this point she may dream that, assisted by an unseen helper, she finds herself taking the plunge. Such a vision could lead her to safety.

Going into the sea in an attitude of trust means, quite simply, to trust the libido, to follow it, and to believe that it can bring one to the very source of life. This principle of honouring the libido as the stream of living energy is therefore the same as honouring God. This is what is meant by the attitude of acceptance. Accepting one's fate means to accept oneself as one is without reservations or conditions. The patient will probably reply 'Make me well first, then I shall be able to take the plunge'. But that condition cannot be satisfied because only the act of faith which takes the leap can start again the flow of vital energy upon which all healing rests.

There is an early Greek cosmogonic myth which puts the whole neurotic problem in a nutshell. Before the world was, we are told, there existed a vast primal egg. This was split into two halves, one half became Eros, the other Phobos. These two coupled like male and female and out of their mating the world was born. This cosmic egg refers to the fact that what conditions or predetermines the whole issue of an event, or indeed one's whole life, is the basic affective attitude with which one goes to meet it. The attitude underlies everything. If it is ruled by Eros one can trust oneself to the unknown adventure and believe in its outcome. One goes to it with assurance and one is singleminded in the service of life. This means that one is going with the libido and accepting one's fate as an intelligible and reasonable experiment. If it is ruled by Phobos the flow of libido is congealed, water becomes ice, and the chill reverse aspect of fate threatens to overwhelm one's whole being. Yet both fear and love, though apparently irreconcilably opposed, are equal servants of life. For without fear no living thing could survive. It is like the dragon who guards the treasure. Tibullus wrote: 'The first thing God made in the world was fear.' It is in very truth the guardian of life and value. Therefore wherever one loves most, fear is greatest. The whole point of the myth lies in the fact that the two must be related together in a loyal partnership. Neither must attempt to rule alone. The love which suppresses all fear exposes the best values of life to every imaginable risk. This is a state of foolhardy unconsciousness. On the other hand, when fear becomes tyrannical, and suppresses all the tasks and purposes of love, it produces a compulsion or anxiety neurosis, thereby bringing the whole of life to a standstill.

Following the libido, therefore, entails the necessity of making fear your friend and ally. I will give you an example from my own experience. When I was a lad I tended to be over-confident and reckless. At my school there was a Swedish master who taught us swimming and gymnastics. He was a superb diver and of course I had to emulate him, particularly in high-diving. One day he took me aside and said: 'Don't imagine, when you are up there on the twenty-foot board, that you are not afraid. You are meant to be afraid because if you just dive off in a hurry you can break your back. But if you know you are scared you can put your fear in front of you and dive over it. That will give you just the elevation you need.'

Fear is necessary, therefore, to warn one of danger, and the overcoming of it brings out the *elan* and power needed for the achievement of a new and dangerous task. Without fear man would assuredly never have attained to consciousness. It provides the vital challenge which makes one think and reflect and find the better way. Thus, once again we arrive at the same truth we discovered before, that the very thing which as an absolute kills and destroys life, when taken as a relative factor becomes an essential ministering function.

I have tried to show that in whatever direction the libido turns, if we follow it steadfastly and follow it through, we shall come to reality. But it is just here that the persona valuation of the way chosen by the libido is liable to undermine the whole attempt. For the persona, you will remember, is largely constructed of average collective views, and collectivity is always against the daring individual venture. The average view will invariably favour the comfortable, the safe and the respectable. Where individuality wants to dare the heights, following untried ways, the collective man prefers the funicular. Considering that both possibilities exist in everyone, it is paradoxical that individuality and the collective persona should be mutually so unsympathetic. But so it is. Before a person will be willing to undertake the experiment of individuation he must first be able to criticize the easy collective formulae beloved of his persona. For unless he is prepared to see the thing through, whatever the cost, it is better that he stay in the sheepfold along with the helpless and the sick. All the slogans of collectivity betray a fundamental distrust of the libido. At the critical juncture, when individual effort is most needed, who has not heard the comfortable voice tempting one: 'It is dangerous to become too interested in anything. Just keep going and trust to luck like everyone else'? It offers cheap love but expensive recreation; cruises, parties and costly distractions. Above all we are urged not to take anything seriously. Or the cynic suggests: 'See what women will do for you.' Always women, mark you, not woman; not the decisive one with whom the heights and depths of the soul will be challenged.

It is this ubiquitous automatic example of the collective man which makes Dr. Fromm's work *The Fear of Freedom* such a terrible social indictment. Yet this cheap voice of the average man has always filled the air, as the radio does to-day. It is the presence of a serious purpose which shuts our ears to the voice of Nietzsche's 'all-too-many'. Can we in truth wish the world otherwise? The mountain of individuation is there, with all the dangers of the climb, for those who are awake to the call to worthy achievement. But even the most daring climber looks to his home in the valley and enjoys the friendly voices of the tavern. Man is at bottom a social animal and his roots are nourished by the community to which he belongs. This need not conflict with the other claim of his nature, which commands him to be himself, and to be whole. If he lets the easy-going collective voice seduce him from the other loyalty he will never know his royal inheritance.

It is this other centre of value which Jung calls the individuality of the Self. When the bottom has dropped out of the world and the voice of the persona can only reiterate outworn clichés, it is this inner centre which now begins to draw the libido away from the object and towards the subject. Perhaps the first thing which strikes the patient is that he begins to remember, and even to reflect upon, his dreams. Perhaps he has an impressive, commanding dream which wakes him up and he feels shaken, as by an awe-inspiring experience. A patient, whose marriage had become a torment to him and who had had a breakdown, dreamed that he was in his bedroom sitting on the side of his bed and looking at himself asleep in the bed. It was growing light and he felt that there was something urgent to be done, but he could not get the self that was sleeping to wake up. He in fact woke himself up in his angry efforts to awaken his sleeping partner in the bed. Such a dream is transparent: its meaning could not possibly be mistaken, even by the patient who, like many very extraverted subjects, assured me that he never dreamed.

The dream tells him that one part of his personality is asleep, i.e. unconscious, while another part is waking up to the urgency of his situation, symbolized also by the moment of dawn. This temporary splitting of the personality in a crisis—depicted in the dream by the doubling of the personality—represents the state of affairs when the libido tends to divide against itself, part remaining with the old extraverted persona and part going over into a new and more conscious attitude. This progressive part is represented by the dreamer in whose mind the reality of his situation is beginning to dawn. This exemplifies the practical point already emphasized, that one cannot empty the existing vessel of its libido-content without first creating a better or more attractive one into which it can go. While the new direction is still an untried possibility, it cannot be wholly convincing. It is only a hope. Hence only a portion of the libido will go over towards the new conception, while the remainder clings with conservative inertia to the existing form. Thus a characteristic conflict develops between the progressive and regressive tendencies; a conflict which may force one in the end to take a definite standpoint. One has then to deal with the contrary standpoint exactly as one would talk to a partner who has become one's antagonist. Such an attempt would always be useless if one merely tried to prove one's own way right and the other wrong. The only way that can work in the long run is the way between the opposites. This means a reconciliation of opposite qualities, which can be achieved only as the vision and enthusiasm of the progressive part attracts the steadiness and conservatism of the other, or vice versa. While the conflict is being actively waged it is presented to the mind as an either-or situation. When the will has been undermined by neurosis the consequences entailed by either choice appear distorted and magnified by fear. The neurotic conflict is not so much a battle between opposing tendencies as the helpless oscillation of a timorous ego seeking to escape any decision which would lead to the tasks of life. But in a man with a resolute will that has not been debauched by escapism, the conflict wears a very different aspect. His primary intention is to make up his mind and to act accordingly, since he knows by experience that the effective deed can only issue from a single-minded purpose. Taking counsel, then, from the unconscious, the father and mother of all experience, he will say to his adversary: 'You and I belong together: we cannot go our separate ways without losing everything. Moreover, the qualities which make you pull in the opposite direction are exactly those we shall need in trying out the new venture. Let us keep our differences and step along together.' Something in that line will help to transform the conflict from an absolute contradiction into a workable collaboration; the whole aim being to preserve the unity of personality and the continuity of spiritual life.

From the mere fact that my patient was conscious of having dreamed, I was able to prove to him that his libido was moving independently towards the opposite pole, and was now illuminating the inner world of the subject. The dream already provided him with a standpoint from which he could see that his attitude to events had been altogether insufficient, too childish, extraverted and wayward. He began to look back and see how his unreflecting extraversion had taken him ever wider in a centrifugal curve, further and further from his base. Until at last, as the dream shows, he was literally beside himself. Thus his dream makes him see his recent breakdown in a new light. Blinded by the hero-mirage of the persona-ideal he had no conception of his real personality, his basic human subject. Therefore to save him from his own blindness the unconscious had to intervene. It does so by making him sick. His nerve gave way and he had to be taken to hospital, his moral completely shattered. It was only after this experience that he first came to me. Even then all he wanted from me was to 'fix him up' so that he could get on with his job. He did not seek to become conscious of himself or to know what he was doing to his soul. Nevertheless, his libido, obeying a wiser direction, turned irresistibly towards the neglected antipodes, and all that was necessary was to show him what was happening and to urge him to follow the direction of his libido.

This peculiar blindness of the conscious ego is, as I said, one of the most ticklish problems to handle. It is quite useless for the doctor, who sees what is wrong, to tell the patient what he ought to do. Because unless the patient's reason is convinced, the front door of his house will remain shut. Doctors used to try and sneak round to the back door, as though one could by-pass the will by means of hypnotic suggestion. This naturally resulted in a mechanical compliance with the doctor's will, but without the sanction of the subject's reason. This was not unlike the condition of Germany under Nazi dictatorship. By using age-old primitive means for hypnotizing the national will, Hitler proceeded to use the vast compliant animal for his own ends.[1] But this method cannot create an effective unity. Hypnosis, after all, is only a protracted sleep. The awakening will inevitably come and then the magician and all his ways will be repudiated; because alien suggestion, by its very nature, is an offence against the individuality of the subject. Accordingly we must abandon the attempt to achieve the unity of personality by psychologically dishonest means.

The blindness of consciousness is primarily due to lack of reflection and self-criticism. This statement needs elaboration. Certain basic views or premisses are normally taken over from the past, or from the environment, without question. Upon this given groundwork one proceeds to plan one's conscious activities. These basic values may have served well for a time, and because they have brought a certain success, there seems no obvious need to question them. A man, for instance, has achieved a certain success at school or university. He adapts to life in the same style and with the same code of ethics; maintaining the same free and easy relationship to his fellows as though his public school code comprised the whole wisdom of life. Or it may be one has been brought up in a certain denomination, or with a set of views which served well enough in the past, but which has long since become obsolete. Many people suffer from trying to face life with the wrong image; but because the ego has become identified with the given hypothesis it seems impossible to change it. To effect a radical change in one's basic attitude is a very disturbing and painful experience. These basic premisses or assumptions are like the earth on which one stands. For doubt or criticism to penetrate this realm is not unlike the experience of an earthquake. One feels as though the very stability of one's house were threatened. It is indeed not uncommon at such times for a person to feel the floor tilting.

Thus the conservatism of the ego is bound up with the maintenance of psychological equilibrium and it would be disastrous to overlook this fact when a radical change becomes due. Before attempting

[1] I have described this process fully in *Germany Possessed* (Jonathan Cape, Ltd., 1941).

deep analysis the doctor should always ask himself whether the patient has a sufficiently integrated consciousness. In the case of my patient I had to deal with a reasonable man with a well-disciplined mind. When such a man is invited to listen to the clear voice of his own being speaking to him in his dreams, it is easy to see how infinitely preferable is the longer way of self-realization to the arbitrary method of hypnotic suggestion, or to the method of the doctor admonishing his patient to follow a prescribed regimen.

People often wonder why the analyst pays so much attention to dreams. How is it possible for the patient to learn something from his dreams which he does not already know?

I will try to tell you. First of all, the dream is a natural statement of the patient's own psychology. Its very frankness, spontaneity and independence of conscious control gives it a peculiar authority. Moreover, it must be granted that the patient's own psyche is a better informed witness concerning the real causes of the trouble than the most knowledgeable expert. The dream-mind undoubtedly has its roots in the physical as well as the psychical make-up of the dreamer. It has emphatically the best inside knowledge and, it always speaks to the point. Furthermore, it is a living experience. The figures of the dream live and move and have their being, are informed with their own indwelling vitality and they act always in accordance with their own principle of independent activity.

With all these self-evident facts in its favour, why has the sage counsel of the dream been ignored by civilized men as belonging to the realm of primitive superstition? Solely from our lack of understanding of the dream language. That, at least, is my view. The idiom of the dream is so irrational that if one behaved in waking life as one does in a dream one would have to be certified as insane. It is this irrationality of behaviour, as well as its scandalous frankness about things which reticence and modesty are at pains to repress, that has given the dream its bad reputation.

But apart from the strangeness of its primitive mode of expression the dream has normally a relatively low content of energy. It is a phantasmal half-light experience compared with the fully illuminated reality of waking life. Naturally this is not always so. But in the case of a very extraverted mentality, such as my patient, who only feels himself to be alive when he is furiously active, the amount of psychical energy available for ordinary reflection, not to mention dreaming, is negligible. Hence, unless something happens to stop the machine, the libido is simply used up in the compulsive system of work and activity. The polite term 'nervous breakdown' happens to be surprisingly suitable for these cases. The breakdown has the character of a forced introversion imposed upon the subject by reason of the fact that his libido suddenly recedes from the tyrannical system. His mind is now in a state very like that of a factory when the fuel has given out, or when a sit-down strike is declared. It simply ceases to operate.

At this point a psychological principle comes into operation which Jung has called *enantiodromia*.[1] It denotes the dynamic principle of opposition in the psyche, whereby, after a certain point has been reached, everything tends to go over into its opposite. Here again is a law which is absolutely necessary for the maintenance of equilibrium. For when any direction or goal has achieved a dangerous absoluteness, the libido tends to recede away towards its natural opposite, in order that balance shall be restored. Thus one of the primary functions of the unconscious is to compensate or counterbalance the one-sidedness of consciousness.

But why should a man want to create a system of work which entails superhuman effort to maintain? What is the motive which compels him? He does not want it. It is the worldly minded personal ideal, his own one-sidedness which compels him. He is in the power of an obsessional demonic system, like a man tied to the tail of a madly careering bull. A man in such a situation might experience a certain precarious sense of power and exhilaration, but he is certainly not free. Some force within him is compelling the subject to live the role of the hero and thus to prove his superhuman powers. But why should he have to do this if he were not somewhere weak and helpless?

The hero is a central mythological figure in a man's unconscious and few men with powerful ambition will escape the danger of being forced to identify themselves with the system, or machine, which their ambition creates. The hero is a half-mortal and half-immortal being who can make the impossible possible. Hence a man who unconsciously identifies himself with the image is riding for a fall, since men are not immortals; they are weak and human. The trap

[1] A term used in the philosophy of Heraclitus. See Jung's *Psychological Types*, chapter on Definitions, p. 541.

that is being prepared by his own consciousness is that the subject falls suddenly into the opposite of the hero, i.e. the victim. Hero and victim are indissolubly united as a primal pair of opposites. They are like the head and tail of a coin, inseparable. When the stream of libido recedes, therefore, from the hero-system it goes over into the victim-neurosis. That was the condition my patient was in when I saw him. He felt helpless and weak. For hours together he sat sobbing like a child. His wife, fate, the doctors, everyone was against him or despising him, and there was no help anywhere. From the viewpoint of the angels it was obvious that the victim role was now being dramatized with the same intensity and absoluteness as the role of the hero had been previously.

If that were the end of the story you might well say 'How stupid life is, first to drive a man on to Scylla and then to suck him down into Charybdis'. But that is not the end. I must explain further that, while my patient was identified with the role of the hero, his attitude to women was flirtatious and trivial: he was merely showing off in the approved style of the superior male animal. Naturally no woman is satisfied for long with displays of male coquetry, or with the role of the barnyard hen, impressed and amazed by masculine prowess. Yet that in fact was what the man expected of the woman he married. Observing his flirtatious demonstrations with other women, and feeling no warmth in his relation to herself, she naturally became devoured by jealousy. This he felt to be wholly unjust, as, in fact, his relations with all women had, as he explained, 'nothing to them'. But after his breakdown, and while he was in hospital, he began to realize that his whole hope of recovery and of restoring belief in himself was centred in the woman who had been working alongside him as his secretary. His conventional philosophy made it impossible for him to admit that he was in love with her. But nevertheless he confessed to me that her image was the one healing and integrating influence which gave him strength to hold on to life and to restore his morale.

This woman was steady and serious, having suffered a great deal without losing faith in life. She had discerned his real quality behind the persona-masquerade and her unquestioning belief in him seemed to him the one real thing on which he could count. Thus she was in every way fitted to personify his feminine inner character or soul, which until then he had treated so scurvily. In his personal myth this woman became the vessel of healing, bearing the values of his soul. She could thus symbolize for him the realizable potential or major purpose of his life.

All this had actually happened before he came to me; but he simply had not realized it. He protested that all he wanted was to 'make a go' of his marriage and to hold down his job, without being haunted by the fear of breaking down again. The persona values were, in fact, still claiming that his life must go for ever along the old lines and that nothing must be changed. But the contradiction existed and could not be denied. All I had to do was to show him, by means of his dreams, that his libido was intent on reality and would not be coerced into bolstering up a sham. His conventionally adapted persona, i.e. the voice of the world in which he lived, knew very well how his life ought to go. If his soul didn't like it, well, so much the worse for her. But the soul will stay with a man, working beside him as a helpful and invigorating power, only so long as his life is real. If a man stubbornly persists in living a boring, artificial life, his soul will surely leave him. Slowly it dawned upon him that to try and follow two absolutely contradictory hypotheses results in hopeless division, like a state of civil war. Life has its own inexorable logic, based upon that completed figure which everyone needs to know. The soul knows it, and that is why wisdom has been defined as the knowledge of the soul. The book of life is recorded in the unconscious, and the best we can do is to learn how to read it.

My patient did not really believe in his persona-philosophy. He merely accepted it, or rather swallowed it, like a dose of medicine ordered by the doctor, without ever questioning whether, in fact, it agreed with him. Thus the conflict forced him to reflect, and to question the basic premisses upon which his psychological house had been built. However upsetting this might be, there was no other way. He saw it as a life and death issue and, indeed, nothing less than an absolutely vital conflict could have brought about the transformation which actually took place in this man's personality.

Perhaps the most distressing thing of all for such a man was the fact that, when at last he had accepted the situation as it actually was, he could not immediately swing back into his extraverted stride. He could see the new direction his life was taking, and he knew he had to follow it faithfully and seriously, but he could not transpose the mental conflict into any ready-made plan of action. He had to learn how to steer his boat by the stars.

In this chapter I have tried to show that following the libido means accepting the real, instead of the artificial. It means accepting the way one's life has to go. This always involves the problem of purpose, and the manner in which one honours the libido is conditioned by one's reply to that problem.

We have also learned something about the pairs of opposites, and the tendency of the libido to recede from a too one-sided standpoint to its opposite. This tendency is called enantiodromia.

Index

Adler, 48
Aetiology, psychological, 75
Alchemy, 2, 3, 4, 6, 7, 8, 10
Alchemy, as the Yoga system of the West, 8; as the forerunner of the individuation process, 8
Anal-erotic fantasy, 120
Analysis, 19, 21, 62, 65, 89, 112, 119, 121, 146, 211
Analytical, experience, 19; method, 108; practice, 19; process, 127; reduction, 48; relationship, 109; talks, 26; therapy, 141; work, 128
Ancestor-worship, 157
Anima, 8, 13, 57, 58
Animus, 58
Archaism, 150
Archetypal, forces, 16; images, 93, 182; pattern, 180; rôles, 59
Archetypes, 65, 117, 123, 150, 182, 201
Astrology, 2; early science of, 3, 7, 8, 11
Astronomy, 3, 4
Attitude, causal-reductive, 135
Autochthonous creation, 180, 181

Book of Changes, 9

Caste-system, 39
Censor, 119
Change of life, 32
Character, English, 39, 44, 50, 51, 54; national, 40, 43
Chemistry, 3, 4, 6, 7
Child, character, 79; mind, 78, 79, 92; neurosis, 89; psyche, 78, 89; soul, 76, 78, 84, 85, 88, 89, 92, 93, 95; study of, 78, 79
Chinese philosophy, 9
Christ, 8, 36, 94, 95; redeeming power of, 9
Christianity, 5, 6, 9, 124
Christian, era, 6; faith, 36; legends, 58; Mass, 6; revelation, 7; spirit, 155; theology, 6; values, 95
Chthonian cults, 6
Church, 35, 36, 94
Cosmogonic, Greek myth, 65
Culture, 1, 2, 180; beginning of, 2; British, 56; Chinese, 9, 78; early, 35, 181; Egyptian, 7; emerging, 117; English, 49; extinct, 57; extraverted, 1; German, 176; history of, 6; Indian, 147; transfusion of, 55

Delirium, 25, 26
Dementia praecox, 49
Descartes, 132, 133
Divination, 9
Divine Kingship, psychological origins of, 180–203
Dream, affective content of, 143; objective character of, 140; consideration of, 139; constellations, 97; of children, 90, 93; as clue to purposive activity, 156; and value of constructive method, 148, 149, 150, 151, 152, 153; objective figures in, 141; formulations of Freud and Jung, 13, 14; and Freud, 99, 103, 104, 105, 106, 107, 108; interpretation, 2, 3, 4, 10, 11, 23, 26, 27, 28, 29, 30, 33, 63, 119, 120, 121, 123, 124, 125; imagery, 2, 13, 99; and Jung, 105; language, 91, 209; life, 162; prophetic, 94, 118; questions solved by, 189; rediscovered by Freud as a possible object of science, 4; and understanding of the unconscious, 17, 18, 22, 231, 232, 234, 237

Eastern systems, 147
Ego, 16, 21, 102, 103, 213
Enantiodromia, 235, 238
Esprit de corps, 44
Extraverted science, 1, 9

Fair-play, British principle of, 43, 51, 55
Fordham, Dr. Michael, 90
Frazer's *Golden Bough*, 11
Freud, mechanistic causality, 108; fundamental conceptions of, 79, 212; contrasted with Jung, 83, 117, 136; criticism of, 98, 99, 100, 116, 118, 125; rigid determinism of, 109, 111, 114; discovery of the mechanism of repression, 101, 102; on dreams, 4, 13, 103, 104, 105, 120, 140; ideas of, 47, 48; Oedipus pattern, 90; researches of, 131; wish-fulfilment concept of, 172

Geisteswissenschaften, 153

Gentleman-idea, 35, 36, 38, 39, 42, 43
Ghosts, 154, 155, 157, 158, 159, 161, 162, 165, 166, 206, 207, 208
Gilgamish, early Sumerian epic, 2, 3, 158, 183, 184, 185, 186, 187, 188, 193, 202
God, 7, 8, 40, 41, 95, 119, 124, 158, 159
Great Plan, 9
Guilt-complex, 119

Haldane, Dr. J. S., 113, 114
Hindu philosophy, 9
Homosexual, associations, 107; frustration, 50
Homosexuality, 52
Hypnosis, 12

Id, 119
Incest-problem, 82
Infantilism, 150
Inheritance, cultural, 77; psychological, 76
Initiation, psychology of, 191, 192, 193; puberty, 188; ritual pattern of, 180; the ritual of coronation, 191; tribal, 188
Intellect, 1
Introverting science, 1
Intuitive sciences, 2, 3, 4, 10

Jeans, Sir James, 4
Jung, 8, 12, 47, 48, 49, 51, 54, 56, 61, 77, 79, 81, 83, 89, 99, 116, 117, 118, 120, 122, 124, 126, 146, 147, 158, 188, 204
Jung, theory of dreams, 13; dementia praecox, 163; the empiricist, 14; enantiodromia, 235; versus Freud, 97; function of libido, 136; individuation, 172; individuality of the self, 230, 231, 232; persona, 214; *Psychology and Pathology of so-called Occult Phenomena*, 175, 176; *Psychological Types*, 127, 128, 129; *Psychology of the Unconscious*, 11, 71, 123, 207; constructive system of, 152; *Weltanschauung*, 110, 125, 172; word-association tests, 108; theory of the basic uniformity of structure of, 181, 182

Kant, 136

Libido, 13, 123, 136, 142, 144, 149, 195, 197, 223, 226, 227, 228, 229, 230, 232, 235, 237, 238
Libido, and nervous breakdown, 235; distrust of, 230; divided against itself, 231; following of, 225, 226, 227, 228, 229, 238; Freud's theory of wish-fulfilment, 13; in children, 223; in puberty, 71; introversion of, 146; recession of, 82, 83; *sexualis*, 142; symbol of, 197; teleological conception of, 136; transformation of, 144, 149; unfulfilled, 67; weaning of, 66, 112

Marriage, 32, 96; failure, 11; meaning of, 95; problem, 62, 73; relationship, 68
Migration, of ideas, 180, 181
Morals, 9
Mother-complex, 67

Naturwissenschaften, 153
Neuroses, 107, 113, 126; incidence of, in man, 82; problem of, 21
Neurotic, alibi, 64; condition, 178; failure, 84; island of fantasy, 69; fears, 64; immaturity, 73; influences, 75; past, 112; patient, 113, 203; stagnation, 121, 123; tendency, 84

Occultism, 3
Oedipus, pattern, 89, 90, 95; complex, 99, 112

Pagan, mystery religions, 6
Parent-child, relation, 76; constellation, 79
Participation mystique, 36, 38, 53, 66, 68, 81
Persona, 229, 230, 236, 237; defences, 221; feminine, 224; ideal, 218, 219, 220; meaning of, 213, 214, 216; the ego, 225, 226
Physics, 9
Politics, 9
Pre-conscious, 118
Prima materia, philosophical theory of, 7
Primitive, nature of psychic activity, 170; communities, 208; culture, 36; mode of expression, 234; forms, 6, 10; labyrinth, 206; man, 2; materials of the unconscious, 22, 174, 187; medicine man, 173, 176; mentality, 172, 194, 195; mind, 169, 209; nature, 186; peoples, 161; psyche, 169; psychic necessity, 196; psychology, 157, 202; religion, 199; societies, 81, 190; state, 185; superstition, 234; unconscious, 22, 174, 187, 198; world, 3
Primitive sciences, 11
Primordial, conception of human

Primordial—cont.
psychology, 65; elements of the mind, 4, 6, 23; instinctual energy, 147; man, 28, 77; masculine and feminine antithesis, 64; natural existence, 183; ocean, 167; psyche, 4; soul, 14; source of life, 80; state of man, 80; strata of the unconscious, 57; unconscious, 186, 187, 188
Primordial, energy of nature, 197, 199; instinctual energy, 147; language, 13; mind, 4, 6, 23; science, 4; unconscious, 3, 8, 15, 17, 157, 186
Primordial sciences, *see* intuitive
Projection, childish, 61; of philosophical ideas, 7; of psychic images, 2; of the unconscious, 8; of instinctual wisdom, 8
Provisional, life, 61, 69
Psyche, 1, 12, 51, 65, 180, 182, 225; antonomous, 141; child, 92; definition of, 143; English, 55; formations of, 139; functions, 113; primordial, 4, 5
Psychic, activity, 135; cause, 35; causality, 136; contents, 163; continuity, 81; constitution, 65; determinism, 59; differentiation, 28; energy, 163; elements, 88; experience, 115; experiments, 163; field, 128; forces,102; identity, 66; inheritance, 149; life, 104; mechanism, 90; motivation, 156; necessity, 36; organization, 88; phenomena, 132, 155; processes, 112, 130, 171; reaction, 45; structure, 78; tendencies, 117, 198; underworld, 52; value, 123; world, 51
Psychical research, 154, 168, 179
Psycho-analysis, 10, 11, 47, 107, 138, 170
Psychological, background, 176; field, 11; groups, 50; metamorphosis, 10; pioneering, 47; research, 10; significance, 35
Psychology, 3, 137, 199, 203; analytical, 1, 34; Adlerian, 48; clan, 44, 46, 47; collective, 190; defined, 97, 110; English, 51; extraverted, 34, 50; of Freud, 77, 83; fundamental, 129; future, 100; of ghost-complexes, 164; human, 82, 89; individual, 31; of initiation, 191; of Jung, 77, 83; medical, 49, 154, 179; modern, 21, 79; national, 53; parental, 79; personal, 144, 190; real object of, 12, 16, 17, 178; savage, 81; unconscious as object of, 15, 57; of values, 88; of woman, 122
Psycho-therapeutic, practice, 85, 161; standpoint, 140; task, 152
Psycho-therapy, 126, 152
Puberty, 71

Rapport, 12
Regression, 83, 99, 100, 101, 102, 103, 109
Religious, 2, 3, 58
Représentation collective, 188
Repressive, conscious influence, 5
Rickman, Dr., 99, 109

Schizophrenia, 140, 151
'Secret society', 52
Self-realization, 234
Sex, primordial energy of, 50
Sexuality, 52, 64, 66, 67, 76, 77, 104, 198
Shadow, 27, 30, 31, 75
Soma, a libido-symbol, 196, 197, 198, 199
Soul, 11, 12, 14, 30, 48, 59, 76, 77, 84, 85, 93, 95, 208, 216
Sublimation, 64, 65, 66, 67, 70
Suggestion, 12, 106, 173, 174, 234
Super-ego, 106, 119
Symbol, 33, 43; cultural, 38; meaning of, 33; of authority, 30; of devotion, 58; of the gentleman, 39, 44, 55; of the national myth, 41, 50
Symbolism, 8; of individuation, 7

Tao, Chinese concept of, 37, 38
Telepathy, 169, 178
Therapeutic principles, psychological variants of, 49
Transference, erotic, 175, 176; purpose and function of, 112; relation, 107

Unconscious, 5, 9, 16, 21, 24, 31, 39, 48, 55, 56, 65, 72, 74, 80, 81, 89, 93, 102, 103, 112, 139, 147, 148, 150, 151, 156, 162, 164, 165, 166, 169, 172, 174, 189, 201, 208, 210, 211, 212, 222, 226, 232, 237
Unconscious, and analysis, 23; archaic power of, 198; collective, 7, 13, 47, 78, 92, 95, 117, 167, 193; *dynamis*, 32; functions of, 235; German, 176; identification, 36; in literature, 58, 59; personal, 15, 17; primitive materials of, 10; primordial, 8, 15, 17, 157, 186; psychology of, 1, 57, 71; characteristic qualities of, 22; racial, 123, 161, 177

Water, classical symbol of, 145

Weltanschauung, 4, 110, 125, 126, 127, 172
Will-to-power, 76
Wish-fulfilment, 4, 13, 141, 142, 212
Witchcraft, 66
Yoga, system, 8, 167
Zarathustra, 30
Zürich School, amplification method 149